INDIA'S TRADE POLICY AND THE EXPORT PERFORMANCE OF INDUSTRY

INDO-DUTCH STUDIES ON DEVELOPMENT ALTERNATIVES-12

Indo-Dutch Studies on Development Alternatives

The present study is the twelfth volume in the series of studies sponsored under the *Indo-Dutch Programme on Alternatives in Development* (IDPAD). This programme grew out of intensifying contacts and cooperation in the seventies between Indian and Dutch social scientists interested in sharing each other's experiences in development research. Led by a common concern about the need to critically assess existing structures and policies from the point of view of meeting basic needs of large masses of people and to conceive alternatives that heighten the capabilities of the latter to serve as creative agents in the evolving world economy and society, a work-plan of joint research was agreed on in 1980 forming the first phase of IDPAD (1981–83).

Since its inception, the programme has been jointly implemented by the Indian Council of Social Science Research (ICSSR), New Delhi, and the Institute of Social Science Research in Developing Countries (IMWOO), The Hague, and financed to a major extent by a grant from the Dutch government and a generous contribution from the Indian government. From January 1992 onwards, IMWOO's role as the Dutch counterpart organisation has been taken over by Nuffic, the Netherlands Organisation for International Cooperation in Higher Education, The Hague. Following the second (1984–89) and third phase (1990–94), the programme is now preparing its fourth phase (1995–98), which will be based on the same principles as prepared by the Joint Committee of IDPAD.

This series of *Indo-Dutch Studies on Development Alternatives* includes only those research results obtained under IDPAD which are considered essentially qualified for wider dissemination. However, the views expressed and the facts stated therein are, of course, those of the authors. The following titles have appeared in the series:

1. H.H. de Haan: *Alternatives in Industrial Development: Sugarcane Processing in India* (1988).
2. Jairus Banaji and Rohini Hensman: *Beyond Multinationalism: Management Policy and Bargaining Relationships in International Companies* (1990).
3. M. Doornbos, F. van Dorsten, M. Mitra and P. Terhal: *Dairy Aid and Development: India's Operation Flood* (1990).
4. Martin Doornbos and K.N. Nair (eds): *Resources, Institutions and Strategies: Operation Flood and Indian Dairying* (1990).
5. Nirmala Banerjee (ed): *Indian Women in a Changing Industrial Scenario* (1991).
6. Nirmal Sengupta: *Managing Common Property: Irrigation in India and the Philippines* (1991).
7. Hein Streefkerk and T.K. Moulik (eds): *Managing Rural Development: Health and Energy Programmes in India* (1991).
8. Willem van Schendel: *Three Deltas: Accumulation and Poverty in Rural Burma, Bengal and South India* (1991).
9. Hans Linnemann (ed): *South-South Trade Preferences: The GSTP and Trade in Manufactures* (1992).
10. T.M. Thomas Isaac, P.A. van Stuijvenberg and K.N. Nair: *Modernisation and Employment: The Coir Industry in Kerala* (1992).
11. Kanta Ahuja, Huub Coppens and Herman van der Wusten (eds): *Regime Transformations and Global Realignments: Indo-European Dialogues on the Post-Cold War World* (1993).

INDIA'S TRADE POLICY AND THE EXPORT PERFORMANCE OF INDUSTRY

Pitou van Dijck

K.S. Chalapati Rao

INDO-DUTCH STUDIES ON DEVELOPMENT ALTERNATIVES-12

Sage Publications
New Delhi/Thousand Oaks/London

First published in 1994 by

Sage Publications India Pvt Ltd
M-32 Greater Kailash Market I
New Delhi 110 048

Sage Publications Inc
2455 Teller Road
Thousand Oaks, California 91320

Sage Publications Ltd
6 Bonhill Street
London EC2A 4PU

Published by Tejeshwar Singh for Sage Publications India Pvt Ltd, phototypeset by Pagewell Photosetters, Pondicherry and printed at Chaman Enterprises, New Delhi.

Library of Congress Cataloging-in-Publication Data

Dijck, Pitou van.
India's trade policy and the export performance of industry / Pitou van Dijck, K.S. Chalapati Rao.
p. cm.—(Indo-Dutch studies on development alternatives; 12)
1. India—Commercial policy. 2. Foreign trade promotion—India. 3. Exports—India. I. Chalapati Rao, K.S. II. Title. III. Series.
HF1589.D54 1994 382′.6′0954—dc20 93–50133

ISBN: 0–8039–9156–8 (US)
81–7036–384–5 (India)

CONTENTS

LIST OF TABLES

PART I

PART II

LIST OF FIGURES

PREFACE

This volume is the outcome of the research project entitled 'The Impact of Multinational Corporations on India's Position in the International Division of Labour'. The project was funded by the Indo-Dutch Programme on Alternatives in Development (IDPAD) and the Indian Council of Social Science Research (ICSSR). The Corporate Studies Group (CSG) of the Indian Institute of Public Administration (IIPA), now the Institute for Studies in Industrial Development (ISID), New Delhi, the University of Amsterdam and the Economic and Social Institute (ESI) of the Free University of Amsterdam were the participating institutions. The data system and the documentation available at the CSG/ISID proved to be of considerable use to the researchers.

The papers in the volume were discussed at a seminar of IDPAD–ICSSR–IIPA held in New Delhi in January 1988. The comments and suggestions by the participants proved useful. We appreciate the encouragement and support of the two project directors and the participating institutions.

In view of the many significant changes in India's policies that have been implemented or announced recently, and the radical transformation of Eastern Europe and the Soviet Union, a post-script has been included at the end of Part II of this volume to make the analysis as up-to-date as possible.

New Delhi
January 1994

PITOU VAN DIJCK
K.S. CHALAPATI RAO

INTRODUCTORY NOTE FROM THE PROJECT DIRECTORS*

The need for enlarged exports by constituents of the Third World is rarely disputed, though the rationale and future perspectives, as well as the policy prescriptions differ widely. In the case of India, there are at least three streams of thought each voicing the urgency to raise the level of exports. But each of these streams looks at exports from a different perspective. Though we may do injustice to individual scholars whose propositions fall somewhere in between, we may label these three approaches the 'self-reliance approach', the 'World Bank approach' and the 'Government of India approach', and we shall describe these approaches consecutively.

Within a few years of the country's political independence Indian leadership realized the need for export promotion to enable the country to replenish the capital stock that got nearly exhausted during the Second World War period. The harsh reality of dependence on petroleum and foodgrain imports made it imperative that the country adopted export promotion policies. The rationale for export promotion received support as India embarked on a development programme with a high priority accorded to the establishment of capital goods and heavy industries. Coupled with the emphasis on export promotion, Indian policy makers sought to establish trade relations with a large number of countries. The inspiration to diversify the origin and destination of foreign trade had its own rationale and perspective. The underlying philosophy for higher exports, regulated imports and a wider geographic

* This note was written much before the new policy package was introduced during the middle of 1991. A postscript to the volume by K.S. Chalapati Rao, one of the contributors to the volume, has been added to present the trends in exports of Indian large private corporations until the time of announcement of the new policies.

diversification was an expression of the desire of a developing nation to seek a new identity that combined national development with self-reliance.

The policy package that emerged from the above perspective included all-out efforts at import substitution, quantitative restrictions on non-essential and consumer imports, and a variety of measures to provide protection to indigenous and infant industries. In order to promote exports, a variety of financial and fiscal incentives were offered along with a policy to encourage technology imports. The focus of this export strategy was governed by considerations of national self-reliant development in a framework of long-term planning.

The second school of thought that places high emphasis on exports is outlined in the 'Policy Agenda for Developing Countries' by the World Bank. The basic premise of the World Bank approach is that inward-oriented countries have been outperformed by outward-oriented countries. It is through increased competitiveness in world markets, it is argued, that an optimal resource allocation, and efficient modes of production, a rational international division of labour can be achieved. The set of policy proposals emanating from the above assumptions is obvious i.e. lowering trade barriers, replacing quantitative restrictions with tariffs and adoption of 'realistic' exchange rates.

The third perspective to export promotion policies is provided in a number of official statements made since the beginning of the 1980s. A basic point of departure from the World Bank perspective is that India is too large an economy to adopt the export-led growth model of the small nations of Southeast Asia. Indian economic development in essence will have to be Indian. After having stated this, it is argued that India in the past four decades has developed an inefficient production system with protected markets offering no challenge to entrepreneurs. As a consequence, the manufacturing systems are ridden with high costs and inefficient and obsolete technologies, and India has developed no aptitude to exploit a wide variety of advantages offered by modern technological revolutions.

The policy thrust of the 1980s, therefore, has been to make a break with the past and opt for a much higher degree of openness than previously accepted. The basic distinction between the World Bank approach and the policy pronouncements of the Government of India lies in the stated objectives and the nature of the arguments put forth. The Government of India perspective is related to the need for administering a 'shock therapy' to introduce a new dynamism so that India could emerge as a powerful economy at the turn of the twenty-first century. The policy implications of the Government of India's perspective are similar, though not the same, as that of the World Bank. Probably, a factor of significance in sustaining the difference is in the historical past that led India to emerge as an important trade partner with the socialist bloc. Second, Indian policy makers would find it hard to accept policies that are seen to be adopted under external pressure. Political reactions born out of national sensitivities in a democratic set-up cannot easily be swept aside.

The two contributions in the present volume review the development of India's trade policy and export performance in the light of the different perspectives described above.** Both contributions result from a research project on 'The Impact of Multinational Corporations on India's Position in the International Division of Labour' which has mainly been financed by the Indo-Dutch Programme on Alternatives in Development (IDPAD) and the Indian Council of Social Science Research (ICSSR). The two contributions in this volume together provide a basis to understand the processes in the evolution of India's export policies. The contribution by Pitou van Dijck is essentially based on international data at the macroeconomic level whereas Chalapati Rao's paper depends heavily on data published in India on the export performance of the top 405 Indian private sector companies. Van Dijck has viewed the Indian economy and her exports performance in terms of a process that could integrate the Indian economy into the world economic system. For Van Dijck, India has traditionally been a major exporter of manufactured products, at least among the developing countries. Following industrial development, India has

** The second volume groups the other contributions to this project. That volume contains contributions by S.K. Goyal, Biswajit Dhar, Nagesh Kumar, M.R. Murthy, K.V.K. Ranganathan and Sudha Sachdeva on the private corporate sector, identification of foreign controlled companies, development of Indian policies with regard to foreign capital, joint sector enterprises in which the public and private sectors join hands to promote new industrial ventures, Indian joint ventures abroad and a comparison of advertisement expenditures by Indian and foreign controlled companies.

a much larger potential and capacity to successfully interface itself with the rest of the world. Since this has not happened, Van Dijck seeks to outline the character of India's export performance in order to identify factors that have facilitated or retarded the country's progress towards securing a more important place in world trade. His focus is primarily on policy induced bottle-necks for a further exploitation of India's trade potential. He discusses several strategies to improve the export performance, not only necessary to improve the country's balance-of-payment position but also to increase the efficiency of domestic manufacturers.

Both Van Dijck and Rao view the need to raise the level of exports as a mechanism to acquire adequate foreign exchange resources to (*a*) support critical imports, (*b*) meet debt servicing and other international obligations, and (*c*) gain the necessary strength to pursue a self-reliant process of sustained growth and national development.

The contributions by Rao and Van Dijck have dissimilarities in perspectives, data and information sources as in their methodology; and yet both have reached the same conclusions with respect to the fact of India's failure on the export front. As regards identification of the reasons for the failure as also the implied policy packages, however, some differences can be discerned.

Van Dijck, for instance, shows that the main reason for India's low export performance and loss of market shares lies in her 'more inward-oriented pattern of total and manufacturing production', which is both due to structural factors such as the size of the domestic market and policies that have consistently favoured production for the domestic markets. The policy prescription in this approach is lower trade barriers, replacing quantitative restrictions with tariffs and to exploit fully the comparative advantages and remove the bias against exports. Rao, on the other hand, shows that over the past four decades the Indian policy towards exports has been substantially guided by internal and external pressures resulting in successive relaxations in the case of imports without insisting on matching efforts at exports by the beneficiary groups. One major reason for India's failure, according to Rao, is the absence of effective monitoring of the foreign trade sector. In his review of the various official committees he underlines that the more influential of them made recommendations without examining hard facts and objective conditions.

This has been the case in spite of the fact that researchers studying the international division of labour have access to data on annual earnings and utilization of foreign exchange by all Indian public limited companies since 1975–76. Companies have been obliged to publish the contribution of exports to total sales as well as the volume of their total imports in their annual reports. The availability of company level data offers an opportunity for a detailed analysis of India's export performance. Rao has compiled information at the company level and data on foreign trade. The two studies reveal that for a closer understanding of the impact of export policies, it is desirable to combine studies at the macro level with studies at the micro level. For policy guidance in the field of export policy, such an analysis cannot be dismissed. The two contributions in this volume are complementary and may help to understand the evolution of export policies in India and contribute to the ongoing debate in India's foreign trade policies.

S.K. Goyal
Institute for Studies in Industrial Development

G. Junne
University of Amsterdam

Part I

EXPORT PERFORMANCE AND COMPARATIVE ADVANTAGE OF INDIA'S MANUFACTURING SECTOR

I

EXPORT PERFORMANCE AND COMPARATIVE ADVANTAGE OF INDIA'S MANUFACTURING SECTOR

Pitou van Dijck

INTRODUCTION[1]

During the 1970s and 1980s some disturbing developments occurred with respect to the performance of India's manufacturing sector in the international market: exports as a share of total sales in most industrial sectors declined, the country lost a substantial share in the international market to newly industrializing countries in East and Southeast Asia and Latin America, and India faced serious balance-of-payments problems. In view of the country's high dependence on manufactures for its foreign exchange earnings, new policies must be implemented to redress these trends and lay the foundation for an optimal pattern of industrialization and a sustainable balance-of-payments position during the 1990s.

The predominantly inward-oriented and protectionist policies that have been pursued for four decades in a country of sheer continental size have limited strongly the role of international trade in the Indian economy. Indeed, India has been one of the very few countries where the export orientation of the industrial sector tended to decline in the course of time. This development is contrary to the worldwide trend in the period following the Second

World War of increasing internationalization of industrial production and a further integration of national economies into world markets.

A critical evaluation of the numerous attempts that have been made by developing countries to liberalize the trade regime and stimulate non-traditional, particularly manufactured exports, reveals that many such attempts failed or enjoyed only short-lived successes. Trade policy is part of a much wider range of instruments that governments use to intervene in markets and to redirect the allocation of resources, and, consequently, the export performance of countries depends on the combined effect of these government policies as well as on the effect of all types of market distortions and the long-term investment strategies of companies. Moreover, a reorientation of production does not simply occur in response to a change in price signals but requires additional and long-term measures to strengthen the competitiveness of industry in the international market. Only a few developing countries have managed to penetrate world markets with a range of industrial products that have been either produced or assembled by domestic companies. In the course of time the Indian government has applied a wide arsenal of incentives and regulations to stimulate domestic companies to export and to attract foreign companies to export processing zones (EPZs). Nevertheless, the country has failed to exploit fully the growth opportunities in the international market.

Transformation of trade policy has frequently led to a heated debate in India as in many other countries. This is particularly so when the reorientation of trade policy is part of an adjustment and restructuring programme orchestrated by multilateral agencies such as the IMF and the World Bank as has been the case in many developing countries during the late 1970s and the 1980s. In such circumstances policy reorientation not only causes a break with a tradition of more interventionist and inward-oriented policies and conflicts with vested interests in such policies, but is also considered an intrusion in national sovereignty with respect to a highly sensitive area of macroeconomic policy. Moreover, when necessary adjustments have been postponed until the balance-of-payments position has become unsustainable, shock-wise, sometimes drastic measures need to be adopted that may lead to high economic, social and political transition costs. These costs to society could have been avoided if adjustments had been introduced at an earlier stage.

There are at least three good reasons to study in some detail India's export policies and performance. First, India has traditionally been one of the major exporters among the developing countries. The history of the country's export industries goes back to the nineteenth century when India was a major exporter of textiles. Although its predominant role as an exporter of manufactures has been displaced by some East and Southeast Asian and Latin American countries, it still is one of the major exporters of manufactures among developing countries, supplying a wide range of products to a large number of foreign markets.

Second, the balance-of-payments problems that have occurred during the 1980s require new policies that go beyond the measures introduced in the past. An investigation of the essential characteristics and weaknesses of the policies pursued in the 1970s and 1980s is a precondition for understanding the new initiatives that have to be taken in this area.

Third, a study of the type of policies India pursues and of its actual trade dependence and export performance may be helpful in understanding the position India takes in international fora and negotiations on the future of the international trade regime such as in GATT, the negotiations on the Multi-Fibre Arrangements and the Global System of Trade Preferences among developing countries.

The study is organized along the following lines.

In the following section the role of trade in India's economy and India's role in world trade in manufactures will be examined. It will be seen that the export orientation of India's manufacturing sector is still very limited notwithstanding many attempts that have been made to stimulate exports of manufactures. Also, it will be seen that India's competitiveness in world markets of manufactures is constantly declining and that the country's export industries are not able to compete successfully with other developing countries. The next section will focus on options for regime transformation. Here an attempt will be made to distinguish several strategies to transform a basically inward-oriented industrialization regime into a regime that stimulates industry to export and opens the domestic market to foreign competition. This will be followed by a review of changes that have taken place in India's trade and industrialization regime and the main characteristics of the trade regime during the 1970s and 1980s. In particular, we will focus on attempts to liberalize imports, stimulate exports through the application of compensating facilities and export promotion measures, and the creation of export processing zones. In the following section we will study India's manufactured export performance and compare the composition and factor intensities of manufactured exports with the composition and structure of imports. Also, we will compare the degree of technological sophistication of India's exports to the markets of developed market economies, developing market economies and of CMEA countries so as to depict the country's position in the hierarchy of nations in world markets. In the last section the main results of the study will be summarized.

THE EXPORT PERFORMANCE OF INDIA'S MANUFACTURING SECTOR

General observations on the export orientation of industry

It holds for all countries that the higher the level of income per capita, the larger the contribution of the manufacturing sector to exports. In that sense, the role of manufactures in total exports is an indicator of the level of development of an economy. However, there is wide variation among countries in the export orientation of the manufacturing sector, and countries at a similar level of development may differ significantly in export orientation.

As will be seen, the export orientation of industry in developing countries is negatively correlated with the size of the domestic market, the availability of natural resources and/or the availability of arable land per capita, and the degree of protection against imports. When the sample is confined to developing countries only, it appears that the level of income per capita as such does not significantly contribute to the explanation of the inter-country variation in the export orientation of the manufacturing sector. Apparently, a low level of income per capita does not necessarily impede an export-oriented pattern of industrialization. Two structural variables, population size and population density (as a proxy for natural resource availability) explain nearly 75 per cent of the variation in the export orientation of the manufacturing sector in developing countries. In addition to these structural characteristics of economies, the trade and industrialization regime has an impact on the market orientation of the manufacturing sector. The relevant variable here is not the degree of government intervention but the type of intervention. The more the mode of intervention favours domestic market-oriented production over export-oriented production, the lower the export-output ratio of the manufacturing sector, other variables being equal.

The role of the variables mentioned earlier in explaining the variation in the export orientation of the manufacturing sector in developing countries is shown below. As a proxy for trade policy we use the percentage ratio of the import duty revenue to the value of imports of manufactures. This variable captures only part of the total effect of government intervention on the market orientation of the industrial sector and, therefore, underestimates the significance of protection. However, it is also true that the bias against exports, created by protection, can be reduced by compensating measures, as will be seen later. The results of the statistical analysis are as follows:[2]

$$E_m/O_m = \underset{(1.2)}{11.4} - \underset{(2.88)}{2.3 \ln P} + \underset{(8.23)}{6.5 \ln Da} - \underset{(1.42)}{2.7 \ln T^m/M_m}$$

$$n = 34 \qquad R^2 = 0.81$$

in which

E_m/O_m = Ratio of the value of manufactured exports (E_m) to the value of manufacturing production (O_m), expressed as a percentage.

P = Size of population in thousands of inhabitants.

Da = Density of population on arable land i.e. the number of inhabitants per km^2 of arable land area.

T^m/M_m = Average tariff rate on manufactures i.e. ratio of total import duty revenue (T^m) to the value of imports of manufactures (M_m), expressed as a percentage.

The independent variables are statistically significant at 95 per cent confidence level. The equation is in semi-logarithmic form. The t-statistics are in parentheses. The data relate to 1980.

These variables underlie the pronounced export orientation of the manufacturing sector in some East Asian economies such as South Korea, Taiwan, Singapore and Hong Kong. They also underlie the more inward-oriented pattern of total and manufacturing production in a country like India which has a large domestic market, limited availability of arable land per capita and a system of government intervention that tends to isolate the economy from the world market.

The role of international trade in India's economy

Key indicators of the role of international trade in India's economy are presented in the upper half of Table 1. As seen in the first two columns of the table, the share of trade in production was extremely small in the beginning of the 1970s, due to the large domestic market and the system of incentives that hampered both imports and exports. The share of trade in GDP approximately doubled in the course of the 1970s. During the 1980s, however, the ratio of exports to GDP fluctuated slightly in the range of 5.9–6.8 per cent while the share of imports fluctuated at a somewhat higher level. The import shares peaked in 1979 and 1980 due to the dramatic rise in oil prices. Thus, during the 1980s no tendency was discernible of a further opening of the economy. It is true that during the 1980s India's exports grew at a much higher rate than the value of imports and as a consequence the resource gap as a percentage of GDP was reduced. Nevertheless, the large number of export incentives and import controls could not prevent the trade balance from being negative nearly every year during the period 1970–87. Moreover, on an average, this gap was wider during the 1980s than during the 1970s.

The highly inward-oriented character of the pattern of industrialization is indicated by the ratio of manufactured exports to manufacturing output and of manufactured imports to the domestic demand for manufactures. Manufactured exports and imports have been defined here as including SITC sectors 5–8 less 67 and 68. Manufacturing output includes the output of ISIC 3 less ISIC 353, 354, 371 and 372. Wolf found that during the 1960–73 period the ratio of manufactured exports to output dropped from 9.7 per cent in 1960 to 8.6 per cent in 1973, 'a virtually unique experience among developing countries'.[3] He also observed that during this period the share of manufactured imports in domestic demand fell from 19.3 per cent to 9.5 per cent. As is clear from our data, this trend was clearly not reversed during the 1970s and the early 1980s. At the end of the decade the export-output ratio of the

TABLE 1
Key Indicators for International Trade and Foreign Debt, 1970–87

	International Trade		*Resource Gap in GDP*[1] *(%)*	*Export-Output Ratio in Industry*[2] *(%)*	*Import-Demand Ratio for Manufactures*[2] *(%)*
	Exports in GDP[1] *(%)*	*Imports in GDP*[1] *(%)*			
1970	3.99	4.79	−0.79	5.99	5.72
1971	3.94	4.91	−0.96	..	..
1972	4.48	4.92	−0.43	..	..
1973	4.49	5.05	−0.55	7.20	6.79
1974	5.22	6.38	−1.16	7.60	7.01
1975	6.57	6.98	−0.40	6.72	8.64
1976	7.58	6.78	0.79	8.39	6.39
1977	7.36	6.82	0.54	8.74	7.46
1978	7.03	8.31	−1.27	8.51	8.09
1979	7.49	9.85	−2.36	8.18	7.43
1980	6.51	10.11	−3.60	7.68	7.98
1981	6.37	9.66	−3.28	7.91	7.81
1982	6.07	8.82	−2.74	6.59	..
1983	6.11	8.42	−2.31	..	..
1984	6.81	9.20	−2.39	8.16	9.78
1985	5.93	9.07	−3.14	..	..
1986	6.21	8.39	−2.17	..	..
1987	6.82	8.80	−1.97	..	..

	Foreign Debt Debt Stock[3] *(US \$ 10⁶)*	*Disbursements of Long-term Loans*[3] *(US \$ 10⁶)*	*Total Debt To GNP*[3] *(%)*	*Debt Service to Exports*[3] *(%)*
1970	7,937	908	14.9	21.5
1971	8,892	959	15.3	21.3
1972	9,805	865	15.9	19.8
1973	10,581	959	14.0	17.1
1974	12,238	1,393	14.0	14.7
1975	13,256	1,901	15.5	11.6
1976	13,998	1,585	15.6	9.6
1977	15,529	1,387	14.8	8.7
1978	16,482	1,259	13.8	9.5
1979	16,856	1,362	12.6	8.1
1980	19,250	2,878	11.1	7.1
1981	21,106	2,401	11.8	7.3
1982	25,627	3,104	13.9	8.1
1983	28,796	3,204	14.4	8.8
1984	31,272	4,386	16.3	8.3

Table 1 *(Continued)*

	Foreign Debt Debt Stock[3] *(US $ 10⁶)*	*Disbursements of Long-term Loans*[3] *(US $ 10⁶)*	*Total Debt To GNP*[3] *(%)*	*Debt Service to Exports*[3] *(%)*
1985	36,625	4,421	17.2	11.6
1986	41,311	4,090	18.1	15.2
1987	46,370	6,191	18.8	16.9

Notes: .. No data available.
Data in the last column relate to debt service on public and publicly guaranteed debt only.

Sources: [1] Exports, imports and resource gap in GDP taken from the World Bank, *World Tables*, 1988–89 edition, Washington DC, 1989.
[2] Values of manufactured exports and imports taken from UNCTAD, *Handbook of International Trade and Development*, New York, various issues.
Values of manufacturing output taken from United Nations, *Yearbook of Industrial Statistics*, New York, various issues.
[3] The World Bank, *World Debt Tables, External Debt of Developing Countries*, 1988–89 edition, Washington DC, 1988, Vols. II and III.

manufacturing sector was 8.2 per cent while the import-demand ratio in manufacturing was 7.4 per cent. This trend follows more clearly from the time series presented in Table 2. The table shows the export-output ratio of 19 manufacturing sectors during the period 1975–76 to 1983–84. In nearly all the manufacturing sectors a clear trend of a declining export orientation is discernible. Only in the pharmaceuticals sector exports assumed growing significance. It is also clear from the table that exports were relatively insignificant in most sectors, the major exceptions being jute textile, electrical machinery, food processing, silk and rayon, pharmaceuticals and other chemicals. (The export orientation of Indian companies is analysed in greater detail by Chalapati Rao in Part II of this volume.)

The foreign debt

In the course of the 1970s and 1980s India's foreign debt and its debt burden increased substantially as shown by the indicators in the lower half of Table 1. The need for fresh foreign loans increased constantly during these two decades and by 1987 the accumulated

TABLE 2

Industry-wise Percentage Shares of Exports in Net Sales of 423 Large Private Companies, 1975–76 to 1983–84

Sector	*1975–76*	*1976–77*	*1977–78*	*1978–79*	*1979–80*	*1980–81*	*1981–82*	*1982–83*	*1983–84*
Tea	11.51	15.02	14.39	9.37	9.77	9.34	8.25	5.37	4.48
Food Processing	9.92	9.52	9.29	9.82	7.84	6.26	7.78	6.86	6.67
Cotton Textiles	6.63	8.84	6.99	5.81	6.96	6.06	4.57	4.42	3.34
Jute Textiles	37.48	40.27	40.08	33.91	34.19	34.48	32.04	25.46	20.78
Silk and Rayon	5.90	3.58	3.75	3.17	3.09	2.37	7.97	7.64	5.92
Breweries and Leather	4.17	5.59	5.16	5.67	5.53	5.37	4.44	3.24	4.76
Metals	5.85	11.10	6.29	2.51	1.30	2.30	0.80	1.41	1.11
Transport Equipment	5.54	7.54	8.60	8.07	7.08	6.66	6.23	5.49	4.16
Electrical Machinery	6.83	6.95	8.68	7.79	6.43	6.67	7.18	7.58	7.01
Non-electrical Equipment	6.97	5.87	4.03	4.67	4.44	4.01	3.90	3.42	2.42
Metal Products	3.87	8.49	7.35	5.32	3.16	1.81	1.80	1.65	1.25
Basic Chemicals	2.21	2.76	2.54	2.97	2.59	2.47	2.16	2.13	1.91
Pharmaceuticals	3.74	4.07	3.22	2.83	3.99	4.42	6.14	6.29	5.86
Other Chemicals	5.37	5.47	5.13	4.65	6.21	6.86	8.22	6.63	5.65
Cement and Asbestos	8.17	12.31	10.83	4.34	3.30	2.48	2.74	2.00	1.19
Glass and Ceramics	2.69	2.59	2.97	1.96	1.75	2.33	3.13	2.12	1.73
Rubber Products	3.17	4.66	5.37	4.03	2.07	2.94	2.21	2.27	2.51
Paper and Wood Products	1.01	1.20	1.09	1.40	0.92	0.85	3.25	1.66	0.47
Other Industries	5.45	5.71	5.48	5.14	5.62	5.63	4.08	3.58	2.03
All Sectors	5.66	6.97	6.34	5.41	4.99	4.81	4.69	4.24	3.59

Note: Companies have over Rs 1.00 crore of risk capital since 1982.
Source: Data system of the Institute for Studies in Industrial Development, New Delhi.

foreign debt was over US $46 billion. Moreover, the structure of the debt became less favourable to India. Up to the end of the 1970s nearly all of the debt consisted of long-term loans, but in the course of the 1980s India increasingly relied on IMF credits and other short-term loans. As a consequence of this shift, the share of long-term debt in the total accumulated debt decreased from 94 per cent in 1980 to 88 per cent in 1987. The ratio of debt service—interest payments and principal repayments—to disbursements of long-term loans increased significantly during the 1980s. By 1980 debt service was equivalent to only 26 per cent of disbursements of new long-term loans while this amounted to 43 per cent in 1987. Thus, by the end of the period net inflow was only 57 per cent of the disbursed flow of long-term loans. These long-term loans are disbursed to a very large extent by official creditors such as governments and multilateral agencies like the World Bank and IDA. While it is true that official creditors still provide most of the fresh foreign loans that India needs, private creditors such as foreign suppliers and particularly financial markets have played an increasingly important role, especially during the 1980s. While disbursements of long-term loans by private creditors were only of marginal and even declining importance in the 1970s, in 1987 they amounted to no less than 58 per cent of the amount disbursed by official creditors, India's traditional suppliers of long-term guaranteed loans. Within the group of official creditors we may notice another significant shift: the contribution of bilateral official flows has tended to decrease and the roles of the World Bank and IDA have increased, as illustrated by the following data. The share of flows from the World Bank and IDA in the total disbursements by official creditors was only 12 per cent in 1970. It increased to 32 per cent in 1975, 37 per cent in 1980 and went up further to 65 per cent in 1987. Consequently, while India relied traditionally for its external financing on bilateral long-term loans from governments in developed countries, the actual situation is very different, with a much more prominent role of the World Bank, IDA and financial markets for long-term loans, and IMF credits for short-term balance-of-payments support. In the last year of the period under study, the disbursement of loans by the financial markets was as sizeable as the sum total of official bilateral flows and IDA. These shifts may have major implications for India's macroeconomic policies and, for that matter, future trade policies. The IMF conditionality attached to short-term balance-of-payments assistance includes measures to liberalize markets, adjust the exchange rate and limit the use of quantitative import barriers, apart from the expenditure reduction measures that are typical of these programmes. Moreover, the World Bank provides loans increasingly as part of sectoral and structural adjustment programmes. These programmes also emphasize the liberalization of the trade regime and export promotion. Following the disastrous developments in Latin America, Africa and some other countries in the 1980s, private banks tend to critically examine the actual policies governments pursue with respect to their balance-of-payments position. Two crucial variables in this respect are presented in the last two columns of Table 1. These columns show the ratio of total debt to GNP and the ratio of debt service to exports respectively. Both ratios tended to decline during the 1970s but in the 1980s there was a strong reversal of this trend. It is clear that India does not belong to the group of heavily indebted countries and that the relative size of the foreign debt and the debt burden are still limited.

However, the policies actually pursued by the Indian government may be unsustainable and dangerous in the longer term. According to the latest data made available by the OECD, India's total debt and liabilities including the use of IMF credits have increased dramatically in recent years and were estimated at US $54.3 billion at the end of 1988.[4] The rapid accumulation of foreign debt, the growing dependence on financial markets and multilateral agencies such as the IMF and the World Bank, and the rise in the debt service ratio are all sound reasons for a critical review of India's trade policies.

India's share in international markets

Although exports are not a major outlet for the manufacturing sector, the sector's contribution to India's total exports and its foreign exchange earnings has been remarkably high and has been continuously increasing as seen in Figure 1. In 1960, no less than 43 per cent of all goods exported by India were manufactures. The contribution of such products increased rapidly during the 1970s and further still during the 1980s. According to the broader definition of manufactures used by the World Bank, nearly 70 per cent of India's exports were manufactured products in 1987. This reflects the country's limited options for alternative foreign exchange

FIGURE 1

Contribution of Manufacturers to Exports (in percentages), 1960–1987

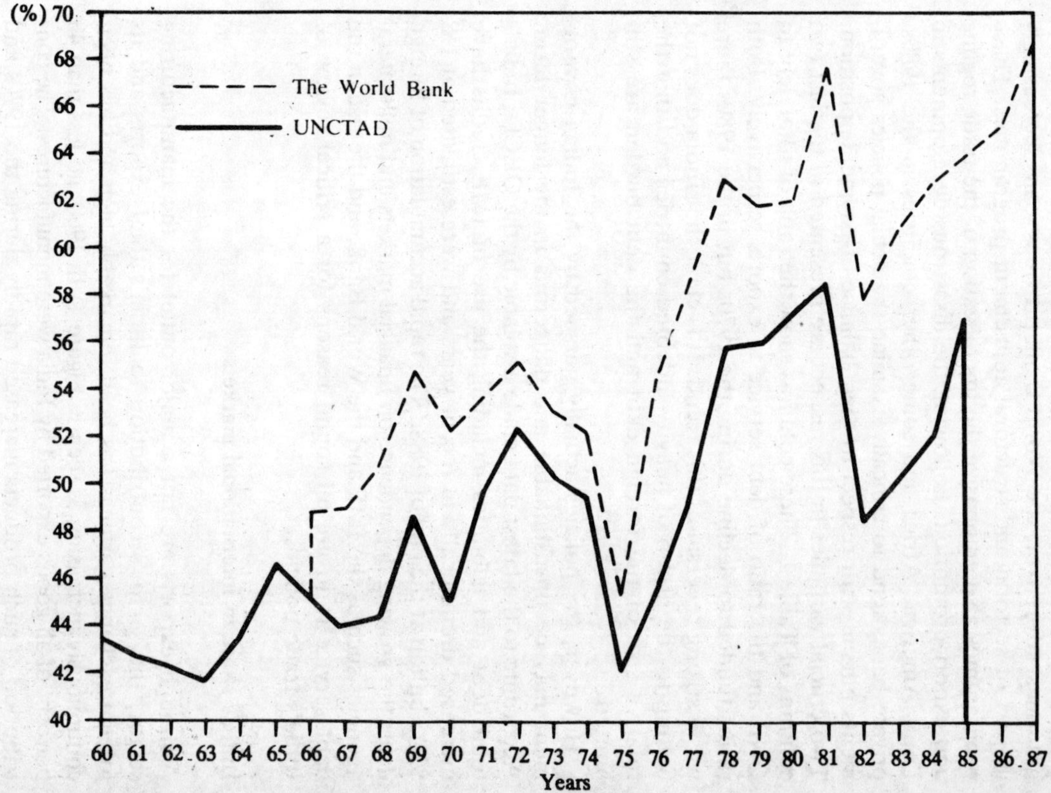

Sources: UNCTAD, *Handbook of International Trade and Development Statistics*, United Nations, New York, various

earnings due to the poor resource base of the economy and the limited availability of arable land per capita. These structural factors tend to make the country highly dependent on the capacity of the manufacturing sector to compete in world markets. A similar situation is seen in a series of small island economies in the Caribbean and in some resource poor Asian countries such as Bangladesh, South Korea and Taiwan. This is in contrast with the experience of most developing countries, particularly low income countries, where manufactures played only a very limited role in total exports during the 1960s and 1970s.

Till the early 1960s India and Hong Kong were the two major exporters of manufactures among developing countries. In the early 1960s South Korea and Taiwan initiated an export-oriented incentive structure for their manufacturing sector. After a relatively short period of import substitution, in which exports of these countries consisted mainly of primary products, the reorientation in the system of incentives led to an expansion of manufactured exports, resulting in a rapid transformation of the export structure and a rapid growth of the share of these countries in total developing countries' exports of manufactures. In the late 1970s and the 1980s, policies to stimulate exports of manufactures were introduced in some Latin American countries as a response to external shocks and serious balance-of-payments problems. While the current value of India's manufactured exports increased by a factor of 4.75 during the 1970s, this could not prevent a dramatic decline in India's share in world trade in manufactures and its share in developing countries' exports of manufactures. Only during the 1975–78 period the general downward trend was reversed temporarily. Notwithstanding the growing emphasis on the stimulation of manufactured exports, the very low share of India in world markets of manufactured products declined even further in the 1980s. The changes in India's share in exports of all developing countries to the OECD markets during the period 1970–87 for all manufactures as well as for some major product groups such as chemicals and related products (SITC 5); manufactured goods classified chiefly by material (SITC 6 less 67 and 68), including leather manufactures, rubber manufactures, cork and wood manufactures, paper products, textiles, non-metallic mineral manufactures and metal products; machinery and transport equipment (SITC 7); miscellaneous manufactured articles (SITC 8), including travel goods, apparel and clothing accessories, footwear, professional and scientific goods, photographic apparatus, optical goods, watches and clocks are presented in Figure 2. The first graph shows a rather dramatic decline in India's share in exports of manufactured goods of developing countries to the markets of the OECD countries. During the 1970–87 period this share dropped from 7.6 per cent to 3.1 per cent. During the 1970s the sector of manufactured goods (SITC 6) registered a rather steep fall in its market share, as did the sector of machinery and transport equipment (SITC 7). The sector of miscellaneous manufactured articles (SITC 8) showed an entirely different trend with a sharply increasing share in the international market during the 1970s, followed by a steep fall during the early 1980s, and a stabilization of its market share from 1983 onwards. The only sector that managed to increase its share during the 1980s was chemicals (SITC 5). Given India's high dependence on manufactured products for its foreign exchange earnings, the country must reverse the overall trend of declining market shares.

OPTIONS FOR REGIME TRANSFORMATION

There are several avenues for countries to liberalize the economy and stimulate exports of manufactures. We will discuss three options: (*a*) across-the-board liberalization; (*b*) partial liberalization, combined with tailor-made compensation and stimulation of export industries to make them overcome the anti-export bias emanating from the prevailing trade regime; and (*c*) a dualistic policy in which import competing industries are protected and the export of manufactures is concentrated in export processing zones (EPZs).

All countries rely on a different mix of instruments to protect their domestic market from foreign competition and stimulate industries to export. Moreover, there is no simple change-over from inward-oriented policies towards more open policies, and conceiving such a change-over as a one-way development process bypasses the complexity of policy reform. Domestic economic and political constraints and external shocks compel countries to change the speed and direction of economic reform. Many attempts to alleviate the anti-trade bias in the regime have failed. Case histories show that periods of liberalization may be succeeded by a return to protectionist policies.[5] However, notwithstanding the many difficulties involved in regime transformation, several countries have implemented new policies to reduce the anti-export bias in the prevailing system of incentives and to stimulate industry to export. The most comprehensive avenue to liberalization and export promotion is at the same time the most difficult to implement. For this reason, most countries opt for a gradual approach of partial liberalization-cum-compensation, sometimes in combination with the creation of export processing zones.

The issue of regime transformation invariably provokes a fierce controversy over its perceived merits and drawbacks. The heated debate that took place at the time India devaluated the rupee in 1966, the controversy over the IMF loan and its conditionality, and the more recent liberalization attempts have revealed the politically explosive character and the social and economic risks of regime transformation. The main points of critique put forward in the debate on liberalization of the trade regime and export stimulation are as follows.

First, it is argued that liberalization and export-oriented industrialization policies increase dependence on foreign markets and foreign companies, and on trade and investment policies designed abroad. Consequently, when such policies are pursued, the structure and volume of production are determined to a large extent by factors beyond the control of domestic decision makers. At the same time, such policies reduce the possibilities of a more self-reliant growth path, based on the growth of the domestic market and the development of indigenous and appropriate techniques.

Furthermore, so the argument goes, the pattern of specialization that results from an export-oriented industrialization strategy in countries with an unlimited supply of unskilled and low wage labour, is at the lower end of the spectrum of technology. The contribution of such a strategy to the creation of a skilled labour force and to technological development is expected to be limited since export production is mainly a kind of non-complex and routine-like assembly activity. The possibilities for upgrading and shifting the comparative advantage towards more skill and capital intensive sectors are considered limited.

Also, the open trade regime and export zones that are specifically designed to stimulate manufactured exports, result in footloose

FIGURE 2
India's Share in the Manufactured Exports of Developing Countries to OECD Countries (in percentages), 1970–1987

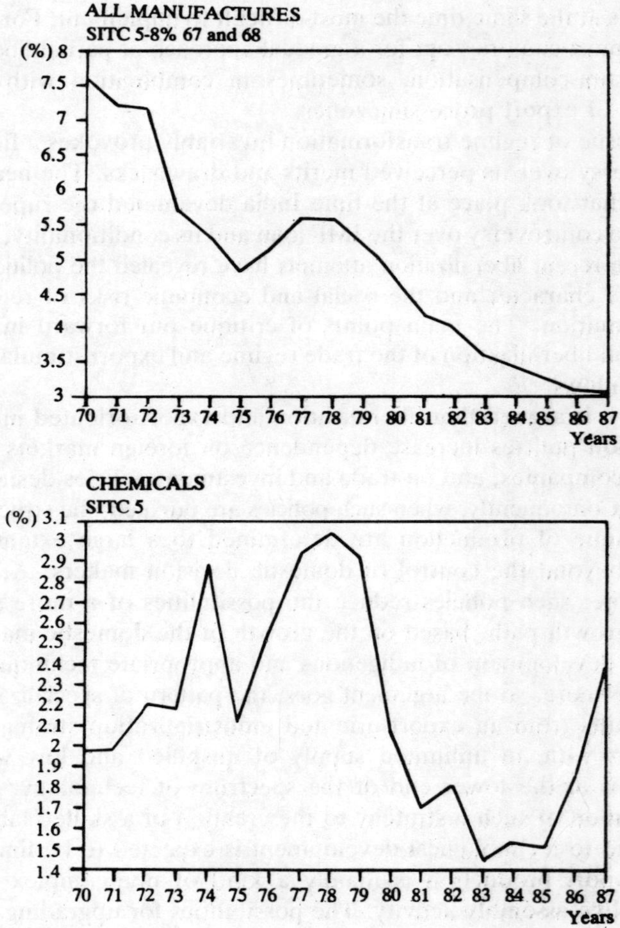

MANUFACTURED GOODS
SITC 6% 67 and 68

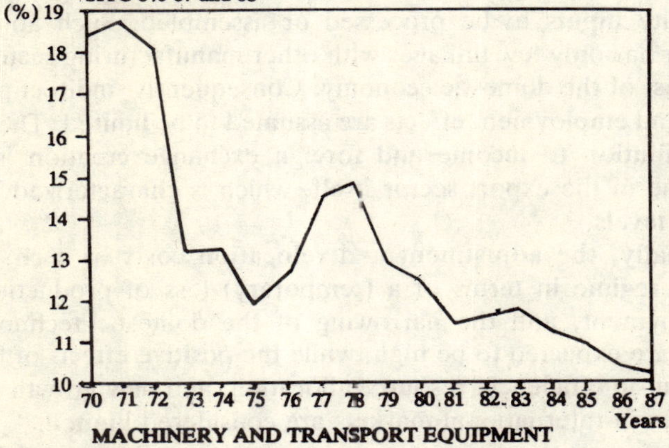

MACHINERY AND TRANSPORT EQUIPMENT
SITC 7

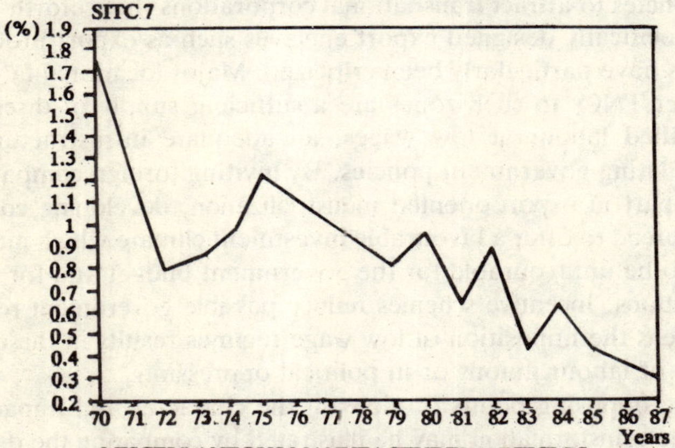

MISCELLANEOUS MANUFACTURED ARTICLES
SITC 8

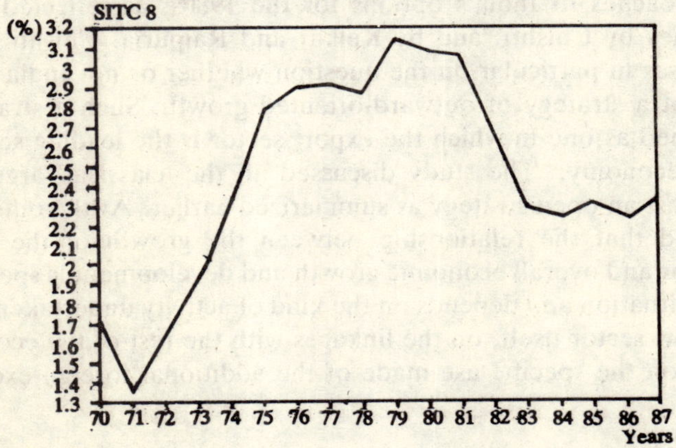

Source: OECD, *Foreign Trade by Commodities, Imports*, Paris, various issues.

export activities, dependent on imports of capital goods and intermediate inputs to be processed or assembled. Such an export sector has only few linkages with other manufacturing sectors and the rest of the domestic economy. Consequently, indirect production and employment effects are assumed to be limited. The major contribution to income and foreign exchange creation is wage income in the export sector itself, which is characterized by low wage levels.

Finally, the adjustment and relocation costs of a change in trade regime in terms of a (temporary) loss of production and employment, and the narrowing of the domestic technological basis are expected to be high, while the positive effects of liberalization on efficiency, resource allocation, and new growth opportunities in international markets are considered limited.

Policies to attract transnational corporations (henceforth TNCs) to specifically designed export enclaves such as export processing zones have particularly been criticized. Major locational factors to attract TNCs to such zones are a sufficient supply of disciplined unskilled labour at low wages, an adequate infrastructure and stimulating government policies. By inviting foreign companies to take part in export-oriented industrialization, developing countries are forced to offer a favourable investment climate which may turn out to be unfavourable for the government budget and for labour conditions. Incentive schemes reduce possible government receipts, whereas the imposition of low wage regimes results in the curtailment of labour unions or in political oppression.

The opposing points of view on the character and impact of a regime transformation may be illustrated by comparing the different approaches to India's options for the 1980s, as reflected in the studies by Chishti, and by Kelkar and Raipuria. Chishti's study focuses in particular on the question whether or not India should adopt a strategy of outward-oriented growth. Such a strategy is defined as one in which the export sector is the leading sector of the economy.[6] The study discussed all the 'classical' arguments against an open strategy as summarized earlier. At the outset it is stated that the relationship between the growth of the export sector and overall economic growth and development is specific to the situation and depends on the kind of activity undertaken in the export sector itself, on the linkages with the rest of the economy, and on the specific use made of the additional foreign exchange earnings. In the Indian context, Chishti rejects such a strategy as either feasible or desirable, for several reasons. First, the export sector is not likely to be a high growth sector. A distinction is made between the prospects for exports of agricultural and mineral products, and for three categories of manufactures. Prospects for agricultural exports such as sugar, coffee, tobacco, tea, rice and beef are assumed to be poor because of price stagnancy and decline, a slow growth of demand for primary products in developed countries and increasing protectionism.[7] Prospects for mineral exports such as iron ore, mica and manganese are considered limited as is inferred from past experience.[8]

Evaluating the prospects for exports of manufactures, Chishti distinguishes labour intensive, resource intensive, and capital and skill intensive manufactures. Three factors diminish export prospects for labour intensive products: low growth of demand in developed countries, increased protectionism, and technological change that reduces the advantage of low wages for a labour surplus economy.[9]

Resource intensive manufactures are expected to grow slowly due to the low growth of demand for intermediates in the present state of the world economy.[10] Growth of exports of capital and skill intensive products such as engineering goods is also expected to be low. Barriers to enter markets are high since production and distribution in the sector of engineering goods is controlled to a large extent by TNCs. Such companies are able to raise additional barriers to enter through trade-supporting services, financial facilities and the introduction of new technologies.[11]

The most significant reason for Chishti to reject an outward-oriented pattern of development is the assumed low export growth prospects for all types of primary and manufactured products that India actually exports. In addition to this, she mentions some other arguments for rejecting such a strategy. Such a strategy renders the economy vulnerable to fluctuations in the world economy and to economic policies of importing countries, and consequently reduces domestic control over resource allocation and growth. Presumably even more important, such a strategy does not lead to development. Development is perceived as a process of growth combined with reduced income disparities and improved living conditions among low income groups.[12] The contribution to development is expected to be limited since employment creation will be limited and exports are promoted by keeping wages low. It should be noted, however, that these arguments refer to different categories of exports. The argument of limited employment effects is based on the observation that the export performance of labour intensive sectors in India has not been entirely successful and that India's exports shift towards capital and skill intensive products.[13] The argument of the crucial role of low wages is related to the creation of a competitive edge in labour intensive products.[14] For these reasons Chishti rejects an outward-oriented growth policy and considers such a policy inferior as compared to a policy focusing on agricultural development and the broadening of the industrial basis of the economy.

Kelkar and Raipuria review the arguments in favour of and against regime transformation. Reviewing the arguments in favour of regime transformation they make a distinction between the balance-of-payments argument and the argument based on the static and dynamic advantages of efficient resource allocation.[15] The balance-of-payments situation may provide a compelling argument for the implementation of export promotion policies in the short run. Sluggish prospects for agricultural and mineral exports or reduced net foreign aid may 'force' a country to enhance the capacity of its industry to export, or to attract foreign companies to contribute to manufactured exports. In addition, increased protection in importing countries against traditional labour intensive imports may 'force' a developing country to diversify and upgrade its manufactured exports. The rationale of liberalizing the trade and industrialization regime, however, rests on efficiency criteria for resource allocation. The rationale of a more open and trade-oriented policy, as compared to the inward-oriented policy pursued in the past, is the exploitation of (dynamic) comparative advantages and economies of scale, the impact of increased exposure to international competition on efficiency and the price level, and on accelerating growth through a more optimal use of the available factors of production.[16]

There is also another effect liberalization may have on the use of resources. In a regime characterized by quantitative import restrictions and import licences, rent-seekers use resources to obtain licences.[17] By liberalizing the import regime and substituting tariffs for quantitative import control measures, such directly unproductive activities cease to generate a rent and the investments in rent-seeking activities are released for more productive kinds of activity.

The point stressed by Kelkar and Raipuria is that the prevailing regime that fosters inward-oriented inefficient production should be transformed into a regime that stimulates efficient industries to compete in the domestic and foreign markets. Efficient import substitution and export production is warranted when the rate of protection of industry and the anti-export bias in the incentive structure have been reduced. The argument—at least in the long run—is not in favour of export-led growth but in favour of neutrality in the incentive system with respect to the market orientation of production. Kelkar and Raipuria differ from Chishti in their assessment of the growth opportunities for exports and the capacity of India's manufacturing sector to exploit opportunities to penetrate foreign markets once the incentive system has been sufficiently adapted. Export pessimism may be in place with respect to primary products, but not so much in the case of manufactures. In their assessment, the institutional framework is adequate and the economy has a diversified basis for exports ranging from simple labour intensive products by small-scale industries to capital and skill intensive products.

INDIA'S TRADE AND INDUSTRIALIZATION REGIME

Introduction

In this section we will highlight the main characteristics of India's trade and industrialization regime in the past and discuss in detail more recent changes in policies. In particular we will focus on the instruments that have been used to stimulate the manufacturing sector to export. In the following section we will highlight the main direction of change in India's trade and industrialization regime up to 1980 by applying the scheme for regime classification proposed by Bhagwati and Krueger. This will be followed by a discussion of import barriers and export incentives. In the next section we will focus on the emerging balance-of-payments crisis and the rising debt servicing problems in the beginning of the 1980s, and on the sets of proposals for changes towards liberalization and export stimulation in order to cope with the external payment position.

Finally, we will review the elements of the new import-export policy for the period 1985–88.

A classification of the trade regime before 1980

The classification scheme proposed by Bhagwati and Krueger is a useful tool to highlight major changes in India's economic policy up to 1980.[18] The scheme distinguishes five phases in the process of liberalization:

- Phase I : Quantitative restrictions are imposed and intensified.
- Phase II : Quantitative restrictions are still intense but various price measures are adopted to offset some of the undesired results.
- Phase III: Attempts are made to systematize the changes which take place in the previous phase.
- Phase IV: If changes in Phase III lead to adjustment in the country so that liberalization can continue: increased foreign exchange earnings and relaxation of quantitative restrictions.
- Phase V : Full liberalization.

Since independence the framework of economic policy has been laid down in a series of Five-Year Plans. The first of these plans, which spans the period 1951–56, was not so much a genuine national development plan but merely a set of projects financed by the public sector. The Second Plan (1956–61), based upon the Feldman-Mahalanobis model, focused on industrial targeting and licencing and exchange control over all current transactions. Imports were controlled through import licences.[19] Import substitution was stimulated while exports were not considered a line of activity to be stimulated. During this period the incentive regime was in Phase I according to the classification scheme of Bhagwati and Krueger.[20] The Third Plan (1961–66) assigned a higher value to improved export performance as indicated by the expressed need for creating an 'atmosphere' more favourable to export industries, diversification of export markets and the development of export-support services such as promotion councils, state trading houses and export houses.[21] Following Bhagwati and Srinivasan, the regime at that time can be classified as in Phase II. A shift towards export subsidization on a large scale took place. The economy entered Phase III (1966–68) with a devaluation in June 1966 to systematize and rationalize the export incentive system. At the same time, export subsidies were reduced and export duties imposed, turning the substantial nominal devaluation of the rupee of 57.5 per cent into a net devaluation of 21.6 per cent for exports and 42.3 per cent for imports.[22] Consequently, the net effect was a further stimulation of import substitution over export production.

However, the devaluation was not a prelude to a phase of comprehensive liberalization and adjustment—the economy moved back to Phase II (1968–70). Nevertheless, during the Fourth Plan (1969–74) liberalization and export stimulation were considered increasingly crucial to enhance efficiency and competitiveness of domestic industry and for balance-of payments reasons.

While scrutinizing export promotion measures, Wolf concluded that these measures were inadequate to have any major impact on export performance for a number of reasons. First, the cash assistance programme, the most important incentive introduced in 1966, suffered from some serious shortcomings. The programme was highly concentrated on only a few products, especially engineering goods, chemicals and cotton textiles. These products accounted for only 17 per cent of total exports but received 70 per cent of total disbursements. Also, cash assistance was announced quarterly which hampered the development of export-oriented investment plans. Finally, disbursement was frequently delayed.[23]

The programme of cash assistance was modified several times. The number of products eligible to receive cash assistance was increased in October 1975 but the rates of assistance for the new products were lower than those for engineering goods. The basis for computing cash assistance was modified in 1975 and again in 1978 with the new rates being effective from 1979–80. The latter change, recommended by the Alexander Committee, probably reduced the effect of the programme for many products. Thus, the programme was still limited to a small number of companies, lacked consistency in time, and hardly provided assistance for infant export activities.

Import Replenishment Licences were also introduced in 1966. Again, there was a strong bias in the programme in favour of engineering goods and chemicals. Moreover, the incentive provided by the licence is unstable since its value fluctuates with the relative scarcity of foreign exchange. The value of the licence is also highly dependent on the transferability of the licence. In 1975–76 import licences were increased by 10 per cent for many exports and by an additional 10 per cent for those products for which licences were less than 50 per cent. The transferability was increased and in 1976–77 the number of items permissible to import also increased.[24] In 1977–78 the licencing system was further liberalized. Restrictions on permissible imports were abolished and licences could be nominated in favour of any manufacturer. However, in 1978–79, the rates and the number of export categories eligible for Import Replenishment Licences were reduced again following the recommendations of the Alexander Committee.[25] In a subsequent change in 1980–81, restrictions on the range of importables were again relaxed if the imported items were used for export production.[26]

A third major element of the export stimulation policy is the Duty Drawback System which provides drawbacks of excise and import duties to exporters of manufactures. There were, however, several export stimulation measures in use other than the three categories mentioned above but these three appear to be the most important, apart from the exchange rate policy. Export stimulation during the period under review resulted mainly from: (*a*) a devaluation of the nominal exchange rate and the purchasing-power-parity-exchange rate; (*b*) an increased incentive rate for manufactured exports through increased spendings on trade promotion (cash assistance); and (*c*) increased duty drawbacks. The trend in the contribution of the system of Import Replenishment Licences appears to be less distinct.[27]

On the whole, export consciousness in policy formulation increased during the 1970s. Despite numerous changes and adaptations in the regime, a tendency is discernible of increased export stimulation while maintaining a high rate of tariff protection for domestic industry and strict import controls, resulting in domestic prices exceeding world market prices.

Import barriers and export incentives

Import barriers

The protectionist nature of the Indian trade and industrialization regime is illustrated by the data on tariff protection presented in

Tables 3 and 4. Columns 1–3 of Table 3 give some proxies for the dependence of government on tariff revenue for meeting its expenses. The contribution of import duties to the tax revenue of the central government increased considerably during the 1970s and 1980s. Thus, while the share of the government budget in total domestic expenditure increased, an increasing proportion of government spending was financed out of taxes on international trade, particularly out of taxes on imports. Taxes on imports and other taxes on international trade such as exchange taxes, taxes on tourism and on travel fares abroad have only limited importance for government revenue.

Column 4 of Table 3 shows the ratio of taxes on imports to the value of total imports which is a proxy for the general level of protection of domestic economic activity. As compared to other

TABLE 3

Taxes on Imports, 1974–1987 (in percentages)

	Import Duties / *Tax Revenue*	*Taxes on International Trade* / *Tax Revenue*	*Taxes on International Trade* / *Total Government Revenue*	*Import Duties* / *Total Imports*
1974	19.3	23.1	19.7	29.7
1975	17.4	19.4	15.8	25.4
1976	16.9	20.0	16.0	29.4
1977	17.8	21.0	16.1	28.4
1978	21.0	22.6	17.9	35.5
1979	23.4	24.4	19.8	37.8
1980	24.8	26.4	21.2	30.3
1981	26.6	27.6	22.0	32.8
1982	28.2	29.8	23.3	34.9
1983	27.4	29.0	22.2	33.7
1984	29.7	30.0	23.4	40.6
1985	32.9	33.2	26.0	47.6
1986	34.5	35.8	27.3	47.9
1987*	34.3	35.2	27.5	51.9

Note: * Provisional data.

Sources: Data on government revenue taken from IMF, *Government Finance Statistics Yearbook*, Washington DC, various issues. Data on imports taken from UNCTAD, *Handbook of International Trade and Development Statistics*, United Nations, New York, various issues.

TABLE 4
Nominal Tariff Rates on Imports of Manufacturers, 1980 (in Percentages)

	Number of Tariff Lines	*Mean*	*Mode*	*Variation*	*Percentage Share of Tariff Lines Affected by Specific Tariffs*
Food Products	42	85.2	100.0	820.7	0
Beverages	13	183.8	100.0	7,242.3	13.3
Tobacco	3	100.0	100.0	0.0	0
Textiles	165	105.9	100.0	1,240.2	0
Wearing Apparel	97	100.0	100.0	0.0	0
Leather and Leather Goods	13	75.4	60.0	410.3	0
Footwear	5	100.0	100.0	0.0	0
Wood and Wood Products	27	57.8	60.0	41.0	0
Furniture and Fixtures	7	100.0	100.0	0.0	0
Paper and Paper Products	50	86.0	100.0	591.8	0
Printing and Publishing	13	53.8	100.0	2,692.3	0
Industrial Chemicals	690	65.8	60.0	452.0	0.1
Other Chemical Products	161	66.8	60.0	235.5	0
Petroleum Refineries and Manufactures	22	44.9	40.0	342.8	15.4
Rubber Products	16	96.3	100.0	225.0	0
Plastic Products	9	100.0	100.0	0.0	0
Pottery, China	3	100.0	100.0	0.0	0
Glass and Glass Products	19	93.7	100.0	224.6	0
Other Non-metallic Mineral Production	29	89.7	100.0	360.6	0
Iron and Steel	83	76.1	60.0	5,585.0	0
Non-ferrous Metals	37	67.6	60.0	452.3	0
Metal Products	87	77.0	100.0	618.9	0
Agricultural Machinery	22	44.5	40.0	73.6	0
Other Non-electrical Machinery	195	49.4	40.0	347.6	0
Other Transport Equipment	44	52.3	40.0	487.7	0
Professional Goods	66	67.3	60.0	684.8	0
Other Manufactures	90	91.6	100.0	458.2	1.1
Non-durable Consumer Goods	343	92.6	100.0	470.1	0.3
Beverages and Tobacco	16	168.1	100.0	6,936.3	11.1

Table 4 *(Continued)*

	Number of Tariff Lines	*Mean*	*Mode*	*Variation*	*Percentage Share of Tariff Lines Affected by Specific Tariffs*
Durable Consumer Goods	35	76.9	60.0	639.8	0
Intermediates	1,347	72.7	60.0	1,029.1	0.4
Capital Goods	387	57.7	40.0	594.6	0
Total Manufacturing	2,128	74.0	60.0	1,065.9	0.4

Source: UNCTAD tape.

countries in the world, this ratio is extremely high in India. Most primary imports, such as food and fuels, however, are imported free of taxes and the ratios therefore underestimate the dependence of protected domestic producers on taxes on trade.

The rate of protection for manufacturing sectors in 1980 is presented in Table 4. Altogether 2,128 tariff lines are applied for manufactured products. A total of 27 product groups have been differentiated according to the International Standard Industrial Classification (ISIC) for manufacturing activities and five major clusters of such activities. For each group the table shows the number of tariff lines, the mean tariff rate and the mode, the variation in tariff rates and the percentage share of tariff lines affected by specific tariffs. According to the mean values, the consumer goods industries have the highest rates of tariff protection while protection is somewhat less substantial in sectors producing intermediates and capital goods. This is in line with the structure of protection that is usually observed in developing countries. The most frequently applied tariff rates are: in the sector of non-durable consumer goods 100 per cent, in the sector of durable consumer goods and intermediates 60 per cent, and in the sector of capital goods 40 per cent. Surprisingly, traditional and labour intensive sectors such as textiles, wearing apparel, footwear, and pottery have nominal rates of tariff protection above the average rate for manufacturing. Most capital goods sectors, which are usually rather capital and skill intensive by nature, such as agricultural machinery, non-electrical machinery and transport equipment, have low rates of tariff protection. International comparisons of the frequency and levels of tariff rates show that India is one of the most protectionist countries in the world, and that both the government and industries are highly dependent on the income effects of these import controls.

Apart from tariffs on imports, non-tariff barriers are frequently applied as well to limit the penetration of the Indian market by foreign competitors, and to keep the balance-of-payments situation under control.

Indicators of the frequency of application of some non-tariff barriers are presented in Table 5. Like the data on tariff barriers presented earlier, these data were obtained from the UNCTAD Trade Information System. The percentages refer to the frequency of incidence of non-tariff barriers relative to the total number of items in the category specified. In the category of primary products restrictive licencing is not applied frequently, the major exception being the group of beverages and tobacco (SITC 1). In the categories of manufactured products, licences are more frequently applied, particularly to regulate imports of machines and transport equipment (SITC 7). Prohibitions are applied only for some food items (SITC 0), notably, oils and fats (SITC 4). Imports of crude materials (SITC 2) and basic manufactures (SITC 6) are canalized through state trading houses to a relatively high degree, but it is not known to what extent such canalization restricts trade.

In 1978–79 the Alexander Committee recommended the application of a negative list system. The items that were not subject to import restrictions or import bans were listed but most of these listed items were not produced domestically and were not foreseen to be produced domestically in the near future. In 1980–81 competitive imports tended to become more restricted due to the balance-of-payments situation.

Export incentives

Given the complexity of the total incentive system and the numerous changes that have taken place, it is difficult to estimate the price effects of the system and its impact on the market orientation of production. In 1982 Wolf concluded that (*a*) export incentives were highly concentrated in only a few industries (especially engineering goods and chemicals); (*b*) they were part of a regime

TABLE 5

Frequency of Non-tariff Barriers (in percentages)

	Food, Live Animals (SITC 0)	*Beverage, Tobacco (SITC 1)*	*Crude Materials (SITC 2)*	*Mineral Fuels (SITC 3)*	*Animal & Vegetable Oil and Fats (SITC 4)*	*Chemicals (SITC 5)*	*Basic Manufactures (SITC 6)*	*Machines, Transport Equipment (SITC 7)*	*Miscellaneous Manufactured Goods (SITC 8)*
Restrictive Licencing	5.8	30.4	13.0	10.3	3.3	23.2	21.0	32.7	17.7
Prohibitions	1.6	0.0	0.0	0.0	23.3	0.0	0.0	0.0	0.0
State Trading Monopolies	0.0	0.0	12.5	5.1	0.0	1.2	16.9	0.8	1.0

Source: D.A. DeRosa, Trade and protection in the Asian developing region, *Asian Development Review*, Vol. 4, No. 1, 1986, p. 41, Table 5.

that was generally conducive to inefficiency; (*c*) there was a substantial burden of administrative costs and delays; and (*d*) uncertainty about the value of incentives made export expansion a risky venture.[28]

The values of export incentives presented in Table 6 are based on the values of export promotion assistance, cash assistance, duty drawbacks, premiums on replenishment licences, less the value of export taxes. The calculated values of net incentives for exports are relatively low compared with the average rate of import duties. This rate varied between 25.8 per cent and 32.3 per cent during the period and was 29.2 per cent on an average. However, the anti-export bias in the incentive system for manufactures was reduced given a rather stable overall rate of import duties and the increasing net positive incentive rates for manufactured exports. Also, it can be observed that the net incentive rate for manufactured exports exceeded the rate for non-manufactured exports throughout the period. Incentives for exports of primary products such as food and beverages, and for raw materials were even negative. Among the groups of manufactured products, chemicals received by far the highest rate of net export incentives, but in the course of time incentive for other product groups increased and the dispersion in incentive rates decreased.

The increased value of export stimulation measures and the reduced concentration of such measures in only a few product groups during the 1970s and the early 1980s can further be substantiated by focusing on the major incentives separately. The role of cash assistance in stimulating exports of 15 product groups is shown in Tables 7 and 8. At the beginning of the period under review, cash assistance was almost entirely concentrated in the sectors of engineering goods, chemicals and allied products: 88.6 per cent of the total value of cash assistance in 1974–75 was allotted to these two sectors. At the end of the period, however, only a little over 50 per cent of total cash assistance disbursements were concentrated in these two sectors. As indicated earlier, major traditional export industries such as food processing, beverage processing, jute products, textiles and garments, hardly received any cash assistance during the first 10 years of the programme. The change in allocation of funds since 1974–75, however, has been significantly in favour of some such industries as shown in Table 7. Processed food has become a major recipient of cash assistance.

TABLE 6

Net Incentive Rates for Exports, 1973–74 to 1978–79 (in percentages)

	All Imports	*Food and Beverages*	*Raw Materials (incl. Fuels)*	*Manufactures*	*Chemicals*	*Machinery and Transport Equipment*	*Other Manufactures*
1973–74	2.6	−2.6	−6.4	6.3	28.8	3.4	3.4
1974–75	2.6	−1.6	−4.9	5.5	18.1	2.8	2.8
1975–76	4.6	−1.4	−4.1	7.2	18.7	5.1	5.1
1976–77	5.9	−4.0	−3.7	7.8	20.1	5.7	5.7
1977–78	5.4	−9.7	−4.5	10.9	30.8	8.1	8.1
1978–79	8.4	−3.7	−4.8	12.5	27.3	9.5	9.5

Source: M. Wolf, *India's Exports*, Oxford University Press, New York, 1982, pp. 100–105, Tables 4.7 and 4.8.

TABLE 7
Distribution of Cash Assistance Over 15 Export Product Groups (in percentages)

	1974–75	*1978–79*	*1983–84*
Engineering Goods	65.5	45.0	42.8
Chemicals and Allied Products	23.1	10.1	8.0
Plastic Products	2.0	1.0	0.8
Sports Goods	3.2	1.1	0.7
Processed Food	0.3	4.7	6.1
Instant Tea, Packet Tea and Tea Bags etc.	..	3.0	0.2
Instant Coffee etc.	..	0.1	1.1
Woollen Carpets, Rugs and Druggets	3.5	8.5	8.8
Jute Products	..	6.0	2.6
Fish and Fish Products	..	0.3	0.4
Finished Leather and Leather Manufactures	2.0	11.5	11.7
Handicrafts	..	4.4	2.9
Natural Silk Fabrics, Garments and Made-ups, Synthetic Fabrics and Garments etc.	0.3	4.2	4.5
Woollen/Blended Knitwear	..	..	0.3
Cotton Handlooms	..	..	9.1

Note: .. Not available.
Source: *Report of the Committee on Trade Policies*, New Delhi, 1984, pp. 110–11, Table 11.

Other sectors which received cash assistance were woollen carpets, finished leather and cotton textiles, including the handloom sector.

Although the absolute amounts of cash assistance disbursements increased substantially during the 1970s and the early 1980s, the ratio of total disbursements to the total value of manufactured exports decreased as shown in Table 8. Engineering products received the highest export stimulation through cash assistance throughout the period under study. Fluctuations in the rate of stimulation are discernible in the case of some traditional export products such as handicrafts, garments, knitwear and leather products. However, it is hard to infer a pattern from these data. At the end of the period, jute products still received a low cash incentive and many of the other traditional exports showed a rate of stimulation below the average for all product groups that are included in the table.

The values and percentage changes in values of four types of

Table 8

Cash Assistance as a Percentage of the F.O.B. Value of Exports, 1970–71 to 1983–84

	1970–71	1971–72	1972–73	1973–74	1974–75	1975–76	1976–77	1977–78	1978–79	1979–80	1980–81	1981–82	1982–83	1983–84
Engineering Products	14.5	15.9	16.7	15.9	16.1	14.8	15.3	14.4	15.3	16.1	14.2	15.1	14.1	14.8
Chemicals and Allied Products	13.7	15.3	15.3	14.4	14.9	13.3	12.7	12.8	13.1	11.4	10.2	10.1	10.0	9.8
Plastic Goods	9.4	11.3	9.3	9.3	9.2	9.7	10.1	9.5	10.0	9.3	9.5	10.1	11.5	9.6
Sports Goods	14.5	19.9	18.9	19.7	19.4	16.2	14.9	14.1	14.5	14.6	14.8	15.2	14.6	12.6
Processed Food	8.5	7.9	9.8	7.4	8.0	13.8	12.8	11.9	10.9	10.0	7.0	8.4	8.3	9.2
Instant Tea, Packet Tea and Tea Bags etc.						10.0	9.9	10.4	9.6	11.3	13.4	12.3	12.7	13.0
Instant Coffee etc.							10.0	10.0	10.0	10.0	10.0	9.9	10.0	5.6
Woollen Carpets, Rugs & Druggets	10.5	10.1	9.3	10.2	5.7	11.0	15.1	17.5	16.9	17.3	16.9	15.9	14.6	14.0
Jute Products						9.8	9.2	9.9	10.0	7.4	7.4	7.5	7.2	4.7
Fish and Fish Products						6.1	4.9	5.6	5.4	5.0	6.5	6.0	6.6	5.1
Finished Leather and Leather Manufactures		8.4	8.5	5.2	5.6	5.2	6.1	2.4	12.9	11.2	11.0	12.3	11.9	11.3
Handicrafts					5.1	8.7	12.1	13.1	14.7	13.1	6.9	9.9	9.4	9.1
Natural Silk Fabrics, Garments and Made-ups, Synthetic Fabrics and Garments etc.		9.9	10.1	..	7.6	9.9	12.6	13.1	13.9	13.1	12.4	11.4	10.8	8.5
Woollen/Blended Knitwear						15.0	12.1	10.1	9.8	10.7	14.3	..	..	7.0
Cotton Handlooms					14.1	13.2	12.2	9.1	13.7	13.2	11.8	12.7	11.9	11.2

Note: .. Not available.

Source: *Report of the Committee on Trade Polices*, New Delhi, 1984, p. 113, Table 13.

export incentives—duty drawback, market development assistance, cash assistance and other kinds of assistance—are presented in Table 9. Market development assistance and cash assistance have become two major pecuniary incentives for export industries, the values of which increased at a considerably higher rate than the value of total exports. The category of other assistance includes disbursements under the export credit development scheme, grant-in-aid to export promotion councils and other organizations, and other kinds of disbursements for export industries. Dividing the value of total assistance to export industries (col. 6) by the values of exports (col. 2), we obtain the relative export incentives (col. 7). The column indicates that exports were increasingly stimulated by the government during the 1970s and the early 1980s. If it holds that protection against imports did not increase by the same rate, this would imply a reduced anti-export bias in India's trade and industrialization regime.

The last two columns of Table 9 relate to the import regime for exporters. The value of import licences issued for registered exporters increased at a much higher rate than the value of exports, indicating that exporters obtained increased access to imports.

Coping with the foreign exchange crisis

In the previous sections we have seen that India's export policy has not been successful when assessed in terms of the export performance of Indian companies or India's share in world markets. The share of exports in the output of manufactures did not increase during the 1970s and the early 1980s, and India's industries did not recapture shares of world markets. Meanwhile, the gap between the value of imports and exports increased and so did the debt service ratio, two developments that made a change in trade policy at the end of the 1970s imperative.

The IMF loan

The setting in which trade policies are formulated changed with the arrangement between the IMF and India, approved on 9 November 1981. The arrangement included an IMF loan to India of SDR 5 billion under the scheme of the Extended Financing

Facility, the largest of such loans approved by the Fund up to that moment and also the largest loan contracted by the Indian government. According to the arrangement, India could draw SDR 900 million up to 30 June 1982, another SDR 1,800 in the next year up to 30 June 1983, and the remainder up to the end of the three-year arrangement. Repayment of each drawing would begin in the fourth year and would be completed within a period of 10 years after the date of drawing. Drawings would be made only to finance the balance-of-payments. The loan would be in several foreign currencies.

The IMF loan changed the setting for trade policy formulation because of the substantial increase in future debt service obligations and because of the conditions on the loan as laid down in the letter of intent of the Indian government. These conditions touch upon all major areas of economic policy. In the context of this study we shall only highlight the conditions pertaining to India's trade and industrialization policies. The most important are those pertaining to import liberalization and export promotion.[29]

According to the letter of intent, the programme of import liberalization would be continued, especially with regard to raw materials, intermediate goods and capital goods. Throughout the duration of the arrangement, no import restrictions would be imposed or intensified for balance-of-payments reasons, and no multiple currency practices would be introduced. Also, the access of exporters to imports would further be facilitated. The key element in the list of intentions is the export promotion programme. Industries with a high export potential would be identified and offered special incentives to export such as cash compensation, fiscal and import concessions, and simplified and more comprehensive procedures for the duty exempt advance licencing scheme for exporters. Disincentives to exporters would be abolished such as domestic and trade taxes, quantitative restrictions and administrative constraints.

The programme of liberalization and export promotion, as outlined in the letter of intent, cannot be considered a break with trade policies as formulated in the earlier years. But the need to implement effective policies and to boost exports of manufactures had become much greater due to the substantial increase in debt service obligations. For that reason, the prevailing trade policies

TABLE 9

Export Stimulation Measures, 1972–73 to 1983–84

	Exports		*Duty Drawbacks*		*Market Development Assistance*		*Cash Assistance*	
	(Rs Crores)	*Change (%)*	*(Rs Crores)*	*Change (%)*	*(Rs Crores)*	*Change (%)*	*(Rs Crores)*	*Change (%)*
1972–73	1,970.83	22.5						
1973–74	2,523.40	28.0	42.3		62.4		52.4	
1974–75	3,328.83	31.9	60.0	41.84	76.4	22.4	59.9	14.31
1975–76	4,026.26	21.3	82.0	36.67	148.3	94.11	123.7	106.51
1976–77	5,142.71	27.4	120.0	46.34	239.6	61.56	226.4	83.02
1977–78	5,407.87	5.2	133.0	10.83	324.4	35.39	310.3	37.06
1978–79	5,726.07	5.9	150.0	12.78	375.2	15.66	359.0	15.69
1979–80	6,418.43	12.1	152.0	1.33	360.9	−3.81	344.1	−4.15
1980–81	6,710.70	4.6	164.0	7.89	399.1	10.58	376.4	9.39
1981–82	7,805.90	16.3	204.0	24.39	476.9	19.49	452.4	20.19
1982–83	8,834.21	13.2	127.0	−37.75	476.3	−0.13	448.8	−0.80
1983–84	9,865.30	11.7	132.0	3.94	461.4	−3.13	429.9	−4.21

	Other Assistance		Total Assistance		Total Assistance Export Value (%)	Value of Issued Import Licences for Registered Exporters (Rs Crores)	Share in Total Imports (%)
	(Rs Crores)	Change (%)	(Rs Crores)	Change (%)			
1972–73						136.0	7.3
1973–74	10.00		167.1		6.6	151.3	5.1
1974–75	16.50	65.0	212.8	27.3	6.4	166.4	3.7
1975–76	24.60	49.1	378.6	77.9	9.4	237.2	4.5
1976–77	13.20	−46.3	599.2	58.3	11.7	415.5	8.2
1977–78	14.10	6.8	781.8	30.5	14.5	741.4	12.3
1978–79	16.20	14.9	900.4	15.2	15.7	1,096.7	16.1
1979–80	16.80	3.7	873.8	−3.0	13.6	1,086.6	11.9
1980–81	22.70	35.1	962.2	10.1	14.3	1,422.0	11.3
1981–82	24.50	7.9	1,157.8	20.3	14.8	1,762.0	12.9
1982–83	27.50	12.2	1,079.6	−6.8	12.2	1,963.5	13.7
1983–84	31.50	14.5	1,054.8	−2.3	10.7	2,294.5	14.7

Source: *Report of the Committee on Trade Policies*, New Delhi, 1984, p. 98, Table 2; p. 109, Table 10; p. 119, Table 17.

were to be critically reviewed and new instruments were to be implemented. Concrete proposals for an improved and more comprehensive set of export promotion measures were made by the Committee on Trade Policies, the so-called Hussain Committee, and by the Narasimham Committee.

Proposals for a new trade policy

The Committee on Trade Policies concluded in its report of 1984 that the existing system of incentives was (*a*) complex, (*b*) did not promote the cause of efficiency, and (*c*) created a bias against exports. The Committee emphasized the need for a reorientation of the incentive structure for the manufacturing sector to enhance efficiency in production and to integrate production for the domestic and foreign markets. Rather than promoting import substitution per se, as done in the past, or export-led growth, which is neither feasible nor desirable for an economy like India, import substitution and export production should be stimulated in a balanced and equal manner by one set of policies.[30] The transition from a dual incentive approach towards a more integrated approach is a long-term objective. The restructuring process would have to be implemented in a planned and selective manner, not in a sudden and across-the-board fashion. The process of restructuring could start in a few leading sectors, selected according to the revealed or potential comparative advantages India enjoyed in the world economy.[31] At the same time, however, specific export promotion policies should be implemented in the short term to compensate for the existing bias against exports in the actually pursued policies. Exports should be stimulated in the short term to finance imports that are necessary for the continuation of economic growth and to service debts.

The fact that India lost its share in world markets of most manufactured products indicates that supply factors hinder export performance. The export promotion system which was in force was inadequate and inefficient. It was, at best, a compensation for the bias against exports that stemmed from the overall trade and industrialization regime, but it hardly provided any incentive for exporters and it did not stimulate infant export industries.[32] The Committee distinguished the following areas of export promotion: (*a*) the Duty Drawback System; (*b*) market development assistance;

(*c*) fiscal concessions for exporters; (*d*) import policies for exporters; and (*e*) EPZs.

Following a critical evaluation of the functioning of export promotion policies, several recommendations were made by the Committee:

1. The Duty Drawback System should provide a full reimbursement of taxes paid on imports that enter export production. The payment system should be simplified, delays in disbursements should be overcome and classification problems should be solved.[33]
2. The Cash Compensatory Support (henceforth CCS) regime should be maintained in its present form. The cash compensation itself should be exempted from income tax. The rates of compensation should not only be reduced but should also be announced for a period of three years. The remaining part of the cash assistance programme should be efficiently used to stimulate temporarily potentially successful infant export industries.
3. The present Import Replenishment Licence system should be revised to provide exporters with complete access to imported inputs at world market prices. Established exporters should be ensured of a permanent replenishment licence that provides them duty free imports of all inputs required for production in anticipation of exports.[34]
4. The real effective exchange rate should not be allowed to appreciate.
5. Half of the profits from exports should be exempted from income tax.
6. Export industries should be exempted from capacity licencing provisions and from restrictions on imports of capital goods and technology so as to increase productivity.[35]
7. There should be an exchange-entitlement scheme for exporters to provide them foreign exchange required for market development.
8. With respect to EPZs — two of which were already in operation and four more were envisaged to be established at the time — the administrative procedures should be facilitated by creating a single fully empowered authority handling the full functioning of all zones. The selection of industries allowed

> to operate in the zones should be based on the criteria of their contribution to technological development and skill creation. The actual practice of entitling companies operating in the zones to sell 25 per cent of their output in the domestic market should be continued.[36]

These recommendations aimed at creating a 'free trade' regime for export industries. Such a regime — characterized by a combination of import protection for domestic market-oriented industries and free trade for export-oriented industries — was only one step in the direction of full liberalization of the trade regime, albeit a crucial step in view of the urgent need for additional foreign exchange earnings. However, both reports offered a series of further recommendations to liberalize the trade and industrialization regime that will briefly be reviewed below. Such steps constituted a much more fundamental deviation from policies pursued in the past and were expected to have a far more significant impact on the functioning of the entire manufacturing sector. For this reason they were likely to be implemented at a much slower pace.

Traditionally, India's system of industrial promotion depends to a large extent on quantitative restrictions i.e. on administrative controls of production, investments and imports. Subsequent to the liberalization measures that had already been undertaken, the Narasimham Committee made recommendations to improve the operation of the licence system, to limit the system and to replace quantitative restrictions by financial measures. The Committee proposed that delicencing should be introduced for (*a*) industries producing products that are allowed to be imported freely; (*b*) industries in which there is prima facie need for capacity creation; (*c*) industries in which technology is rapidly changing, particularly producer goods industries and the energy sector; (*d*) industries producing specific mass consumption goods; and (*e*) industries producing exports.

For industries in which licences would be required, it was recommended that the efficiency criteria play a decisive role in the issuance of licences. The proposed criteria include: (*a*) the size of investment should allow an optimal exploitation of economies of scale; (*b*) inefficient import substitutes should not be encouraged; and (*c*) licenced capacity should be defined broadly so as to allow for flexibility in changing the product mix in accordance with the changes in demand and technology.

Regarding further liberalization of imports, a reduction of the role of import licences through its replacement by tariffs, lowering of import protection, and a reduction of the canalization of imports were recommended. With the growth in the volume of imports over time, the administration of the import licence system has become more complex. A system of import licencing may thus become opaque with respect to the availability and costs of licences and may lead to delays and misuse.[37] Import control through price measures is superior to discretionary control. The Narasimham Committee made some detailed recommendations on the transformation of the system of import protection of capital goods industries:

1. New industries should be granted tariff protection only.
2. The existing industries should be divided into three groups:
   (*a*) Industries where quantitative restrictions can immediately be replaced by tariffs with a maximum rate of 150 per cent.
   (*b*) In industries where (*a*) is relevant — provided that their inputs are delivered at competitive prices — a transitionary regime should be implemented in which protection is reduced with the lowering of protection for their input supplying industries.
   (*c*) Industries that have to be protected by quantitative controls for the time being. This may be the case for strategic reasons. For industries that are highly inefficient a transitionary regime should be implemented in which quantitative restrictions are gradually replaced by tariffs.
3. Tariffs on non-competing imports should be low.[38]

State Trading Houses play a critical role in the control and management of trade, particularly of imports. The canalization of imports increased significantly over time. By the early 1980s, 60 to 66 per cent of imports were canalized through such trading houses. The Committee on Trade Policies stated that canalization should only be applied exceptionally in case better terms of trade could be obtained in such a way that economies of scale could be realized in trade operations, or management of the supply of essential or strategic products was required. At the same time the Committee suggested that the number of trading houses be limited and operations concentrated in a small number of well diversified trading houses that have the capacity to be transformed into institutions with a potential for export promotion activities.[39]

The new import-export policy: 1985–1988

On 12 April 1985 a new import-export policy was announced, aiming at the stimulation of traditional and non-traditional exports, and at the liberalization of imports. By formulating — for the first time — a policy for a three-year period, an attempt was made to create a more stable and less opaque framework of regulations and incentives. However, this new import-export policy should not be seen as a break with policies pursued in the past or a shift towards export-oriented industrial growth. It is rather an articulation of previous policies with the inclusion of some new instruments. The objectives of the new import-export policy include the assurance of continuity in policy-making, facilitation of production through improved access to imports, strengthening the basis of export production, savings in imports, stimulation of technological upgrading, and a reduced dependence on quantitative measures such as licences. Many of the recommendations made by the Committee on Trade Policies were incorporated in the new import-export policy.

The Import-Export Passbook

A new instrument that was expected to play a key role in the new import-export policy is the Import-Export Passbook. The scheme which was intended to be effective from 1 October 1985, actually came into force on 1 January 1986. Its aim is to streamline the import procedures for exporters by providing duty free access to imported inputs for exporters of manufactures. The scheme is wider in scope and more flexible than the previous advance licencing scheme.

By January 1986, imports used for export production were exempted from customs duty as well as from additional duties on imports on the condition that the importer had been issued the necessary Import-Export Passbook incorporating the import licence. Moreover, the imports should be taken directly to the manufacturing plant and used for the purpose specified in the Passbook. Exports should take place within the period specified in the Passbook. Products should be imported in specified ports, and the products specified in the Passbook should not be sold or otherwise transferred to any other person without official approval. The validity of the Passbook for the purpose of import is 18 months and for the purpose of export 27 months. The Passbook is applicable only to registered manufactured exporters who have been regularly producing for export for at least three years and are eligible for an import licence. Other exporters including export (trading) houses are not eligible. The eligibility to imports is based on the annual average exports of the product concerned during the preceding three years plus 25 per cent thereof or the best year's exports of that product in any of the preceding three years plus 10 per cent thereof. The maximum entitlement for import is 150 per cent of this annual entitlement.

Supply to companies operating in EPZs or EOUs is considered 'deemed exports'. Exports to fulfil the export obligation in the Passbook are, of course, not eligible for Import Replenishment Licences but exports in excess of the obligatory value are. Finally, the importer is required to execute a bond with a bank guarantee for 10 per cent of the face value of the imports or 25 per cent of the customs duty payable thereon, whichever is higher. But a legal agreement could be reached with companies that have been exporting during the preceding five years with a minimum export value of Rs 50 lakhs in the preceding year.

After about six months, in August 1986, it was suggested to increase the number of companies eligible to a Passbook by lowering the export obligation from 75 per cent, the prevailing export share obligation, to 45 per cent, since only a few companies—about 25 at the time—had the capability to achieve such high export levels.

A new round of import liberalization of capital goods

In 1986 a number of important measures to liberalize imports took effect. After a long period in which domestic producers of capital goods had been protected and users had been isolated from foreign supply of technology and equipment through a rigid regime of import licences, tariffs and other import barriers, changes in import policy were implemented to stimulate technological development and the competitiveness of the Indian manufacturing sector. We will now highlight the most important elements of the new import policy for capital goods.

To begin with, the list of banned imports was, in fact, already done away with by 1984. Barring animal tallow, there was no ban on the import of any item. Import licencing had substantially been reduced by abolishing the category of automatic licences and shifting most of the items in that category—some 90 per cent of them—to the category of Open General Licence (henceforth OGL): 467 products on the list of automatic licences were on OGL and 60 on the limited permissible list. In total, the OGL list was expanded by about 600 items. In the new policy since 1986, government departments were allowed to import their requirements under OGL subject to specific conditions, instead of having to obtain a licence.

The canalization of trade had been reduced following decanalization of 53 items. This implies that the role of government to control external trade through state trading houses was reduced.

A general permission to import specifically mentioned capital goods and other essential production inputs was offered on the condition that (*a*) the importer was the actual user, (*b*) by importing, the production did not exceed the licenced or authorized capacity; (*c*) the imported equipment was new or, in the case of second-hand equipment, not older than seven years. Measures to liberalize imports of capital goods and other essential production inputs are as follows:

1. A general permission to import spare parts for manufacturing capital goods including accessories, ancillary equipment, control and laboratory equipment and safety appliances, installed or in use on 1 April of the licencing year (order 37).
2. Products supplied free of charge by foreign companies are permissible to import such as trade catalogues, blueprints and drawings relating to machinery and plant sites, work and building research data, technical and trade samples, advertisement material, all up to a specified value (order 38).
3. Instruments, accessories, tools and spares required by any research and development unit, scientific or research laboratory, institution of higher education and hospital (order 39).

4. Goods listed in Appendix 5 of the Import-Export Policy 1985–88 (Vol. I) by the designated public sector canalizing agencies mentioned in the Appendix (order 40).
5. Jigs, fixtures, dies and patterns, moulds, press tools (order 41).
6. Raw materials, components, consumables, machinery equipment, instruments, accessories, tools and spares, by the Oil and Natural Gas Commission, Oil India Limited, Gas Authority of India Limited and Bharat Gold Mines Limited (order 42).
7. Materials for Air India, Indian Airlines and other IATA members, such as spare parts, tyres and tubes, manuals, technical drawings, and technical literature (order 43).
8. Imports of medical instruments, spare parts of motor vehicles and agricultural tractors. All persons are eligible to import computers and computer-based systems below Rs 10 lakhs (cif) (order 44).
9. Raw materials, capital goods, components, consumables and spares for repairing of ocean-going vessels (order 45).
10. Any goods by government departments, central and state (order 46).
11. Machinery equipment, testing apparatus, tools and instruments required for the gem and jewellery industry by registered exporters and cooperative societies of goldsmiths and artisans (order 47).
12. Selected goods imported by government departments, government industrial undertakings that are departmentally run, railways, state electricity boards, undertakings, projects in the public sector, and public sector industrial undertakings under the ministry of defence (order 48).
13. Teaching aids; instruments and equipment required by blind; educational, scientific and technical books and journals; life-saving equipment; family welfare equipment; finished drug preparations; homoeopathic medicines; crude drugs required for making Ayurvedic and Unani medicines; pulses, spices (cinnamon, cassia, cloves); dates (wet or dry), imported by Indian sailing vessels; rock salt; X-ray films (medical); lubricating oils for watches, clocks, time-pieces and house-service meters; fishing hooks; non-fictional

educational and instrumental films including video films; photographic film (colour); photographic colour papers; photographic films (black and white) other than 120 and 620 size rolls; records for learning languages; rudraksha beads; cinematographic films 8 mm colour and black and white; dental items; items of ophthalmic use; ozone generating apparatus; smoke meters; exhaust gas analysers; energy saving/conservation equipment; spares of printing machinery, machine tools for cutting; forming, abrading and polishing metals, wood, glass and plastics; outboard motors up to 10 HP; laboratory and reagent chemicals; gibberellic acid (order 49).

14. Poultry vaccines required by poultry farms, hatcheries approved by the department of agriculture. Imports by permissible organizations, direct users of the intermediates, of medical gas cylinders of 10.2 litres water capacity and below; CO_2 gas cylinders up to 15 litres water capacity for fire extinguishers; broken electric motors; magnetic and electromagnetic water conditioning systems; grape guard paper; photographic chemicals; 3/4 inch U-matic and 1 inch video cassettes/tapes (order 50).
15. Capital goods required by mining and coal companies (order 51).
16. Raw materials, capital goods, components, consumables and spares required by actual users under the facilities available to non-resident Indians, purchased out of the importer's foreign exchange earnings and resources abroad with no remittance from India, for use in an (industrial) enterprise in India.

The new CCS policy

As seen earlier, the Import-Export Passbook is a major element of the new liberalization-cum-export stimulation policy. Besides, some measures have been adopted to improve the functioning of the CCS. The Committee on Trade Policies recommended that the CCS should be maintained but its functioning should be improved by exempting the CCS from income tax and by reducing the multiplicity in rates. Rates should continue to be announced for a period of three years and assistance for product or market development should be selective.[40] Essentially, the objections against the scheme before changes had been implemented related to the cumbersome administrative procedures, the delays in disbursements and the limited financial consequence of the scheme for many exporters. Textile exporters in particular felt that the export incentive provided under the CCS was inadequate as compared to the incentives offered in competing countries such as Pakistan and China.

The renewed CCS, announced on 1 April 1986 for a period of three years, covered 10 product groups: engineering goods, chemicals and allied products, plastic goods, leather and leather goods, sports goods, marine products, processed food and agricultural items, handicrafts, textiles, jute goods and coir products. As compared to the previous scheme, 30 items were added to the list. However, the scheme for cotton textiles was expected to come into operation in January 1987 and was to remain in effect till December 1988. The main element of the scheme was the reimbursement of unrefunded indirect taxes. Thus, this scheme was not one of export subsidization. The incidence of indirect taxes would be worked out on the basis of unrebated indirect taxes paid on inputs directly used in the production of exports, and the unrebated indirect taxes paid in the intermediate production stages. The scheme was simplified by reducing the number of rates from 17 to 7. The new range of rates would be between 5 and 20 per cent except for two products. The average CCS rates are shown in Table 10. It should be noted that engineering goods received the highest rate which is in keeping with the observations made earlier that the Indian government stimulates exports of such products in particular. Agricultural products and processed food items received a relatively low CCS rate. However, the new scheme included a special compensation for high domestic transportation costs for perishable agricultural products. In the textile and jute sectors the CCS rates are likely to be modified annually since these sectors supposedly require a more flexible approach.

Export processing zones

The rationale of establishing EPZs is that export production can be initiated without adjusting or transforming the regime of protection for companies producing for the domestic market. The implementation of a dual system of incentives allows a continuation

TABLE 10
Average CCS Rates (in percentages)

Engineering Goods	13.60
Chemicals and Allied Products	11.02
Plastic Goods	7.07
Agricultural Products and Processed Food Items	6.22
Leather Goods	10.68
Sports Goods	12.92
Textiles	11.49
Handicrafts and Carpets	12.74

Source: *Report of the Committee on Trade Policies*, 1984, p. 84.

of protectionist industrialization policies or the retarded implementation of a liberalization and restructuring process that is required to increase the efficiency and competitiveness of domestic manufacturing industry. By confining the export sector to a secluded area, this sector may contribute to foreign exchange earnings and employment opportunities while domestic industry continues to produce for domestic demand. In view of the numerous economic and political difficulties involved in liberalization, the strategy of creating EPZs to stimulate export is an attractive option for many governments.

Given the high level of protection offered to the Indian industry, the low efficiency and international competitiveness of large sections of the manufacturing sector and its rather poor export performance, the option of creating separate export enclaves appears to be an attractive one in the Indian context. Indeed, India was the first developing country to establish an EPZ. In 1965, one such zone was established in Kandla while in 1974 a second zone was set up—the Santa Cruz Electronic Export Processing Zone (SEEPZ) near Bombay. Although a special scheme for 100 per cent export-oriented units has been in force since 1980, the government has continued in its efforts to create additional EPZs. The fear of an increased deficit on the current account and of an unmanageable debt service situation, the continuous loss of international markets, and the rather limited success of the EOU scheme have been three important reasons for the government to step up its efforts to create new zones in the mid-1980s. Such a policy had also been recommended by the Tandon Committee Report on Export Processing Zones, released in 1980. The decision to create four zones was taken in 1983. The new zones are located in Madras and Cochin, and near New Delhi (NOIDA) and Calcutta (Falta). Plans have been made to develop still other zones in Chandaka near Bhuvaneswar and in Jallandhar in Punjab.

The 90 acres zone in Madras located in the heart of the city has been planned as a model for the entire Southeast Asian region. It was expected that by the end of 1985 production in this zone as well as in the Falta zone would formally begin since customs and excise notifications governing the conditions of duty exemptions had been issued. The NOIDA zone of 82 acres was declared an EPZ on 20 January 1986. By mid-1986 plans were developed to extend the zone by 200 acres. The first phase of the Falta zone of 280 acres was expected to be completed by April 1987. The Cochin zone of 112 acres experienced delays in construction. The response of domestic and foreign investors has been below expectations. It seems likely that it would take some more time before the zones in Madras, NOIDA and Cochin make significant contributions to export earnings.

In the Kandla and the Santa Cruz zones, the first two zones to be established, many more units were in operation than in the more recently established zones, but nevertheless the contribution of these zones to India's export of manufactures has been limited till now. It took nearly 10 years for the Kandla zone to start exporting. By the middle of 1986, over 110 production units were in operation, six of which are TNCs. However, about 50 per cent of the zone's exports were produced by only 10 units. Over 87 per cent of total exports were destined for the market of the former USSR.

The Santa Cruz zone of 100 acres was the only single product zone in India, exporting exclusively electronic products and components such as computer components, peripheral and other electronic components. Recently, attempts have been made to develop exports of consumer electronics and computer software. Two-thirds of India's exports of electronics are concentrated in the zone. The major export markets were the Far East (50 per cent), the USA (35 per cent), Western Europe (10 per cent) and the former USSR and Eastern Europe (8 per cent). Out of 59 electronic export units in operation in the zone, 25 were in collaboration with foreign companies. The export performance of the zone, however, was strongly concentrated in one Indian company that contributed 45 per cent of total exports. Since August 1986, however, the

Santa Cruz zone is no longer a single product zone as gold jewellery units have been allowed to operate. The area of the zone was expanded by 50 acres that house the 100 per cent export-oriented jewellery complex.

Supposedly, an EPZ creates a free trade environment, allowing for duty free imports of capital goods and intermediate inputs, tax free exports of manufactures and, at least for the initial period, tax free profit remittances. Also, it overcomes the problem of administrative control and bureaucratic intervention. Ultimately, the objective is to attract foreign companies to establish export units. For a long period, however, the Indian zones did not provide adequate incentives and a sufficiently efficient administrative system to turn them into attractive export platforms for TNCs.[41]

To improve the functioning of the zones the Tandon Committee and the Committee on Trade Policies made a series of recommendations. Both Committees stressed the need of a single fully empowered commercially-oriented administrative body handling the total functioning of all zones. The lack of smooth and limited administrative procedures had been identified as one of the causes of slow progress of the zones. Also, both Committees stressed the need to allow companies to sell 25 per cent of their production in the domestic market. In addition to this, the Tandon Committee recommended a tax holiday of 10 years. A comprehensive draft bill providing for a modal authority with discretionary financial powers for overseeing the zones was prepared by the Commerce Ministry in April 1985. Also, it was proposed to expand the existing five-year tax holiday to 10 years and to allow free sale of products from the zones to the domestic market as opposed to the prevailing practice of sales against valid import licences.

On 8 August 1985, a special group of cabinet ministers decided to accept the recommendations of the Committee on Trade Policies and a central free trade zone authority was planned. This high powered statutory authority would manage and control all EPZs, and would have the status of a holding company. In April 1986, it was expected that a legislation would be passed in the ongoing session of Parliament and that the authority would come into operation soon after parliamentary approval. Also, by July 1986, the tax holiday in the zones was extended by three years.

The most important incentives provided to companies operating in the zones included 100 per cent foreign ownership units or joint ventures of foreign and Indian companies with a majority of foreign equity which was under consideration; up to 25 per cent of production could be sold in the domestic market; a five-year tax holiday during the initial production period of eight years; exemption from taxes on profits; permission to repatriate profits; imports of capital goods and intermediate inputs under the OGL scheme and exemption from import duties; administrative attempts to reduce redtapism.

Although the contribution of the EPZs to total exports of manufactures has been limited till now, expectations are rising as witnessed by the targets for the EPZs during the Seventh Five-Year Plan (1985–90) presented in Table 11.

TABLE 11
Targets for EPZs During the Seventh Five-Year Plan, 1985–1990

EPZ	*Value of Manufactured Exports*		*(Rs Crores)*
	1984–85	*1985–86*	*1989–90*
Santa Cruz	75	140	345
Kandla	200	250	400
Falta	..	64	256
Madras	15	..	250
Cochin	5	..	100
NOIDA	..	5	350

Note: .. No data available.
Source: I.C. Singhal, Free trade zones, *Economic Times*, 1 July 1985.

Export-oriented units

Having reviewed the reactivated policy of establishing EPZs, some remarks are in place with regard to the scheme for 100 per cent EOUs. This scheme was implemented in 1981 to provide duty free access to imports of all inputs for such export-oriented companies and to create a single point clearance with regard to industrial licencing and foreign collaborations. A company is required to fulfil three conditions to be eligible as an EOU: (*a*) its output should entirely be exported; (*b*) the domestic value added content of the export value should be 20 per cent at least; and (*c*) export production should be under a custom bond for 10 years, or five years for products facing rapid technological change. However, compared to companies operating in the EPZs such EOUs are at a distinct disadvantage. The advantages EOUs enjoy were considered limited anyhow, particularly after the implementation of the Import-Export Passbook. For this reason an increasing number of companies pleaded to be debound, and the scheme virtually collapsed. The scheme was never really successful. As by September 1985, 453 companies held valid letters of intent to become 100 per cent EOUs, but only 80 of them were reported to be in production and exporting at the end of June 1985. About 80 per cent of total exports of these companies were generated by four units that exported bulk items such as iron ore, charged chrome and minerals. The contribution of EOUs to total exports was low and decreased further. While the targeted value of export of these companies during the period 1981–85 was Rs 5,000 crores, the realized value was only Rs 355.41 crores. The contribution of EOUs to total exports excluding oil was 2.65 per cent in 1983–84, 3.06 per cent in 1984–85 and 0.41 per cent in 1985–86.

A disadvantage facing the EOUs is that these units have to pay themselves for the customs staff in service at the plant site to administer import, export and processing activities. This contribution has been reduced in the course of time from 250 per cent of the annual salary of such officials to 150 per cent, and further reduction is envisaged. To accommodate the relative disadvantage of the EOUs, it has been considered to offer them incentives equal to those offered to companies in the EPZs by extending the tax holiday, and further reducing excise and customs duty. Also, it has been proposed to allow the EOUs to sell 25 per cent of their sales in the domestic market as allowed to companies operating in the EPZs since September 1986.

The seventh plan: 1985–1990

We have seen that during the Sixth Plan period, a series of instruments was applied to stimulate exports of manufactures. Nevertheless, exports and imports grew more slowly than was anticipated and the overall trade deficit (at constant prices) was about 18 per cent higher than anticipated. Also, the growth rate of industrial production was 5.5 per cent which is well below the targeted rate of 7.2 per cent and below the realized growth rate of 6 per cent in the previous three decades.

The Seventh Plan aimed at a revitalization and modernization of the industrial sector, particularly of the capital goods sector, a reduction of quantitative control of production and trade, a containment of imports and a boost of exports. The annual growth of gross value added at factor costs in the manufacturing sector was targeted to grow at 5.5 per cent annually during the period 1985–90. Targeted growth rates were particularly high for the sectors of non-electrical engineering goods (8.2 per cent) and electrical engineering (9.5 per cent). Liberalization of imports of capital goods was expected to lead to an upgrading of technology, a reduction of domestic resource costs and enhanced international competitiveness of the sector.

The system of quantitative controls had become complicated and difficult to operate and consequently led to inefficiency and delays. Therefore, the Plan aimed at substituting tariffs for quantitative restrictions and also at reducing the variability of protection among the sectors.

The possibilities for increasing efficient import substitution on a large scale were expected to be limited. Given the need to enlarge imports of capital goods to modernize the manufacturing sector, and the reduced possibility to obtain foreign exchange on favourable terms through grants and soft loans, the Plan aimed at boosting exports of manufactures, particularly of engineering goods. In order to realize this goal, it was proposed that the export sector should not be treated as a separate enclave distinct from the rest of the manufacturing sector, but an integrated policy for all industries should be implemented to enhance export performance. More particularly, the bias against exports should be further reduced. Although the new import-export policy created a more liberal regime for exporting companies by facilitating imports and by reducing the tax burden, the heavily protected domestic market still offered an opportunity for companies to realize sales and profits more easily than foreign markets do. This relative attractiveness of the domestic market probably accounted for the limited success of many export promotion measures adopted till now, including the EPZs, the EOUs and the Import-Export Passbook. The actual exports in 1984–85 and the targeted exports for 1989–90 at constant prices are presented in Table 12.

The table illustrates that according to the export targets for the Seventh Plan a substantial share of the absolute increase in the

TABLE 12
Export Targets for the Seventh Plan

Product Group	*Rs Crores at 1984–85 Prices*	
	1984–85	*1989–90*
Tea	718	770
Coffee	221	232
Tobacco Manufactured	212	258
Cashew Kernel	217	312
Processed Food	328	424
Spices	217	270
Marine Products	388	446
Jute Manufactures	207	222
Iron Ore	438	608
Leather and Leather Manufactures	533	577
Cotton Textiles	380	440
Garments	875	1,336
Engineering Goods	879	1,862
Chemicals and Allied Products	760	1,224
Gems and Jewellery	1,367	1,663
Other Handicraft	415	494
Others	1,816	2,693
Total	9,971	13,831

Source: Government of India, Planning Commission, *The Seventh Five Year Plan, 1985–1990*, Vol. 1, New Delhi, October 1985, pp. 63, 64, Table 5.3.

value of exports was expected to be realized by the engineering goods and chemical goods sectors. Although exports of engineering goods were stimulated for a very long period of time, the export performance of this sector continued to be poor. Most large companies in this sector did not have any corporate strategy for export and did not consider export an integral element of their sales promotion. Nearly 80 per cent of engineering exports were produced by small- and medium-scale companies. It has been reported that the international competitiveness of the engineering and steel sectors has been weakened by domestic steel prices and energy prices being far above world market prices, and by the adoption of energy intensive absolute technology. Consequently, the Indian industry lost its share in world markets to new competitors such as South Korea and Taiwan.

In order to stimulate exports of engineering goods, special facilities have to be provided for 'thrust' industries, including easy access to imported raw materials and accessories, permission to import non-competing capital goods at either very low rates of duty or duty free, and lower prices for energy (diesel) for companies with an export-output ratio of at least 25 per cent that want to install captive power generating units.

The new import-export policy: 1988–91

The main elements of the trade and industrialization policy have been incorporated in a second scheme to liberalize import and promote exports. This comprehensive system of import regulations and export incentives sets the stage for the export performance of India's industry during the final years of the Seventh Plan period and the first part of the Eighth Plan (April 1988 to March 1991).[42]

The evaluation of the first import-export policy during the period 1985–88 indicated that the formulation of trade policies for a three-year period was indeed preferable over the earlier practice according to which policies were frequently changed, thus creating an opaque and unstable climate for investment and trade. It is true, however, that during the period of the first import-export policy, import controls and export incentives were adjusted, and undoubtedly this would have to be done again in the future. It should be noted that the main objectives of the new import-export policy, as formulated by the Ministry of Commerce, were not trade promotion as such but, first and foremost, stimulation of industrial growth by providing access to essential capital goods, raw materials and intermediate goods. Second, promotion of efficient import substitution and self-reliance. Third, to give 'a fresh impetus to export promotion' by improving the functioning of the incentive system and its administration. Finally, trade policies should be simplified and rationalized.

The combined objectives of self-reliance and export promotion are also at the centre of India's technology policy. In view of the rather difficult balance-of-payments position and the political problems that have occurred during the previous liberalization programme, the essential elements of the new policy are as follows.

First of all, the import regime is characterized by a tight control of imports of a large number of goods the import of which is considered not to be vital, such as non-durable and durable consumer goods, means of transportation (mainly vehicles), and many capital goods that are also produced domestically. The import of many capital goods not included in the OGL list requires approval of the concerned Capital Goods Committee. Raw materials that are inputs for industry can be imported but there are many restrictions on the import of intermediate products. Import of technology as well as foreign investments are permitted only on a selective basis when such import is considered necessary to stimulate technological development and exports, and when no indigenous technology is actually available or will become available in the near future.

The number of goods allowed to be imported under the OGL has been increased. This holds true for capital goods, instruments and several types of products that are considered of particular significance for the stimulation of technological development and upgrading of production. Import conditions for several categories of exporters have been liberalized such as registered exporters, producers of 'deemed exports', export and trading houses, EOUs and companies operating in the EPZs.

This does not imply that exporting companies are allowed to import freely capital goods that are also indigenously produced. The list of restricted items of machinery and equipment covers about 150 categories, but there are several facilities for exporting companies that permit them to import machinery and equipment from abroad. Two aspects of liberalization are to be distinguished here: availability of licences to import, and exemption of import duty. The main improvements in the new policy are, *inter alia*, the extension of the OGL list of products, the modification of the Import Replenishment Scheme to increase its flexibility and diversity, a wider recognition of indirect exports as 'deemed exports', widening of the scope of the Intermediate Advance Licencing scheme, and the simplification of the scheme of export houses and trading houses.

The import policy for registered exporters aims at providing them with the necessary imports. According to the Import Replenishment Scheme, the higher the ratio of exports to sales during the period immediately preceding the licencing period, the higher the value of permitted imports. It should be noted that these licences are transferable and that substantial benefits of such transfers may accrue to the exporting company in an economy characterized by quantitative import controls. Evidently, the more import liberalization proceeds, the less rents can be obtained from transferring import licences. The direct relationship between export performance and the permission to import may induce companies to increase the value of their exports, if necessary without producing the exported goods themselves as will be substantiated in detail in Part II of this volume.

Arrangements to permit exporters to import without paying import duties are made under the Duty Exemption Scheme and the Import-Export Passbook. The first of the two schemes allows imports made against an advance licence, intermediate advance licence or special import licence to enter the domestic market duty free. Licences are issued only if the registered exporters hold export orders, are able to realize the foreign exchange under their own name, and if the raw materials imported under the scheme would undergo substantial industrial processing domestically.

The Import-Export Passbook, introduced in 1985, has been continued in the second period of the import-export policy. This scheme allows registered exporters of manufactures to import free of import duties intermediate inputs for industrial export production such as raw materials, components and consumables. Import of consumables, however, is limited to only 10 per cent of the value of the licence.

A review of the main elements of India's system of import controls and export incentives shows that in the course of time the effort to promote manufactured exports has become more comprehensive and that some important limitations and disadvantages of policies pursued in the past have either been reduced or abolished. Of course, this does not mean that the policies have become fully effective in terms of their stated aims and that they have a significant impact on the behaviour of companies. Given the complexity of India's trade regime and the many variables involved, the question of the efficacy of policies is one of the most difficult to handle. Some aspects of this crucial question, however, will be dealt with in the following sections and in Part II of this volume.

THE STRUCTURE OF COMPARATIVE ADVANTAGE

Introduction

In the previous sections we have studied a wide range of efforts to stimulate manufactured exports and liberalize the trade regime. If successful, such a change in economic policy would turn the manufacturing sector from a secluded and inward-oriented sector into a more import dependent and export-oriented sector and would bring the composition of manufacturing production more in line with the comparative advantages the Indian economy has *vis-à-vis* its competitors.

The study of India's comparative advantages is organized along the following lines. First, we will distinguish manufactured goods according to their factor intensities. For this purpose, 26 groups of manufactured products will be differentiated and their factor content studied according to several variables. This will be followed by a brief discussion of hypotheses of trade theories regarding India's trade structure. Finally, we will study factor intensities of India's imports and exports with its trading partners and try to relate factor intensities of bilateral trade flows to differences between trading partners in factor endowments.

Factor intensities of manufacturing sectors

The concept of factor intensities of products is crucial to the explanation of comparative advantage and the structure of trade. An analysis of the relationship between factor intensities of traded goods and factor availability of trade partners requires a characterization of products according to their factor content. For the concepts of labour intensive and capital intensive products to be meaningful there must be significant differences between products in terms of their factor content.

Data on factor intensities of manufacturing sectors may be obtained from the Annual Survey of Industries (henceforth ASI). In the ASI of 1980–81, 18 major manufacturing sectors and 170 manufacturing sub-sectors have been distinguished. The ASI provides data on values of fixed and (physical) working capital, numbers of workers, employees and persons engaged, number of mandays worked, values of wages and net value added. Following Lary's approach to factor intensities, factor intensities are measured by flow proxies. Total capital intensity is approximated by net value added divided by the number of mandays of workers, skill intensity by the value of wages to workers divided by the number of mandays of workers, and physical capital intensity by the value of fixed capital divided by the number of mandays of workers. As an alternative proxy we have used the value of fixed capital divided by value added. Fixed capital represents the depreciated value of fixed assets owned by the factory while fixed assets are those which have a normal productive life of more than one year. Not all of these assets, however, are used directly in productive activities.

It should be noted that the classification of sectors according to their factor intensities is not independent of the classification criterion that is used. Bhalla has shown that the ranking order of sectors as measured by several flow proxies for factor intensity is affected by the choice of proxy for factor use.[43] Fels has shown that the ranking order of sectors according to the stock concept of capital differs from that according to the flow concept which is used in our study.[44] The data in the ASI have been rearranged into a division of 26 manufacturing sectors according to the ISIC classification scheme. The link between the Indian National Industrial Classification (NIC) and the International Standard Industrial Classification (ISIC) is presented in the Annexure.

The factor input coefficients for 26 manufacturing sectors according to four proxies and the consequent rankings of sectors according to total capital intensity, skill intensity and physical capital intensity are presented in Table 13. Whereas Table 14 shows which sectors are at the lower half of the ranking of sectors according to the four classification criteria. Some remarks are in place with respect to the factor input coefficients used in this analysis.

First, it should be noted that the factor input coefficients as derived from the ASI data are not strictly 'technical' coefficients but are distorted by the impact of the trade and industrialization regime. As discussed earlier, government intervention creates a discrepancy between the value of production measured in world market prices and in domestic prices. Apart from this distortion in the product market, government intervention may also distort factor use. However, the full impact of these distortions on the coefficients is not known.

Second, within-sector variation in factor inputs may be substantial given the level of aggregation of manufacturing sectors used here. Companies in each sector use different techniques, vary in efficiency and in the mix of products they produce.

The intra-sectoral variation in total capital intensity (value added per manday) in the largest manufacturing sector in terms of net value added, textiles, is illustrated in Table 15. Cotton textiles

TABLE 13

Factor Intensities of Manufacturing Sectors

ISIC Code	Ranking Order	VA/L	Ranking Order	W/L	Ranking Order	K/L	Ranking Order	K/VA
311–12	4	429.66	3	144.359	13	734.558	21	1.710
313	22	974.723	11	180.080	19	1,205.483	17	1.237
314	1	187.446	1	85.029	1	51.434	1	0.274
321	9	493.148	16	240.328	6	416.458	8	0.844
322	6	452.952	5	152.826	3	258.210	4	0.570
323	7	463.562	6	156.061	12	686.100	19	1.480
324	12	538.743	21	282.469	4	264.334	2	0.491
331	3	376.448	2	118.018	5	378.987	13	1.007
332	2	294.202	4	152.091	2	232.414	5	0.790
341	16	752.139	13	229.396	23	2,149.982	23	2.858
342	13	593.346	15	239.943	10	490.673	7	0.827
351	26	1,542.986	26	349.432	26	9,251.361	25	5.996
352	25	1,344.640	19	266.945	22	1,370.486	14	1.019
355	21	955.672	18	256.844	21	1,271.568	18	1.331
356	15	727.953	7	163.607	14	808.659	16	1.111
361	8	475.383	9	170.536	8	444.388	11	0.935
362	5	436.603	10	176.134	7	427.482	12	0.979
369	11	513.240	8	169.786	17	985.049	22	1.919
371	20	936.152	23	309.750	24	3,062.313	24	3.271
372	10	512.599	22	303.021	25	3.754.321	26	7.324
381	14	602.901	12	185.963	11	496.423	6	0.824
382	23	1,043.186	20	274.766	16	930.020	10	0.892

383	24	1,304.774	24	311.861	18	1,107.286	9	0.849
384	17	775.111	25	319.482	20	1,244.619	20	1.606
385	19	840.717	14	239.792	15	918.450	15	1.092
390	18	815.646	17	243.888	9	450.532	3	0.552

Notes: VA/L = net value added/mandays (10^6) in Rs lakhs.
W/L = wages to workers/mandays (10^6) in Rs lakhs.
K/L = fixed capital/mandays (10^6) in Rs lakhs.
K/VA = fixed capital/value added in Rs lakhs.

Source: Government of India, Central Statistical Organisation, Department of Statistics, Ministry of Planning, *Annual Survey of Industries, 1980–81, Summary Results for Factory Sectors*, New Delhi, 1984, Tables 5 and 6.

TABLE 14
Typology of Sectors According to Four Criteria[1]

ISIC Code	*Sector*	*VA/L*	*W/L*	*K/VA*	*K/L*
311/2	Food Products	*	*		*
313	Beverages		*		
314	Tobacco	*	*	*	*
321	Textiles	*		*	*
322	Wearing Apparel	*	*	*	*
323	Leather and Products	*	*		*
324	Footwear	*		*	*
331	Wood Products	*	*	*	*
332	Furniture and Products	*	*	*	*
341	Paper and Products		*		
342	Printing and Publishing	*		*	*
351	Industrial Chemicals				
352	Other Chemical Products				
355	Rubber Products				
356	Plastic Products		*		
361	Pottery, China	*	*	*	*
362	Glass and Products	*	*	*	*
369	Non-metal Products	*	*		
371	Iron and Steel				
372	Non-ferrous Metals	*			
381	Metal Products		*	*	*
382	Machinery n.e.c.			*	
383	Electrical Machinery			*	
384	Transport Equipment				
385	Professional Goods				
390	Other Industries			*	*

Note: [1] Indicates that the sector is at the lower half of the ranking of sectors.
Source: Same as Table 13.

(NIC 23) accounted for over 64 per cent of the production in the textile sector. The production process in this sub-sector was somewhat below the average labour intensity of the overall production in the textile sector. Techniques used in the sub-sector at the lower end of the range of techniques, made-up textile goods (NIC 266), are over two and a half times as labour intensive as the techniques in the most capital intensive sub-sector, threads, cordage, ropes, twines and nets (NIC 261). A certain degree of inaccuracy in measuring the technology embodied in export specialization and

TABLE 15
Intra-sectoral Disparities in Labour Productivity in Textiles (ISIC 321)

NIC Code	*Sector*	*Share in Net Value Added (%)*	*Relative Productivity*[1]
23	Cotton Textiles	64.17	0.85
24	Wool, Silk and Synthetic Fibre Textiles	18.31	1.18
25	Jute, Hemp and Mesta Textiles	14.52	0.68
260	Knitting Mills	0.93	1.04
261	Threads, Cordage, Ropes, Twines etc.	0.83	1.32
262	Embroidery, Crepes, Laces and Fringes	0.33	0.74
263	Wearing Carpets, Rugs etc.	0.47	0.81
266	Made-up Textiles Goods (Export Garments)	0.04	0.57
268	Coir and Coir Products	0.25	0.77
269	Textiles Not Elsewhere Classified	0.15	1.23

Note: [1] As compared to unweighted sectoral average level of labour productivity.
Source: Same as Table 13.

import dependence may result from these intra-sectoral differences in technology.

Third, a certain degree of arbitrariness in positioning India in the international division of labour may stem from the fact that the order of ranking of manufacturing sector in India does not necessarily match perfectly with the order of ranking in the countries that India trades with. Comparisons of the ranking orders of sectors in a series of countries invariably show that the ranking order of sectors is not stable across countries. No two countries have an identical ranking order of sectors and only a few sectors—usually those at the extreme ends of the ranking order—are without exception labour or capital intensive in all countries. Most sectors interchange their positions, being labour intensive in one country and capital intensive in another. However, it holds at the same time that there is a fairly stable ranking of sectors across countries and that strong deviations are rather exceptional. The Spearman rank correlation coefficients of the ranking of 26 manufacturing sectors according to the total capital intensity in India with the ranking in six other developing countries are as follows:

	Spearman Rank Correlation Coefficient
Chile	.53
Colombia	.52
Hong Kong	.21
South Korea	.32
Peru	.64
Turkey	.49

Elsewhere we have seen that the position of countries in the international division of labour according to their specialization in labour intensive products is not independent of the choice of definition of labour intensive products.[45] Consequently, India's position in the international division of labour may differ when measured in terms of its factor input coefficients from its position when measured by the factor input coefficients of one of its trading partners. This point is illustrated in Table 16 in which the order of ranking of manufacturing sector in India is compared with the USA.

It follows from the table that agro-based industries such as food products (ISIC 311–12) and tobacco manufacturing (ISIC 314) are labour intensive in India while this is not the case in the USA. Textiles (ISIC 321) are definitely not at the labour intensive end in India but occupy a position close to the average of the range of techniques in terms of total capital intensity. In the USA, however, this sector scores low in terms of total capital intensity. Many other sectors occupy remarkably different positions in the two countries as a consequence of which the sample of labour intensive industries in India differs from the sample in the USA. Although factor intensity reversals do occur and indeed complicate the analysis of India's comparative advantage in world trade, we will use the classification of sectors as presented in Tables 13 and 14 in the statistical analysis below.

Trade theory hypotheses of India's comparative advantage

We will now briefly review the trade theory hypotheses regarding India's structure of comparative advantage. According to the Heckscher-Ohlin-Samuelson model of trade and specialization, the most important factor that determines the pattern of production and trade is a country's relative factor endowment. In a two-country, two-factor and two-product framework this implies that,

TABLE 16
Comparison of the Ranking of Manufacturing Sectors According to Total Capital Intensity in India and the USA

ISIC Code	*Sector*	*Order of Ranking*	
		India	*USA*
311–12	Food Products	7	19
313	Beverages	22	23
314	Tobacco	1	24
321	Textiles	11	3
322	Wearing Apparel	4	1
323	Leather and Products	9	5
324	Footwear	13	2
331	Wood Products	3	6
332	Furniture and Fixtures	2	4
341	Paper and Products	17	15
342	Printing and Publishing	10	21
351	Industrial Chemicals	26	26
352	Other Chemical Products	25	25
355	Rubber Products	23	12
356	Plastic Products n.e.c.	14	9
361	Pottery, China, etc.	5	7
362	Glass and Products	6	11
369	Non-metal Products n.e.c.	8	13
371	Iron and Steel	19	16
372	Non-ferrous Metals	21	20
381	Metal Products	16	10
382	Machinery n.e.c.	20	17
383	Electrical Machinery	24	14
384	Transport Equipment	15	18
385	Professional Goods	18	22
390	Other Industries	12	8

Note: Data relate to 1979. The ranking order in India presented here has been based on UN data for 1979 and does not correspond with the ranking order presented in Table 13 that has been based on data taken from the Indian Annual Survey of Industries, 1980–81.

Source: United Nations, *Yearbook of Industrial Statistics*, New York.

given the validity of the assumptions underlying the model, production and exports in a labour abundant country will be concentrated in labour intensive products while the opposite is true for a capital abundant country. This model has been extended to a multi-country, multi-commodity, two-factor framework indicating that trade structures differ among countries in line with differences in factor endowments of the trade partners.[46] The more capital abundant the trading partner, the more labour intensive exports to that partner. However, distortions in factor and product markets—particularly those emanating from interventions in the trade regime—and differences between countries in community indifference curves may have a significant impact on the composition of a country's trade i.e. they may result in trade patterns inconsistent with the hypothesized pattern.

Linder's approach to the composition of trade is entirely distinct. In this approach the relationship between a country's level of development and the composition of domestic demand is crucial. The most important factor that determines international competitiveness is the size of domestic demand since production functions differ due to the scale of production. Production for the domestic market is a precondition for exports. Thus, the lower the level of income per capita, the more domestic demand and potential exports are concentrated in simple, so-called low income products that differ from their substitutes in high income countries in quality, design and sophistication. Since such products are mainly in demand in countries at similar levels of development, export opportunities for low income countries to high income countries are considered limited. In other words, the structure of potential exports in low income countries does not match the composition of potential import demand in high income countries.

Linder has distinguished some important exceptions to what he considered the normal conditions for trade. Such exceptions may occur '(1) where it is easy to become aware of the foreign demand in spite of the non-existence of home demand for the product; (2) where the product as such is available without inventive effort; and (3) where little or no product development work is needed.'[47] In such cases production for the domestic market is not a necessary precondition for efficient export production, and footloose export production may take place in a low income country for the market of a high income country.

Another approach to the composition of trade is the product cycle theory. The first such approach was formulated by Hufbauer who distinguished two kinds of trade flows: technological gap trade and low wage trade. The lower the level of technological development of a country, the more exports are concentrated in standardized and mature products, the production of which does not require high inputs of skilled, high wage labour. The product cycle approach, as developed by Vernon and Hirsch, distinguishes three stages in the development of a product: the introductory phase, the growth phase and the mature phase. Mature products, particularly labour intensive mature products, offer an opportunity to developing countries; such products are characterized by higher inputs of unskilled labour and of physical capital as compared to the earlier phases in the life cycle of a product.[48]

The characteristics of potential export products of a low income economy, as depicted in the theories summarized above, are not mutually exclusive: labour intensive products are, generally, low wage products, the production of which requires only limited inputs of skilled labour.

The technological characteristics of India's exports and imports

India's large domestic market and its long tradition of inward-oriented industrialization and stimulation of key or core manufacturing sectors have resulted in a diversified manufacturing sector which is able to satisfy domestic demand for nearly all products to a high degree. Tariff protection and a strict control of imports through licences have created an opportunity for domestic producers to supply the large domestic market under favourable conditions. Given the many ways in which government intervenes in market forces, the actual performance of India's industries in the domestic and foreign markets cannot be considered an accurate reflection of the competitiveness of industries and of India's comparative advantage. For instance, the strong support for engineering companies in their export efforts may have created a bias in the composition of exports away from the more labour intensive sectors. Thus, the technology embodied in India's foreign trade, as shown by the subsequent analysis of India's trade structure, is not an unbiased reflection of the 'real' and undistorted structure of its comparative advantage. Nevertheless, the study offers an insight into India's 'revealed' or 'apparent' competitive strength *vis-à-vis* its competitors in world markets and the degree to which the country is dependent on outside suppliers.

Before we present our analysis of India's trade performance, we will discuss the results of Khanna's study on the composition and factor content of India's exports in the 1970s.[49] Our study — like so many other studies on the trade performance of countries — is organized along similar lines. The main hypothesis tested in Khanna's study is that the composition and factor content of India's exports of manufactures differ in a systematic fashion between destinations according to the factor endowments of the partner countries. The higher the level of capital accumulation in the partner country, the more India's exports would be concentrated in labour intensive products.

In his model Khanna has specified 50 partner countries and tested the hypothesis in several ways. The factor content analysis of trade flows distinguishes products according to direct and total—direct plus indirect—inputs of human and physical capital per unit of value added. The direct coefficients were taken from the ASI and the total coefficients from an input-output table of 1973–74. Partner countries were differentiated according to their physical and human capital endowments. Khanna's results are presented in Table 17. Data relate to the factor content of manufactured exports in 1978. In all regressions in which only one explanatory variable has been used, the coefficient significantly differed from zero at the 1 per cent level of significance. When both explanatory variables have been used their significance levels dropped (standard errors in parentheses), but the overall explanation of the variation in the factor content of trade flows improved. It is striking that the application of coefficients that relate to the direct plus indirect factor inputs in production did not yield superior results as compared to the results obtained from analyses in which only direct factor inputs have been used.

The commodity composition version of the analysis consists of two steps, similar to the stages in Balassa's approach to comparative advantage. First, the revealed comparative advantage of India in the market of a partner country is related to the capital intensity of the products. Thus, partner-wise, India's comparative advantage is related to the product composition of exports. Second, the obtained coefficients for the factor intensity variable are related to the capital endowment variables for the partner countries. The results of this two-step analyses are presented in Table 18. Again, it appears that only a very small proportion of the variation is explained by the model.

The empirical analysis undertaken here focuses on the factor content of India's imports and exports with trading partners, not on the product composition of trade at a disaggregated level.

TABLE 17

Factor Content Analysis of Manufactured Exports of India to 50 Destinations, 1978

India's Exports	*Partner Country Endowments*			
	Constant Term	*Physical Capital*	*Human Capital*	R^2
Direct Physical Capital: Labour	4.215	−0.157 (0.033)		0.317
Direct plus Indirect Physical Capital: Labour	4.393	−0.071 (0.020)		0.210
Direct Human Capital: Labour	3.726		−0.014 (0.004)	0.198
Direct plus Indirect Human Capital: Labour	3.378		−0.006 (0.002)	0.161
Direct Total Capital: Labour	8.033	−0.223 (0.073)	−0.012 (0.011)	0.327
Direct plus Indirect Total Capital: Labour	7.932	−0.087 (0.038)	−0.007 (0.006)	0.254

Note: Standard errors in parentheses.

Source: A. Khanna, *Testing for the Direction of Exports, India's Exports of Manufactures in the 1970s*, World Bank Staff Working Paper No. 538, World Bank, Washington DC, 1982, pp. 11, 12, Tables 1 and 2.

TABLE 18

Factor Intensities of India's Comparative Advantage, 1978

India's RCA	*Partner Country Endowments*			
	Constant Term	*Physical Capital*	*Human Capital*	R^2
Physical Capital Intensity	−0.247	−0.58 (0.016)		0.210
Human Capital Intensity	0.703		−0.010 (0.003)	0.192
Total Capital Intensity	−0.025	−0.074 (0.024)	−0.002 (0.004)	0.275

Source: Same as Table 17, p. 17, Table 3.

Attempts to relate the product composition of trade to factor endowments and other structural variables of economies have never been very successful in statistical terms.[50] The proportion of variation in the product composition of the exports and imports of countries explained by inter-country differences in structural variables is usually very limited, even when product groups are clustered into very broad categories. In general, it holds that the more disaggregated the category of traded goods, the less satisfactory the explanation of its contribution to imports and exports. Attempts to explain the factor content of trade have been somewhat more successful.

Here we analyse the contribution of four categories of products to total exports and imports of manufactures: labour intensive products as measured by *VA/L*, *K/L* and *K/VA*; low skill i.e. low wage products as measured by *W/L*. Sectors included in the four categories are presented in Table 14. The shares of these product groups in exports and imports are related to the level of development of the trading partner. This is essentially a 'stages' approach to comparative advantage. As a proxy for the overall—physical and human—capital endowment of trading partners, we use GDP per capita. The level of income per capita is significantly related to the availability of human capital, as follows from the well-known study by Harbison and Meier; it is also significantly related to electricity consumption per employee in manufacturing production, which, in turn, is a proxy for capital use per employee. In another study of patterns in trade this variable was replaced by a proxy for capital availability for the manufacturing sector (value added per labourer in manufacturing) but it appeared that the statistical results did not improve significantly by using the latter variable.[51]

As indicated earlier, India's large domestic market and its long tradition of an inward-oriented industrialization policy with a strong emphasis on self-reliance and the development of key industries have resulted in a diversified industrial structure. The country is self-reliant to a very high degree in the supply of labour and capital intensive consumer and capital goods. However, domestic resource costs in many of these lines of production are relatively high as compared to world market prices, as indicated by the frequency of high tariff rates and non-tariff barriers presented earlier. This implies that in many lines of production the country is not internationally competitive and that the composition of manufactured exports would be much less diversified than the composition of the manufacturing sector itself, as will be discussed later.

According to the ASI of 1980–81, by far the single most important sector in terms of domestic value added creation is textiles. As is clear from Table 19 this sector accounted for 17.34 per cent of total manufacturing production. The most important activities in this sector are manufacture of cotton textiles (NIC 23), wool, silk and synthetic fibre textiles (NIC 24), and manufacture of jute, hemp and mesta textiles (NIC 25). The other important sectors are

TABLE 19
India's Production and Trade in Manufactures, 1980

ISIC Code	*Sector*	*Share in Net Value Added (%)*	*Share in Exports (%)*	*Share in Imports (%)*
311–12	Food Products	5.93	2.83	2.52
313	Beverages	0.65	0.50	0.01
314	Tobacco	1.29	0.00	0.00
321	Textiles	17.34	28.79	3.23
322	Wearing Apparel	0.48	14.53	0.00
323	Leather and Products	0.33	10.24	0.03
324	Footwear	0.25	1.14	0.00
331	Wood Products	0.48	0.50	0.07
332	Furniture and Fixtures	0.05	0.15	0.02
341	Paper and Products	1.95	0.19	4.18
342	Printing and Publishing	1.69	0.21	0.36
351	Industrial Chemicals	3.85	2.51	22.64
352	Other Chemical Products	7.90	5.63	3.80
355	Rubber Products	1.55	0.79	0.37
356	Plastic Products	0.61	0.32	0.08
361	Pottery, China	0.31	0.02	0.00
362	Glass and Products	0.44	0.56	0.31
369	Non-metal Products	2.63	0.71	2.71
371	Iron and Steel	9.81	2.11	15.69
372	Non-ferrous Metals	0.53	0.43	4.91
381	Metal Products	2.78	5.61	1.56
382	Machinery n.e.c.	7.45	6.42	18.94
383	Electrical Machinery	6.99	3.14	4.45
384	Transport Equipment	7.17	6.05	10.43
385	Professional Goods	0.61	0.78	3.03
390	Other Industries	0.48	5.47	0.65

Note: ISIC 353 and 354 have been excluded.

Source: Data on net value added as of Table 13. Data on trade flows taken from UNCTAD tape.

machinery and transport equipment (ISIC 382, 383 and 384) which accounted for 18.61 per cent of manufacturing value added, and chemical industries (ISIC 351 and 352) which accounted for 11.75 per cent of production. The latter two clusters of industries typically belong to the key industries that are capital and skill intensive and have substantial backward and forward linkages.

Focusing on the composition of manufactured exports to all destinations in 1980 it can be observed that exports are far more concentrated in only a few product groups than is production. Textiles and wearing apparel (ISIC 321 and 322) accounted for 43.32 per cent of total manufactured exports. The next important export sector is leather and products which is also a labour intensive product group. The share of labour intensive sectors in exports to the OECD markets is more substantial than their share in exports to other destinations as will be seen later. However, the contribution of the clusters of capital intensive sectors mentioned earlier is rather substantial as compared to their contribution to exports in many other developing countries. Chemical products accounted for 8.14 per cent of total manufactured exports while machinery and transport equipment accounted for 15.61 per cent. Their contribution is especially significant in exports to non-OECD countries.

Imports of manufactures are highly concentrated in a number of capital intensive sectors, notably, chemicals, machinery, iron and steel, and transport equipment. These products accounted for 67.7 per cent of total imports of manufactures and 73.58 per cent of imports from the OECD countries.

The UNCTAD tape with trade data that has been used for this analysis includes 237 trade partners. Many bilateral flows show zero values. It is clear from Table 20 that 23 partners accounted for 79.05 per cent of the total value of India's exports of manufactures while 15 partners accounted for 83.96 per cent of the country's imports of manufactures. The three major Indian export markets were OECD Europe, the former USSR and the USA. As compared to the size of its domestic market, Japan's imports from India were remarkably small. A cluster of countries in the Middle East, notably, Egypt, Iran, Kuwait, Saudi Arabia and the United Arab Emirates, became quite an important outlet that absorbed 9.12 per cent of India's exports of manufactures. Quite remarkably, the relatively large markets of Latin American countries such as Brazil,

TABLE 20
Destinations of Exports and Origins of Imports, 1980

Country	*Value of Exports (10^6 US $)*	*Share in Total Exports (%)*	*Value of Imports (10^6 US $)*	*Share in Total Imports (%)*
Egypt	65.819	1.67		
Nigeria	56.246	1.43		
Canada	51.967	1.32	165.710	3.11
USA	423.796	10.74	1,151.584	21.64
Brazil			112.636	2.12
Japan	67.241	1.70	665.547	12.51
Iran	42.554	1.08		
Kuwait	47.659	1.21		
Saudi Arabia	133.332	3.38		
United Arab Emirates	70.420	1.79		
Bangladesh	68.252	1.73		
Sri Lanka	71.240	1.81		
South Korea			153.700	2.89
Malaysia	44.658	1.13		
Nepal	52.639	1.33		
Singapore	51.567	1.31		
Belgium and Luxembourg	46.565	1.18	78.335	1.47
France	127.558	3.23	244.656	4.60
German Fed. Rep.	348.026	8.82	687.502	12.92
Italy	151.216	3.83	175.226	3.29
Netherlands	78.473	1.99	127.835	2.40
United Kingdom	270.955	6.87	486.814	9.15
Sweden			90.552	1.70
Switzerland			107.989	2.03
Romania			75.803	1.42
USSR	708.157	17.95	144.125	2.71
Australia	82.857	2.10		
Countries Included in the List		79.05		83.96
Total	3,945.205	100.00	5,321.816	100.00

Source: UNCTAD tape.

Mexico and Argentina had only limited importance to India's export industries.

On the import side we may notice an even stronger concentration of trade relations with OECD Europe and the USA and a much more pronounced role of Japan. Japan was the third largest exporter of manufactures to India, after the USA and the Federal

Republic of Germany. While the former USSR was the single largest outlet for India's manufactured exports it had only limited importance as a supplier of manufactures for the Indian market. The most important exporters among developing countries were Brazil and South Korea.

The next step in the analysis is to investigate to what extent there are significant differences between the technological characteristics of India's manufactured exports to and imports from partner countries at different levels of income per capita. This question has been tackled in several ways.

To start with, we relate the share of four clusters of product groups, distinguished earlier, in manufactured exports to and imports from India's trade partners to the level of income per capita of the partner countries. Subsequently, we relate the share of some selected product groups in trade flows to the level of income per capita of India's trade partners. Next, we present the technological characteristics of trade flows to and from some selected trade partners or groups of countries. Finally, a time-series analysis is presented of the changing composition of India's manufactured exports to the OECD markets. We will now discuss the regression results presented in Tables 21, 22 and 23.

TABLE 21

Structure of Manufactured Exports

India's Exports	*Constant Term*	*ln GDP/P*	R^2	*n*
Share of Sectors with:				
Low *VA/L*	1.028 (0.079)	7.306 (4.211)	0.112	142
Low *W/L*	−21.913 (2.035)	7.269 (5.120)	0.168	132
Low *K/L*	−9.748 (0.815)	10.278 (6.451)	0.224	146
Low *K/VA*	47.571 (4.410)	3.457 (2.395)	0.037	153

The analysis shows a highly significant impact of the variable income per capita of the partner country on the factor intensities of exports and imports of manufactures, as shown by the t-statistics that are in parentheses. Nevertheless, this variable explains

TABLE 22
Structure of Manufactured Imports

India's Exports	*Constant Term*	*ln GDP/P*	R^2	*n*
Share of Sectors with:				
Low *VA/L*	102.393 (4.530)	−9.490 (3.396)	0.168	59
Low *W/L*	95.060 (4.343)	−8.964 (3.261)	0.155	60
Low *K/L*	80.036 (4.526)	−8.005 (3.614)	0.174	64
Low *K/VA*	76.643 (3.821)	−6.015 (2.382)	0.076	71

TABLE 23
Composition of Manufactured Exports, Disaggregated Analysis

India's Exports	*Constant Term*	*ln GDP/P*	R^2	*n*
Share of Sectors with:				
321 + 322 + 323 + 324	−5.313 (0.380)	7.479 (4.031)	0.104	142
384	56.674 (5.311)	−5.792 (4.115)	0.140	106
382 + 383 + 384	96.019 (7.363)	−8.848 (5.039)	0.169	127

Note: ISIC 321 Textiles
322 Wearing apparel
323 Leather and products
324 Footwear
351 Industrial chemicals
371 Iron and steel
382 Machinery n.e.c.
383 Electrical machinery
384 Transport equipment

only a small proportion of the variation in the composition of trade flows. Thus, there are significant differences indeed between the technological characteristics of India's trade flows to trade partners at different levels of development. The more developed the trade partner, the more India's exports to it are concentrated in simple, labour intensive products, and the more India's imports from it are concentrated in capital and skill intensive products.

As expected, the relationship between the share of some selected product groups in total trade flows from and to partner countries, and the level of income per capita of the partners is very weak and often shows an insignificant impact of the variable income per capita (see Table 23). As follows from most statistical studies of the export and import structure, it is more difficult to explain the structure of imports than the structure of exports. In our study no significant relationship could be established between the level of development of India's foreign suppliers and the type of products India imported from them.

The technological characteristics of India's manufactured exports to and imports from all countries, OECD countries, Middle East, the USA and the erstwhile USSR are presented in Tables 24 and 25. In all cases it is seen that products at the lower end of the technology range, as defined earlier, dominate export performance to all destinations and play a minor role in imports. Notwithstanding the strong bias in the export incentive structure in favour of the more capital and skill intensive sectors, it appears that India's basic structure of comparative advantage is in labour intensive industries while its import dependence is concentrated in capital

TABLE 24

Composition of Manufactured Exports (in percentages)

India's Exports to:	*All Countries*	*OECD*	*Middle East*	*USA*	*USSR*
Share of Sectors with:					
Low *VA/L*	60.51	76.10	37.76	56.27	66.10
Low *W/L*	36.54	43.99	35.18	56.89	35.40
Low *K/L*	70.44	87.85	57.65	78.55	68.77
Low *K/VA*	66.93	76.42	63.59	73.99	58.50

TABLE 25

Composition of Manufactured Imports (in percentages)

India's Exports to:	*All Countries*	*OECD*	*Middle East*	*USA*	*USSR*
Share of Sectors with:					
Low *VA/L*	14.17	8.62	30.33	8.74	3.11
Low *W/L*	11.50	7.43	0.15	5.69	17.00
Low *K/L*	8.76	7.35	0.23	6.48	1.21
Low *K/VA*	29.60	32.85	0.62	24.34	52.93

and skill intensive industries. It should be noted that the trade flows between India and the group of OECD countries in particular reflect such wide differences in comparative advantages. However, India's exports to the Middle East and the erstwhile USSR are much less concentrated at the lower end of the technology range.

The changing structure of India's comparative advantage: 1965–87

The final part of our study of India's export performance deals with changes in the composition of India's exports to the developed countries in the course of time. As discussed in the previous sections, India's export policy stimulated some capital intensive sectors over a long period of time. It is true that a successful development programme of EPZ could boost the contribution of labour intensive assembled products but the programme has only been partially successful so far. We expect therefore that in the course of time the contribution of the strongly favoured sectors to total exports will increase and that the time-series study will reveal a shift in India's comparative advantage.

The analysis focuses on the composition of India's exports to all OECD countries taken together in six selected years during the period 1965–87. All product groups that are of major significance at the end of the period have been included at the two-digit level in order to obtain a somewhat disaggregated view of the shift in composition. The results are presented in Table 26.

The major finding is that a significant change in the composition of manufactured exports indeed took place and that the composition of exports diversified during the period under study. At the beginning of the period nearly 75 per cent of exports were concentrated in the sector of textile yarns and fabrics. The only other sector of some importance in India's exports at that time was leather manufactures. The contribution of both sectors and particularly of textile yarns decreased dramatically. We have seen that India lost a substantial share of world markets in these product groups to newly industrializing countries, particularly those in East Asia. It is noteworthy that articles of apparel and clothing accessories, the production of which is extremely labour intensive, play a marginal role in the export performance. Only in the course of the 1970s and 1980s this sector became a major exporter supplying over 25 per cent of India's manufactured goods shipped abroad.

TABLE 26

Composition of Manufactured Exports to OECD (in percentages), 1965–1987 (Selected Years)

SITC Code	*Sector*	*1965*	*1970*	*1975*	*1980*	*1985*	*1987*
5	Chemicals	2.57	2.91	3.41	2.61	2.74	3.59
51	Organic Chemicals	0.37	0.62	1.08	0.75	0.56	1.27
53	Dyeing, Tanning and Colouring Materials	0.06	0.20	0.57	0.59	0.55	1.01
6	Manufactured Goods Excl. SITC 67 and 68	93.26	84.64	66.25	64.07	62.94	60.78
61	Leather Manufactures and Dressed Fur Skins	11.60	12.75	14.51	9.04	10.60	8.80
65	Textile Yarns and Fabrics	73.67	57.99	32.25	30.13	20.97	21.07
66	Non-metallic Mineral Products n.e.s.	6.58	10.93	14.33	18.15	26.42	26.87
69	Manufactures of Metal n.e.s.	1.14	2.30	4.39	5.58	3.83	3.29
7	Machinery and Transport Equipment	1.17	3.43	5.70	5.14	4.46	3.29
71	Power Generating Machinery	0.24	0.66	1.18	0.51	0.63	0.56
74	Industrial Machinery and Parts	0.15	0.56	1.40	1.04	0.73	0.66
77	Electrical Machinery, Apparatus and Appliances	0.14	0.70	0.80	0.65	0.69	0.64
78	Road Vehicles	0.01	0.12	0.38	0.53	0.45	0.36
79	Other Transport Equipment	0.18	0.08	0.11	1.42	0.87	0.40
8	Miscellaneous Manufactured Articles	2.97	9.00	24.62	28.16	29.83	32.32
83	Travel Goods, Handbags etc.	0.01	0.36	0.93	0.94	1.33	1.51
84	Articles of Apparel and Clothing Accessories	1.04	4.27	18.59	22.13	23.37	25.80
85	Footwear	0.60	1.58	1.41	1.89	1.30	2.02
89	Miscellaneous Manufactured Articles n.e.s.	0.95	2.02	2.75	2.02	2.90	2.25

Source: OECD, *Foreign Trade by Commodities, Imports*, Vol. II, Series C, Paris, various issues.

Capital intensive goods such as engineering goods and chemicals play a very limited role in India's exports to developed countries. Such products are of greater importance in exports to developing countries. Nevertheless, in the course of time India has managed to penetrate the markets of machinery and transport equipment in some developed countries. Another remarkable development is the high growth rate of some non-metallic mineral products, particularly pearls and precious stones as well as some other products; in 1987 the contribution of these products to total manufactured exports was nearly 27 per cent. In summary, exports to developed countries have become more diversified in the course of time but are still largely concentrated in labour intensive products.

CONCLUSIONS

The review of India's economic policy presented here shows that attempts to stimulate non-traditional exports have a long history and have been made since the 1960s. Already during the Third Plan (1961–66) the need to create 'an atmosphere' more favourable to export industries was recognized. In the course of time the number of instruments to stimulate exports increased and so did export consciousness, particularly since the IMF loan in 1981. Nevertheless, the export policy has definitely not been entirely successful when evaluated according to a number of indicators. The trade deficit increased considerably. Also, the export-output ratio of only a few companies increased substantially. In fact, the ratio did not increase significantly in most manufacturing sectors and even declined in many cases. Moreover, the country lost market shares in international trade in most major product groups to its competitors, notably, East and Southeast Asian countries and some Latin American countries.

It is remarkable that the export promotion efforts of the government have had such a limited impact on the export performance of the manufacturing sector, given the substantial role of state enterprises in the manufacturing sector and the many instruments that the well-developed government bureaucracy had at its disposal to steer the manufacturing sector.

Our review suggests that the export promotion measures suffer from several shortcomings. They do not sufficiently compensate for the anti-export bias rooted in the overall regime of inward-oriented industrialization. Also, export incentives have been concentrated rather strongly in only a few sectors such as engineering goods and chemicals. Moreover, the programme of EPZs has not been very successful in attracting foreign export companies, while the programme of EOUs has not contributed substantially to the growth of manufactured exports. The administrative complexity of the incentive system, the long implementation periods of policies and the high rate of uncertainty due to the ambivalence that is characteristic of government's attitude towards international trade, do not contribute either to a successful export performance of the manufacturing sector.

At the heart of the first and second new trade policies are a series of measures that should facilitate the modernization of the manufacturing sector and help solve the balance-of-payments problem. During their stage of implementation, however, these policies shared some shortcomings with the earlier policies. Nevertheless, the new policies appear to be a more ambitious and less ambivalent attempt at liberalization and export promotion.

Notwithstanding the traditional bias in export incentives in favour of some fairly capital intensive sectors such as engineering goods and chemicals, traditional labour intensive products dominate the manufactured export performance. Indeed, over half of total manufactured exports were textiles, wearing apparel and leather products. However, the contribution of some capital intensive sectors to exports has been rather substantial as compared to their role in the export performance of many other developing countries that are at a much higher level of economic development. The contribution of such products has been notably substantial in India's exports to other developing countries. Trade flows between India and the group of developed countries, however, reflect a traditional division of labour, India being a supplier of labour intensive, simple, low wage products and an importer of capital intensive technologically advanced products. Our time-series analysis shows that in the course of time exports have become more diversified and that the contribution of chemicals and engineering goods to total manufactured exports has increased.

NOTES

1. The author is grateful to the staff members of the Institute for Studies in Industrial Development, New Delhi, for their contribution to the analysis of the export orientation of Indian firms. Their data system of India's corporate sector has been a valuable complementary source of information on the role of trade in the Indian economy. Also, their system of information on trade policies and trade practices has helped in obtaining an overview of the many changes in India's trade and industrialization regime during the 1970s and 1980s. The financial assistance given by IDPAD is gratefully acknowledged, and the assistance of Mrs Berenst-de Bruijn at the Economic and Social Institute of the Free University of Amsterdam is highly appreciated.
2. P. van Dijck, *Causes and Characteristics of Export-Oriented Industrialization in Developing Countries*, Free University Press, Amsterdam, 1986, p. 66, Table 3.7.
3. M. Wolf, *India's Exports*, Oxford University Press for the World Bank, New York, 1982, p. 17.
4. OECD, *External Debt Statistics—The Debt and Other External Liabilities of Developing, CMEA and Certain Other Countries and Territories*, Paris, 1989, pp. 12, 13, Table 1.
5. A.O. Krueger, *Foreign Trade Regimes and Economic Development: Liberalization Attempts and Consequences*, National Bureau of Economic Research, New York, 1978, pp. 12–41.
6. S. Chishti, *Foreign Trade and Economic Development of India*, IDPAD-IVO, Tilburg, 1985, pp. 14, 15.
7. *Ibid.*, pp. 55, 77–80.
8. *Ibid.*, pp. 80, 81.
9. *Ibid.*, pp. 82–85.
10. *Ibid.*, p. 85.
11. *Ibid.*, p. 86.
12. *Ibid.*, p. 13.
13. *Ibid.*, p. 108.
14. *Ibid.*, p. 120.
15. V.L. Kelkar and K.M. Raipuria, *Manufactures Exports in India's Development*, IDPAD-IVO, Tilburg, 1985, p. 20.
16. *Ibid.*, pp. 72–81.
17. T.N. Srinivasan, Neoclassical political economy, the state and economic development, in *Asian Development Review*, Vol. 3, No. 2, 1985.
18. J.N. Bhagwati, *Foreign Trade Regimes and Economic Development: Anatomy and Consequences of Exchange Control Regimes*, National Bureau of Economic Research, New York, 1978, pp. 53–63. See also, A.O. Krueger, *op. cit.*, pp. 22–28.
19. J.N. Bhagwati and T.N. Srinivasan, *Foreign Trade Regimes and Economic Development: India*, Columbia University Press for the National Bureau of Economic Research, New York, 1975, pp. 4, 5.
20. J.N. Bhagwati and P. Desai, *India: Planning for Industrialization, Industrialization and Trade Policies Since 1951*, Oxford University Press for the

Development Centre of the Organisation for Economic Cooperation and Development, London, 1970, pp. 368, 369. See also, V.L. Kelkar and K.M. Raipuria, *op. cit.*, 1985, p. 24.

21. V.L. Kelkar and K.M. Raipuria, *op. cit.*, 1985, p. 27.
22. M. Wolf, *op. cit.*, p. 79.
23. M. Wolf, *op. cit.*, pp. 80, 81.
24. M. Wolf, *op. cit.*, p. 113.
25. M. Wolf, *op. cit.*, p. 116.
26. M. Wolf, *op. cit.*, p. 117.
27. M. Wolf, *op. cit.*, p. 116.
28. M. Wolf, *op. cit.*, p. 92.
29. For a discussion of the IMF loan and the main elements of its conditionality see, R.B. Saxena, *IMF Loan to India, An Economic Assessment*, Anmol Publications, Delhi, 1986, pp. 114–65; C. Gwin, 1983.
30. Government of India, Ministry of Commerce, *Report of the Committee on Trade Policies*, New Delhi, 1984, pp. 3, 4.
31. *Ibid.*, p. 3.
32. *Ibid.*, p. 35.
33. *Ibid.*, pp. 5, 36.
34. *Ibid.*, p. 37.
35. *Ibid.*, p. 39.
36. *Ibid.*, p. 33.
37. *Ibid.*, p. 47.
38. Government of India, *The Narasimham Committee Report*, 1986.
39. Government of India, 1984, *op. cit.*, p. 46.
40. Government of India, 1984, *op. cit.*, p. 84.
41. See, N. Kumar, Foreign investment and export-orientation: the case of India, in S. Naya *et al.* (eds), *Direct Foreign Investment and Export Promotion: Policies and Experiences in Asia*, East West Resource Systems Institute, Hawaii, 1987.
42. Government of India, Ministry of Commerce, *Import and Export Policy, April 1988–March 1991*, Vol. 1, *Imports and Export Promotion*, 1988.
43. A.S. Bhalla, The concept and measurement of labour intensity, in A.S. Bhalla (ed), *Technology and Employment in Industry, A Case Study Approach*, ILO, Geneva, 1981, pp. 35–39.
44. G. Fels, The choice of industry mix in the division of labour between developed and developing countries, in *Weltwirtschaftliches Archiv*, Band 108, 1972, pp. 77–90.
45. P. van Dijck, *op. cit.*, pp. 141–44.
46. A.O. Krueger, *Trade and Employment in Developing Countries*, Vol. 3: *Synthesis and Conclusions*, National Bureau of Economic Research, The University of Chicago Press, Chicago, 1983.
47. S.B. Linder, *An Essay on Trade and Transformation*, John Wiley and Sons, New York, 1961, p. 188.
48. See, G.C. Hufbauer, The impact of national characteristics and technology on the commodity composition of trade in manufactured goods, in R. Vernon (ed), *The Technology Factor in International Trade*, National Bureau of Economics Research, New York, 1970; S. Hirsch, *Location of Industry and*

International Competitiveness, Clarendon Press, Oxford, 1967; R. Vernon, International investment and international trade in product cycle, in *The Quarterly Journal of Economics*, Vol. LXXX, No. 2, May 1966.

49. A. Khanna, *Testing for the Direction of Exports, India's Exports of Manufactures in the 1970s*, World Bank Staff Working Paper No. 538, World Bank, Washington DC, 1982.
50. See R.A. Batchelor, Development patterns and the basis for trade, in R.A. Batchelor, R.L. Major and A.D. Morgan, *Industrialization and the Basis for Trade*, The National Institute of Economic and Social Research, Cambridge University Press, Cambridge, 1980; P. van Dijck, *op. cit.*, pp. 157–66.
51. P. van Dijck, *op. cit.*, pp. 164, 165.

ANNEXURE: LINK BETWEEN THE INTERNATIONAL STANDARD INDUSTRIAL CLASSIFICATION (ISIC) AND THE INDIAN NATIONAL INDUSTRIAL CLASSIFICATION (NIC)

ISIC Code	*NIC Code*
311–12	20, 21
313	220, 221, 222, 223, 224
314	225, 226, 227, 228, 229
321	23, 24, 25, 260, 261, 262, 263, 266, 268, 269
322	264, 265, 267
323	29-/-291
324	291
331	270, 271, 272, 273, 274, 275, 279
332	276, 277
341	280, 281, 282, 283
342	284, 285, 286, 287, 288, 289
351	310, 311
352	312, 313, 314, 315, 316, 317, 318, 319
355	300, 301, 302
356	303
361	322, 323
362	321
369	320, 324, 325, 326, 327, 328, 329
371	330, 331, 332
372	333, 334, 335, 336, 339
381	34
382	35
383	36
384	37
385	380, 381, 382
390	383, 384, 385, 386, 387, 389

Part II

AN EVALUATION OF EXPORT POLICIES AND THE EXPORT PERFORMANCE OF LARGE PRIVATE COMPANIES

II

AN EVALUATION OF EXPORT POLICIES AND THE EXPORT PERFORMANCE OF LARGE PRIVATE COMPANIES

K.S. Chalapati Rao

INTRODUCTION[1]

The primary objective of this part of the study is to promote an understanding of the export sector in India and the issues involved. More particularly, the aim of the study is to assess the response of the large private corporate sector to the mix of industrial policy liberalization and export incentives offered by the Indian government. This has been attempted by tracing the evolution of the export promotion policies and the export performance of selected large companies. Reference to individuals and companies is considered necessary to place the issues in their proper perspective.

Foreign exchange problems of developing countries described in general terms in the next section provide the background for the subsequent discussion and analysis. The following section discusses in detail the evolution of India's export policies by reviewing the main policy recommendations of the many committees that have been involved in the reorientation of India's trade and industrialization regime. The next section throws light on India's export performance at different levels of product group disaggregation and presents data on the role of the small-scale sector and the central public sector enterprises in India's export performance. The remaining part of the study focuses on the role of large private sector companies in India's export performance and their response to the export incentives. The next section deals with the two Acts that have played a vital role in this context, the Monopolies and Restrictive Trade Practices Act, 1969 and the Industries (Development and Regulation) Act, 1951. Drawing on the data system of the Institute for Studies in Industrial Development, the results of empirical studies of the export orientation of large companies and their contribution to net foreign exchange earnings are discussed. The main results of the study are summarized in the final part. A postscript presents the trends in exports of Indian large private companies until the introduction of the new policies in 1991.

FOREIGN EXCHANGE AND DEVELOPING COUNTRIES

Developing countries depend heavily upon the industrially advanced countries, irrespective of their colonial heritage. For long it has been a widely shared belief that the initiation of the process of industrialization is a prerequisite to rapid socio-economic growth and development; and for this, developing countries could find it advantageous to learn from the experiences of the industrially advanced nations. The need for a closer interface between the developed and the underdeveloped world was further emphasized through the existence and operation of international organizations.[2] While it may be debatable if the present system of financial and technical aid—bilateral and multilateral—has really assisted and strengthened the long-term process of socio-economic development in all the developing countries, the system has certainly brought the developed and the underdeveloped world more 'face to face' than was the case during the period before the Second World War.

The struggles for independence in the former colonies were invariably motivated by the ideals of national independence and economic development.[3] With the acceptance of the assumption that industrialization is synonymous with development, different variants of planning were adopted in the developing countries to achieve rapid economic growth. However, due to the low levels of economic activity and other factors, most developing countries which adopted planning experienced severe resource constraints in the process of implementing their growth plans. While low levels of savings inhibit internal resource mobilization, these countries have little to offer apart from primary goods to fund their imports of raw materials and services necessary for development. Given these circumstances, foreign capital—whether in the form of loans, aid or direct investment—was considered necessary to support initial higher investment.[4] Also, developing countries depend on external sources for technology and equipment and quite often for a variety of raw materials.[5] Invariably their knowledge and competence to exploit fully even their own natural resources are limited.[6] It is not uncommon to see that many countries continue to depend on imports because of inadequate and delayed action to exploit their national resource endowment.

Moreover, many developing countries happen to be deficient in food availability.[7] In order to avoid food scarcity and the consequential human misery, political unrest and adverse international attention, developing countries are obliged to import foodgrains and other essential goods. Conflicts with neighbouring countries due to historical reasons or the international political situation, over which developing countries generally do not have any influence or control, add another dimension to their problems and consequently a strain on their already limited resources. With a none too developed industry their arms requirements are met through imports. In view of the rapid advancement of the defence industry in the developed world, these nations are constantly on the lookout for more and more sophisticated arms to maintain the balance with their adversaries.[8] This puts further strain on their limited internal and foreign exchange resources which otherwise could have been available for education, health and development.[9]

Developing countries have to pay for shipping and other services as their own sea and air transport infrastructures are either not developed or are non-existent. Finally, the external assistance obtained over a period of time places still other demands of a separate kind. Developing countries also have to plan for repayment of loans and the interest accrued on them. Since the aid/loans are used within the limitations of the socio-economic environment and the preferences of and constraints placed by the aid giver, aid may not result in adequate and expected returns and may affect the repayment capabilities of the recipient.

Given these conditions, it is not surprising that most developing countries depend on foreign aid, assistance and loans on the one hand and pursue a variety of policies to augment foreign exchange resources, on the other. These include policies aimed at export promotion, tourism development and attracting remittances from their nationals working in other countries. Exports from the developing countries are generally composed of primary commodities and manufactured products involving low technology and higher labour intensity. The scope for such exports is, however, limited. Also, developing economies are not able to take full advantage of the export efforts due to their weak bargaining capabilities. The international prices of primary commodities are known to be rising at a much lower rate than the prices of manufactures originating from the advanced countries.[10] The fact of better coordination among developed nations is quite normal. This is particularly true when exports from the industrialized world originate from transnational corporations. In contrast, most of the suppliers among developing countries are pitted against each other and unhesitatingly resort to mutual undercutting. Some developing countries also adopt administrative, fiscal and other mechanisms to promote exports. A variety of incentives and concessions are offered to exporters. In nearly all cases, the costs and benefits of such policies remain unassessed. Developing countries invariably are obliged to export unprocessed raw materials and natural resources to earn foreign exchange. In one case it may be crude oil, coal, iron ore, bauxite or sulphur and in another fruit, vegetable oils and other agricultural produce.

To meet the pressure on foreign exchange resources, most of the developing countries are obliged to adopt measures to conserve foreign exchange by imposing physical restrictions on low priority or non-essential imports. Such policies, however, are not viewed with favour by the industrially advanced nations as they are seen as restrictions on the free interplay of economic forces which are considered as the ideal for rapid economic development of the world.[11] Import substitution policies of the developing countries are long-term measures to reduce imports. Such policies also have the additional advantage of providing the necessary protection to infant and indigenous industries. However, policies directed towards import substitution do involve a risk that they might lead to the establishment and continuance of an inefficient production system under which economies of scale are not fully exploited and the country is saddled with high cost industrial enterprises. Similarly, the absence of international competition could result in inefficient, high cost and low quality process of industrialization that thrives at the cost of the consumer and the national economy at large. This is particularly so since such industrial structures cannot withstand international competition in terms of quality as well as prices, unless accompanied by appropriate policies. The existence of wide disparities in incomes and wealth, which is quite normal in developing countries, implies the presence of a small elite section which supports the consumption of a large variety of goods which are often referred to as 'luxury' products. Restrictions on imports of such items coupled with the non-availability or low quality and high costs of the indigenously manufactured consumer products, give rise to smuggling.

In short, majority of the developing countries need large foreign exchange resources. A good part of the import demand may in fact be treated as inelastic. For instance, food scarce nations cannot afford to postpone their food imports. Similarly, defence requirements have a high priority and the demand is inelastic in nature; the same holds true of imports of capital goods and basic and essential raw materials. Also, the social reality has to be recognized that the rich, vocal and influential sections of the developing countries cannot be deprived of a lifestyle which, though cannot be supported from the viewpoint of national priorities, has active support in policy-making circles. Combined with the international order in which policies in developing countries are considerably influenced through negotiations, exchange missions and the so-called friendly advice (and sometimes insistence on conditionality clauses in international agreements) there always appears to be a plea for escalation of imports. To promote imports, international loans do become available. Arguments for restrictions on imports are invariably dubbed as unrealistic. Since the size and nature of imports is not critically questioned, policy efforts are mainly directed towards enlargement of national exports. The problem of foreign exchange gets identified as that of export promotion and not of regulation or judicious imports.

EVOLUTION OF EXPORT POLICIES IN INDIA

After India attained independence in 1947, the country opted for a broad model of economic development that emphasized rapid development of indigenous capabilities to manufacture capital goods and a general process of industrialization.[12] However, a model which accorded high priority to human capital formation and adoption of structural changes in the socio-economic system was not emphasized upon.[13] Regarding the question of equity it was stated that mere distribution of existing wealth would not make any significant difference to the people as it amounted to 'distribution of poverty'.[14] In order to implement the strategy of planned industrialization a number of regulatory policies were adopted. These regulations were similar to the ones proposed by the Bombay Plan.[15] The Second Five-Year Plan (1956–61) strategy necessitated large critical and maintenance imports.[16] As a consequence, a variety of restrictions on import of non-essentials and low plan priority goods were imposed and a policy of import substitution was promoted to reduce recurring strain on the scarce foreign exchange reserves. This became imperative in view of the fact that the accumulated sterling balances were nearly exhausted by the time the Second Plan came into operation.[17] Import substitution became a key element in the strategy for industrialization. Technical collaborations in the public and private sectors were encouraged. The Second and Third Plan periods also witnessed substantial food imports.[18] While a part of the food imports was initially met through PL 480 and other forms of foreign aid, India continued to face the need to mobilize higher levels of foreign exchange.[19] The reasons have varied but not the basic problem—foreign exchange. It may have been the 1962 conflict with China, the two wars with Pakistan, the continuing strained relations requiring import of sophisticated weaponry[20] or the consequence of liberalized import policies. The foreign exchange constraint has been a long standing problem for Indian policy makers. The importance attached to export earnings was realized and the strategy to be adopted for meeting the foreign exchange requirements was initiated as early as in 1962–63. It was observed that a progressive increase in the country's export earnings should be a major consideration in any scheme for achieving a viable external payments position. To achieve this, it was recognized that it would require: (*a*) a reorientation of the pattern of investment in the light of the nature of demand abroad, (*b*) restraints on domestic demand to have export surpluses, (*c*) promotional measures to cultivate foreign markets abroad, (*d*) liquidation of relative handicaps of indigenous exporters, and (*e*) implementation of high quality standards.[21]

Evolution of export promotion policies

A number of committees have been appointed by the government to identify appropriate incentives as well as to suggest other policy measures to promote Indian exports. A beginning was made with the appointment of a committee under the chairmanship of A.D. Gorwala in 1949.[22] The Gorwala Committee, while recognizing the country's dependence on imports of foodgrains, petroleum and capital goods, favoured a regulatory policy in relation to imports in order to achieve a balance in international payments. The Committee criticized the government's policy of allowing imports of consumer goods to contain inflation as it led to frittering away of the sterling balances and worsening of the balance-of-payments situation. According to the Gorwala Committee, a reduction in the general price level in the domestic economy was a prerequisite for a successful export drive. Its recommendations included:

1. Relaxation and/or removal of regulations on exports.
2. Reduction of export duties.
3. Improvement in the quality of manufactured goods.
4. Abolition of sales tax on goods exported.
5. Income tax concessions.
6. Cost advantage in freight to the ports.

In the face of the foreign exchange crises of the mid-1950s,[23] the government appointed another committee in 1957 under the chairmanship of V.L. D'Souza, to make a 'comprehensive study of all aspects of trade promotion'.[24] The D'Souza Committee observed that the only recourse left for the country was 'to go all-out for an export drive to enable it to pay its way and reinforce its foreign payments position'.[25] The Committee's recommendations included:

1. Simplification and extension of the duty drawback system.
2. Relief from income taxes.
3. Incorporation of export requirements into licencing targets.
4. Production and processing of goods in bond for export purposes.
5. Upgradation of technology and production methods.
6. Diversification of exports and export markets.

7. Setting up of new export promotion councils for commodities which were not already covered.
8. Development and extension of services like shipping, banking, internal transport and insurance.
9. Formation of cooperatives by small producers and exporters.
10. Launching a weekly trade journal and the publication of a directory of exporters.
11. Organizing industrial and commercial exhibitions and fairs.
12. Liberal foreign exchange allowance to exporters to enable them to travel abroad to conclude export deals.
13. Development of facilities for tourists.[26]

The D'Souza Committee's recommendations appear to have laid the foundations of the export policies and strategy of the country. These measures were aimed at ensuring that (*a*) Indian products became more competitive abroad, and (*b*) exports were less unprofitable to domestic manufacturers. As we will see later these measures still appear to be followed, though with wider coverage and variety. The approach towards export promotion was further elaborated by another committee chaired by A. Ramaswami Mudaliar, appointed by the government in 1961. A number of representatives of the private sector, especially big business, were nominated on the Committee, with the chairman himself being one of them.[27] The Committee observed:

> The government will have to carry the business community with it in its effort to make a break-through in the world market. The promotion of our trade depends upon the efficiency of our merchants and manufacturers. It is the business community that would have to shoulder the main burden of responsibility of augmenting the country's export trade.
>
> The mercantile community cannot be expected to be guided by *altruistic or patriotic motives* and will expect to receive, for its efforts in the export market, a return which stands in a reasonable relation with the profits on domestic sales. It would be Government's responsibility to compensate the trade for its export effort through selective concessions, fiscal reliefs and other incentives to make the export business worthwhile over the long haul (emphasis added).[28]

A couple of years after the submission of the Mudaliar Committee report, the government appointed another committee under the chairmanship of T. Swaminathan to recommend measures to speed up industrial approvals.[29] In its interim report the Swaminathan Committee identified certain industries as key industries and recommended that a special procedure should be evolved for dealing with all other clearances required while granting industrial licences such as approval of foreign collaboration terms, approval to issue capital and issue of import licences, special preferential treatment in respect of release of foreign exchange. The Committee recommended the setting up of a separate cell in the Ministry of Industry to receive applications for licences and other clearances and to coordinate with other ministries. The special procedure was expected to cut delays in investment approvals by the government and provide an in-built preference and advantage to key industries. In its final report the Committee recommended that the same facilities as granted to key industries should be extended to import saving and substantially export-oriented industries. The recommendation was accepted by the government and *export-oriented industries were given equal status as that of 'key industries'*.[30]

In June 1966, India devalued its rupee by 57.5 per cent mainly at the instance of the Aid India Consortium and the IMF who insisted on it as a precondition for resumption of aid to India. The devaluation was expected to boost India's exports as Indian goods became cheaper for foreign buyers. Though export incentives were drastically reduced following the devaluation of the rupee, they were soon introduced once again.[31]

An assumption which has gained general acceptance both in India and many of the international institutions in the capitalist world is that transnational corporations (TNCs) with their vast international linkages and control over trade channels and market structures of the industrially advanced countries, are in an advantageous position to help the developing countries in their export efforts. TNCs, it is argued, know the tastes, preferences, and requirements of the foreign consumers. Their brand names are already well established in international markets. In recognition of such arguments, Indian policy makers have treated TNCs, which have high export potential, as a special category. In addition to placing a premium on TNCs, in the hope of export promotion, the technology import policy of the government has also been linked to export potential.

Normally, foreign collaborations were permitted only in high priority areas and in areas where import of technology was found necessary. However, in case the collaborator was able to convince the government of good export potential, foreign collaborations were allowed even in low priority areas. This relaxation appears to have followed mainly from the acceptance of the recommendations of the Committee on Foreign Collaboration (1967) headed by A. Ramaswami Mudaliar which advocated that a 'liberal approach in regard to foreign collaboration would be worthwhile' in respect of 'industries which are substantially export oriented'.[32] Further, according to the Mudaliar Committee, 'The question of international standards is of paramount importance in connection with our need to expand our export markets'.[33] The Committee recommended joint venture collaborations as it believed that Indian manufacturers would have access to 'foreign collaborators' established overseas network of distribution and agents'.[34] However, the conclusions arrived at by the studies undertaken by the Industrial Licensing Policy Inquiry Committee (ILPIC) 1969 did not find empirical justification for the Mudaliar Committee assertions. The ILPIC noted that:

> One reason why foreign firms are interested under conditions such as those obtaining in India in entering into collaborations is that with the existing import restrictions, the only way in which they can have a foothold in the Indian market is through collaborations. On the other hand, having their own interests to pursue in the markets provided by other countries, they would not be normally interested in encouraging exports from India of the products whose production develops through their collaboration.[35]

Of the 270 foreign collaborations studied by the ILPIC, in only 95 (35 per cent) cases exports were freely permitted. The remaining agreements were subjected to varying degrees of restrictions on exports. The imposition of export obligations for new industrial licences has been in practice for a long time. The ILPIC noted that whenever there were doubts about the advisability of the government undertaking foreign exchange commitment involved in foreign collaboration approvals and capital goods imports, or when the items of production were of low priority, conditions used to be attached to the industrial licences for export of a certain proportion of production over a specified period of time.[36] The ILPIC, however, noted that the export obligations existed only on paper. The obligations had no legal or administrative back-up and support.

A comprehensive policy statement on exports was issued in 1970. The policy statement expected the people to view export effort as one of the highest national commitments and sought them to extend to it their wholehearted support and accord due recognition to those engaged in it. The statement added that:

> . . . in pursuing the aim of creation of new export capacities every effort will be made to assist export oriented units in the private and public sectors to achieve economies of scale, improve efficiency of production, reduce costs and adopt production to meet the requirements of their customers abroad. To this end, the procedures relating to foreign investment, licencing of creation or expansion of industrial capacity, licencing of import of capital goods and raw materials or other inputs, will be suitably adapted. Every effort will also be made to secure that indigenous industrial raw materials required for export production are made available in right quality and quantity, and at fair prices.[37]

It also reiterated the need to impose temporary restrictions on domestic consumption in order to retain export markets, whenever such a situation arose.

In 1974 a committee under the chairmanship of M. Sondhi was appointed to suggest means to step up exports of engineering goods. The Sondhi Committee stated that there should be a provision for automatic growth of licenced capacity by 5 per cent per annum or up to 25 per cent in a plan period of five years in 16 specified industries.[38] The Committee noted the fact that licencing of capacity for export purposes was generally freely allowed. This included companies registered under the Monopolies and Restrictive Trade Practices Act (MRTPA) and those covered by the Foreign Exchange Regulation Act (FERA).[39] The Sondhi Committee suggested that the foreign investment policy be relaxed in the case of 100 per cent export-oriented units so as to allow foreign share up to even 100 per cent. For ascertaining the market dominance, for purposes of the operation of the MRTPA, it recommended the exclusion of exports from the company's production. Exploring the possibilities of export of technology and machinery to some of the developing countries, particularly those in Africa and the oil-exporting countries, was another important recommendation of the Committee.

The Committee on Import-Export Policies and Procedures which was appointed in 1977 under the chairmanship of P.C. Alexander submitted its report in 1978.[40] Based on a 'limited examination' of the relationship between cash assistance and exports, the Committee concluded that 'the ratio of incremental cash assistance to incremental exports was not unfavourable'.[41] The Committee was of the opinion that cash assistance should be available for only a limited period during which the disadvantages faced by the exporters should be eliminated. The Committee recommended that export houses be given more facilities such as additional import licences, permission to deal in all types of machinery and equipment (which are permissible under the general import policy) for stocking and sales etc. The Committee also recommended that the policy of canalization be restricted to selected items where the advantages of bulk operations and the need for preventing unfair practices and assurance of long-term supply were significant. A number of items were identified by the Committee for decanalization. One of the main recommendations of the Alexander Committee was the need for a stable export policy for a period of three years. The Committee stated that there was a case for exposing Indian industry to an environment of effective and fair international competition so that its production could be improved thus reducing costs and enhancing quality.

Export promotion policies in the 1980s

In view of the interdependence of a number of issues involved, and in particular, the role played by the industrial licencing policy under the Industries (Development and Regulation) Act of 1951 in determining industrial capacities, the latter has also been altered periodically in response to the recommendations of the different committees which examined the question of export promotion. One view that appears to have gained increasing acceptance in recent times is that Indian industry has become inefficient and lacks dynamism due to the protective industrial policies of the past.[42] The licencing system as it had operated gave rise to monopolies and due to the inefficient structure and consequent high prices, the domestic market had been yielding monopoly profits which in turn had acted as a disincentive for manufacturers to enter into more competitive export markets. The licencing system was also held responsible for stunting the growth of large companies in creating production capabilities for exports and the slow rate of technological advancement and poor quality of manufactured goods. The inefficient Indian industry, thus protected all along, is not in a position to face stiff competition in the international market on the one hand, and on the other would be more than willing to remain in the lucrative domestic market.[43]

These assumptions seem to have influenced the thinking and recommendations of the committees which examined the export policies for the 1980s. The report of the Committee on Export Strategy: 1980s, headed by P.L. Tandon, is an important document in terms of its impact on the approach to the recent economic policies in India.[44] The Committee made a number of recommendations on specific aspects of export promotion including:

1. Extending the automatic escalation in the licenced capacities facility, which was introduced in 1975 subsequent to the Sondhi Committee recommendations, to all units exporting more than 10 per cent of their production (excluding MRTPA and FERA companies).
2. No restrictions to be imposed on the setting up of units in urban areas in the case of units exporting more than 10 per cent of their production.
3. Industrial units exporting more than 25 per cent of their production continuously over a period of three years to be allowed to import capital goods duty free.
4. Rationalization of the indirect tax structure for export-oriented units to exempt them from excise duties on raw materials.
5. Encouraging the emergence of TNCs from India.
6. Reservation of footwear manufacture for the small-scale sector not to be applicable to large exporting units, and export obligations to be introduced in a phased manner.
7. A new category of export houses, namely, trading houses to be introduced.
8. To continuously update technology so that Indian products gain acceptance abroad—for this the technology import policies and procedures should be considerably liberalized.

The changes in industrial policies and economic environment advocated by the Committee were bound to have a far-reaching impact on the economic policy frame of India. The Committee desired to rationalize the 'structure of protection afforded to industry and gradually move to a situation in which the structure of incentives is more evenly balanced between the production of import substitutes and production for exports'.[45] The Committee explained that: 'Licencing restrictions, MRTPA restrictions and restrictions on imported technology all tend to limit the growth of creation of capacity in areas with export potential. Relaxation of these restrictions could provide a considerable stimulus to export'.[46]

The Committee made detailed recommendations on export management at the national, state and sectoral levels. Further, the Committee suggested that in order to offset the disadvantages faced by exporters in the form of non-availability of imported raw materials and components and the high costs and poor quality of domestically available substitutes, the import policy for exporters should be based on the principle of achieving a 'free trade regime for exporters'.[47] The Committee appeared to have made its impact. The Industrial Policy Statement of 1980 announced after a change in the central government, attributed the inability of Indian industrial products to compete in the international markets to the low scales of production and lack of advanced technology. The statement expressed the government's readiness to encourage 100 per cent export-oriented units (henceforth EOUs).[48]

The Tandon Committee report was not unanimous. There were sharp differences on the recommendations and assumptions. Two members recorded a note of dissent.[49] They stated: 'It seems that this Committee on Export Strategy has interpreted its task as one of recommending a series of schemes and methods for promoting exports *without being concerned too much about the economic costs and social consequences of such promotional schemes*' (emphasis added).[50]

The 'quantum jump' in exports, visualized by the majority report, was described 'illogical' in view of the recession in developed countries. The dissenting members saw a distinct prejudice against social justice in the majority view. The dissenting members also disagreed with the assumption of import inflexibility. In support of their argument they outlined the policies that were unsuccessful. Some of these were: (*a*) absence of curbs on the growth of wasteful consumption of petroleum; (*b*) stagnation in coal production; and (*c*) non-implementation of policies to clear infrastructural bottle-necks which could reduce the maintenance imports of steel, cement, paper and other items. They also attributed the problems of the economy to the slowing down and postponing of the import substitution programme.

The dissenting members held that changes in industrial policy had been suggested by the Committee without 'empirical study or analysis to justify such drastic policy changes'.[51] They also pointed out that the Committee's recommendations were biased 'in favour of multinationals'.[52]

In spite of the sharp differences and controversial nature of the Committee, Tandon was nominated by the Government of India to chair another committee in 1981.[53] The second Tandon Committee was appointed to recommend policies regarding export processing zones and 100 per cent export-oriented units. While calling for a new approach to the free trade zones in India, the second Tandon Committee noted that there was a promise, of late, 'of releasing and opening up of the Indian economy and its approach'.[54] In the view of the Committee the free trade zones were to be centres of transnational production. According to the Committee, one of the special attractions of these zones for foreign companies was the access to the Indian market besides the expected markets of their home country and other export markets. The Committee recommended for allowing 25 per cent of the production of the units, located in the EPZs, to be sold in the domestic tariff area. Another important recommendation of the Committee was with regard to trade union activity in the EPZs. The zones, the Committee recommended, could *safely* be exempted from most of the restrictive legislation as there was practically 'little fear of any exploitation of labour in the zones'.[55] The other recommendations of the Committee included:

1. Encouragement of trading activities in the zones.
2. Provision of land free of cost or at nominal rates, and the fixation of rates for the supply of water, electricity etc. on a costs recovery basis.
3. Setting up of new zones.
4. Establishment of a new type of zone for raising fruits, vegetables, flowers and meat.

5. Flexibility in approving the level of foreign equity.
6. Increasing the period of tax holiday from five to 10 years with a provision for the re-examination of the issue at the end of the period.

In 1984, three official committees were at work examining trade, industrial policies and the possible alternatives to controls and regulations: (*a*) the Committee on Perspective Plan and Strategy for Export of Engineering and Capital Goods headed by D.V. Kapur; (*b*) the Committee on Trade Policies constituted under the chairmanship of Abid Hussain; and (*c*) the Committee headed by M. Narasimham to study the possible shifts from physical to financial controls. Their deliberations and recommendations had a direct bearing on the evolution of economic policies of the government.

The Committee on Trade Policies (1984) observed that the earlier combination of economic policies had resulted *inter alia* in creating an environment which was not conducive to a competitive reduction in costs. This had, in turn, led to low quality and high prices. According to the Committee, it was 'necessary to change the nature and quality of state intervention in the economy'. In the perception of the Committee, 'a complete solution cannot be found in the realm of trade policies alone; rationalisation of other economic policies is also necessary'.[56] The Committee on Perspective Plan and Strategy for Export of Engineering and Capital Goods, the Kapur Committee, emphasized the need to modernize Indian industry to improve the engineering industry's competitiveness. The Committee stated that the large houses were not utilizing their resources and capabilities on the export front due to the availability of a protected domestic market. The Committee called for identifying certain 'thrust' industries where liberal technology imports should be allowed and entry by MRTPA–FERA companies be exempted from the special approvals needed under the respective Acts. The incentives and benefits available to exporters, the Committee recommended, should be extended to thrust industries both for their domestic and export operations.[57] A list of sectors chosen for special thrust in export markets is as follows:[58]

1. Tea, especially in packaged and value added forms.
2. Cereals, in particular wheat.
3. Processed foods, including fruits and juices, meat and meat products and fresh fruits and vegetables.

4. Marine products, especially in value added form.
5. Iron ore.
6. Leather, particularly leather manufactures.
7. Handicrafts and jewellery.
8. Capital goods and consumer durables.
9. Electronic goods and computer software.
10. Basic chemicals.
11. Fabrics, piece goods and made-ups.
12. Readymade garments.
13. Woollen fabrics and knitwear.
14. Projects and services.

Thrust industries were also to be allowed to import technology under the Open General Licence (OGL). The Kapur Committee, after having recommended a set of thrust industries and a variety of incentives, felt that:

> With various incentives being considered in this report, there should be *certain amount of interest* shown by the large companies in increasing their export activity, but *in case, this does not happen in practice* the Empowered Committee (the setting up of which was recommended by the Kapur Committee) should take the initiative of asking the larger manufacturing units to draw up long term export plans as well as medium term targets and this should be watched periodically through the mechanism of [the] Empowered Committee. This should be with a view to *urging larger companies* to go into meaningful export thrusts rather than be lured by the domestic market[59] (emphasis added).

The data on the relative profitability of export and domestic markets for 17 selected industries, on which the Committee relied, were prepared by the World Bank.[60]

The restrictive nature of the industrial licencing system has been viewed by many vocal sections of the economy as the main cause for the lack of competitiveness of Indian industry and, consequently, for the poor performance of Indian exports. An alternative scheme was proposed by the Committee to Examine Principles of a Possible Shift from Physical to Financial Controls (henceforth the Narasimham Committee).[61] A review of the report of the Narasimham Committee is necessary, though it did not address itself directly to the problem of export promotion, due to the fact of the close interlinkages between the policies examined by this Committee, the D.V. Kapoor Committee and the Committee on Trade Policies. A little earlier, the Committee on Trade Policies under the chairmanship of Abid Hussain had emphasized the need for a change in the nature of state interventions. The Narasimham Committee was expected to examine the whole gamut of physical regulations and suggest possible alternative financial controls.

While commenting on a wide range of issues the Narasimham Committee did not seem to have any study to go by. The appendices published later are more in the nature of executive summaries of policy statements. The Narasimham and the Abid Hussain Committees reached similar conclusions with regard to repetitive imports of technology. The Narasimham Committee was of the view that there was an element of repetitiveness in the foreign collaborations approved during the past four years in the light commercial vehicle industry, but supported the same as such import of technology, 'helps prevent emergence of monopoly or oligopoly condition and is justified as long as this is not carried to the extreme of free import of such technology'.[62] The Abid Hussain Committee stated: 'The multiplicity and periodicity of technology imports should not be over regulated in so far as it limits competition between firms in the economy'.[63] The real costs to the economy in terms of foreign exchange outgo or the needless 'competition' for imported technology for the sake of remaining in the market were not examined by either of the Committees,[64] nor did they offer any concrete solution to the vexatious problem of the negative effects of imported technology on indigenous research and development.

The style of the Narasimham Committee report makes an interesting reading. For example, regarding industrial licencing the Committee observed that: '. . . a change to a system of licencing by exception would be logical but also far reaching. However, on *practical and administrative considerations*, we feel that it would be difficult to go over to such a system at the present time' (emphasis added).[65]

The Committee did not spell out the administrative considerations in support of its recommendation of 'delicencing certain industries' instead of, as per the Committee, maintaining a negative list excluding the rest of the industries from the scope of licencing.[66] Similarly, on the one hand the Committee expressed satisfaction over the operation of capital issues control, in particular the quick disposal of applications; on the other hand, it recommended a hike in the exemption limit from Rs 1 crore to Rs 3 crores.

Much has been said about the policy regarding reservation of items for production in the small-scale sector, their lack of quality, high cost etc. The Narasimham Committee specifically mentioned some articles of mass consumption and consumer durables being reserved for the small-scale sector neglecting the economies of scale. However, the Committee overlooked the fact that many large companies marketed consumer durables and other components manufactured by small-scale manufacturers under their own brand names. Large companies find it more advantageous to trade than to manufacture those items.[67]

The Narasimham Committee suggested that foreign technical collaboration should not be permitted in light consumer industries, where brand names were more important than technology, with exceptions for exports. On other collaborations, which satisfy the prescribed limits with regard to royalty and lump sum payments, the Committee suggested that these should be taken on record by the administrative ministries instead of being sent to the Foreign Investment Board for prior approval. The Committee stated that all foreign collaboration proposals *including those not requiring prior approval* should contain plans for research and development. If, however, some collaborations were going to be taken only on record, it becomes difficult to understand how collaborations in consumer goods industries and low priority industries could be avoided and research and development plans insisted upon. Also, while admitting that export obligations have remained obligations on paper, the Committee recommended the imposition of such obligations in the case of collaborations in consumer goods industries. The safeguard suggested is that in case the export obligations were not met, this fact 'would be taken into account' while considering fresh collaboration proposals of either of the two parties *i.e.* the recipient as well as the supplier.[68] It is difficult to anticipate the success of this measure. There are many questions which remain unanswered.[69]

It is difficult to understand why the Narasimham Committee did not discuss the relative advantages of financial controls over physical controls before recommending them. The Committee only 'believed' that greater use of excise duties and tariff policy would protect specific industries or industrial sectors like the small-scale sector and also prevent the flow of resources to low priority industries.[70] The administrative steps required to implement this suggestion were not deliberated upon.

The policy for export promotion has been subjected to constant review. A number of official committees made recommendations to help achieve higher level of exports. The recommendations of these committees were generally accepted by the government. There appears to be a similarity and commonness of approach among the recommendations that have been made more recently.[71] Not much empirical examination seems to have been done to support the recommendations in spite of their touching upon a number of issues of fundamental importance. The organized private industrial associations such as FICCI and ASSOCHAM have consistently maintained that the government should give more and more concessions to larger national enterprises who alone can compete internationally. The concessions sought are broadly of two types: liberal fiscal concessions, and exemptions from the economic regulatory mechanisms. Government policies have been generally receptive to such demands. Export promotion plea has in fact been used as an excuse to initiate all types of administrative and economic regulations in India.[72]

As a result of the recommendations of successive export promotion committees, a variety of incentives and facilities are now being offered to Indian exporters. Simultaneously, institutional support has also been developed.

TRENDS IN INDIA'S FOREIGN TRADE

The opening up of the economy and policies toward liberalization are the culmination of the trends in policies initiated in 1961. The extent of direct financial assistance provided by the government is reflected in the fact that subsidies on export promotion occupy the third highest position in the subsidy structure of the central government and the size of subsidy has been rising rapidly. Against the budgeted amount of Rs 555 crores for the year 1986–87, the revised estimate of export subsidies was Rs 788 crores. The corresponding budgeted amount for 1987–88 was Rs 870 crores. The share of export subsidies in total subsidies increased from 11.04 per cent in the 1986–87 budget to 15.52 per cent in the 1987–88 budget.[73] With export promotion occupying an important place in Indian economic policy and this being the guiding force behind a number of changes in policies it would be relevant to examine the present status of Indian exports.

The growth of Indian exports, the corresponding growth in imports and the share of Indian exports in world exports are shown in Table 1. One notable feature is that while there has been a steady growth in the value of exports, the import bill has risen much faster and as a result trade deficit has increased. Indeed, there was a steep increase in the trade deficit during 1980–81 which has remained consistently above Rs 5,000 crores since then. The picture was more dismal during 1985–86. While exports declined in value terms, imports shot up by more than Rs 2,500 crores. As a

TABLE 1
The Growth of India's Foreign Trade (in Rs. crores)

Year	*Exports (Rs Crores)*	*Imports (Rs Crores)*	*Balance of Trade (Rs Crores)*	*India's Share in World Exports (%)*
1972–73	1970.83	1867.44	103.39	0.58
1973–74	2523.40	2955.37	−431.97	0.51
1974–75	3328.83	4518.78	−1189.95	0.47
1975–76	4036.26	5264.78	−1228.52	0.50
1976–77	5142.71	5073.79	68.92	0.56
1977–78	5407.87	6020.23	−612.36	0.56
1978–79	5726.07	6810.64	−1084.57	0.51
1979–80	6418.43	9142.58	−2724.15	0.48
1980–81	6710.70	12549.15	−5838.45	0.42
1981–82	7805.91	13607.55	−5801.64	0.42
1982–83	8803.37	14292.74	−5489.37	0.47
1983–84	9770.71	15831.46	−6060.75	0.48
1984–85	11743.68	17134.20	−5390.52	0.46
1985–86*	11011.96	19759.43	−8747.47	..

Notes: * Provisional.
.. No data available.
Figures on India's share in world exports refer to the corresponding calendar years. For example, 0.58 shown against 1972–73 is actually based on the data for 1972.

Sources: Government of India, Ministry of Commerce, *Report of the Committee on Trade Policies*, 1984, for the period 1972–73 to 1981–82; and Government of India, Ministry of Commerce (Dept of Commerce), *Annual Report: 1986–87*, p. 12, for the remaining years.

result, the trade deficit increased by nearly 65 per cent over the preceding year's deficit. It is significant to note that the worsening of trade deficit coincided with the initiation of the current liberalization drive that was introduced in the early 1980s.[74]

During the period 1975–76 to 1984–85 India's exports rose from Rs 4,036.26 crores to Rs 11,743.68 crores representing an increase of Rs 7,707.42 crores. This increase was mainly accounted for by the manufacturing sector which contributed Rs 4,459 crores. Other sectors which contributed to this increase were mineral fuel and lubricants (Rs 1,787.36 crores) and agriculture and allied products (Rs 1,502.70 crores) (see Table 2). Since non-manufactured exports do not necessarily reflect the economic strength and competitiveness of a country's industry, and the emphasis in the proposals for a New International Economic Order is on manufactured exports of developing countries, we will examine in some detail the composition of India's manufactured exports.

In the case of manufactured exports there appears to be some confusion in the published data on exports of engineering goods. The total exports of manufactured goods are less than the reported sub-group totals within the manufactured sector for the period since 1982–83. The footnote provided to the tables is also not of much help.[75] Till 1981–82 it appears that exports of some of the engineering items were being clubbed with 'other' exports. This is indicated by a sudden decline in the exports of 'others' from Rs 531.46 crores in 1981–82 to only Rs 70.15 crores in the subsequent year. It is somewhat inexplicable, why the totals for manufactured exports were not adjusted for the changed groupings. The problem of identifying engineering exports becomes more complicated if one takes note of the figures provided by the Committee on Perspective Plan and Strategy for Export of Engineering and Capital Goods in 1984. There is a wide gap between the export figures referred to by the Committee for the period 1981–82 to 1983–84 and what one finds in the official publications. For instance, according to the Committee, India's exports of engineering goods were Rs 1,060, Rs 1,250 and Rs 1,170 crores during 1981–82, 1982–83, and 1983–84, respectively. The corresponding export figures as provided in the *Economic Survey* (1984–85) were Rs 945.67, Rs 841.91 and Rs 734.70 crores, respectively.[76] Why is there such large variation in the engineering exports of the corresponding years? Could it be that the Committee took all the exports of companies classified by it, or any other agency on which it relied, as 'engineering companies', irrespective of the composition of their exports? In some of the years even the inclusion of exports of chemical industry would not be able to bridge the gap between the two estimates. However, the gap between the two sources for earlier years was marginal. For instance, the Committee gave an estimate of engineering exports of Rs 408.22 crores for the year 1975–76, while the *Economic Survey* estimated Rs 408.66 crores (excluding iron and steel prime) as engineering exports for the same year. This factor needs to be investigated further.

In view of the non-uniformity of data, the totals for manufactured exports were recalculated using the given sub-group totals. The results of this exercise are presented in Table 3. It can be seen that exports of manufactured goods increased by nearly three times from Rs 1,682.12 crores in 1975–76 to Rs 6,583.18 crores in 1984–85. Of the total increase of Rs 4,901.06 crores an amount of Rs 1,969.85 crores was accounted for by textiles and their manufactures (or 40.19 per cent of the increased exports). This was followed by handicrafts with Rs 1,431.16 crores (29.20 per cent). The share of leather manufactures including footwear was Rs 520.72 crores (10.62 per cent). Taking into consideration other traditional exports such as jute and coir products, the share of sectors that use traditional technology was 82.09 per cent of the total increase in manufactured exports during the period 1975–76 to 1984–85. Thus, the combined share of engineering and chemical industries was 17.91 per cent only.

Traditional items accounted for nearly two-thirds of India's manufactured exports in 1975–76. However, due to their higher share in increased exports at 82.09 per cent, their share in the total increased substantially in 1984–85 to 78.15 per cent, which means that the share of the non-traditional sector was just 21.85 per cent. The sectors which mainly gained in the process were textiles (from 24.19 per cent to 36.10 per cent) and handicrafts (from 13.32 per cent to 25.14 per cent). These results indicate that the non-traditional or modern manufacturing sector is losing its significance in India's exports. This is particularly true with regard to exports of engineering items. Their position becomes worse if one takes into consideration the fact that until 1981–82, not all engineering exports were being reported as engineering goods in the official statistics.

TABLE 2

Composition of India's Exports

	Item/Sub-group	*Value of Exports (Rs Crores)*			*Share in Total (%)*		
		1975–76	*1980–81*	*1984–85*	*1975–76*	*1980–81*	*1984–85*
I.	Agriculture & Allied Products	1493.63	2056.66	2996.33	37.01	30.65	25.51
	Coffee	66.55	214.24	210.22	1.65	3.19	1.79
	Tea and Mate	236.81	425.50	766.69	5.87	6.34	6.53
	Oil Cakes	86.12	125.08	136.92	2.13	1.86	1.17
	Tobacco	98.37	140.68	178.34	2.44	2.10	1.52
	Cashew Kernels	96.13	140.13	179.68	2.38	2.09	1.53
	Spices	70.96	11.36	206.67	1.76	0.17	1.76
	Sugar and Sugar Preparations	472.33	35.96	36.13	11.70	0.54	0.31
	Raw Cotton	39.24	164.87	59.73	0.97	2.46	0.51
	Rice	13.04	223.86	169.19	0.32	3.34	1.44
	Fish & Fish Preparations	126.56	217.02	381.37	3.14	3.23	3.25
	Meat & Meat Preparations	10.28	55.49	82.50	0.25	0.83	·0.70
	Vegetable Oils	37.15	21.95	55.18	0.92	0.33	0.47
	Fruits, Vegetables & Pulses	37.27	79.58	183.13	0.92	1.19	1.56
II.	Ores and Minerals	296.32	413.56	637.61	7.34	6.16	5.43
	Manganese Ore	17.51	12.69	23.61	0.43	0.19	0.20
	Mica	14.63	17.68	19.57	0.36	0.26	0.17
	Iron Ore	213.79	303.33	459.44	5.30	4.52	3.91
III.	Manufactured Goods	1750.97	3746.81	6210.09	43.38	55.83	52.88
	Textile Fabric & Manufactures	406.89	932.58	2376.74	10.08	13.90	20.24
	of which						
	(i) Cotton Piece Goods	158.74	276.49	450.50	3.93	4.12	3.84
	(ii) Cotton Apparel	146.40	378.18	919.23	3.63	5.64	7.83

	Coir Yarn and Manufactures	19.02	17.26	27.85	0.47	0.26	0.24
	Jute Manufactures incl. Yarn	248.31	329.95	341.26	6.15	4.92	2.91
	Leather & Leather Manufactures	201.30	337.13	694.83	4.99	5.02	5.92
	Footwear	21.20	40.07	48.39	0.53	0.60	0.41
	Handicrafts	224.11	935.40	1655.27	5.55	13.94	14.09
	of which						
	(i) Pearls & Precious Stones	122.94	601.92	1153.27	3.05	8.97	9.82
	Chemical & Allied Products	84.45	224.80	482.86	2.09	3.35	4.11
	Engineering Goods	408.66	815.01	880.25	10.12	12.14	7.50
	Iron & Steel (Prime)	68.18	11.68	75.73	1.69	0.17	0.64
IV.	Mineral Fuel & Lubricants	35.58	27.85	1822.94	0.88	0.42	15.52
V.	Others	459.76	465.82	76.71	11.39	6.94	0.65
	Total	4036.26	6710.70	11743.68	100.00	100.00	100.00

TABLE 3

Composition of India's Manufactured Exports

Product Group	Value of Exports (Rs Crores)			Share in Total Exports (%)		Export Increase (Rs Crores)	Share in Increase (%)
	1975–76	*1980–81*	*1984–85*	*1975–76*	*1984–85*	*1975–85*	*1975–85*
1. Textile Fabric & Manufactures	406.89	932.58	2376.74	24.19	36.10	1969.85	40.19
Cotton Piece Goods	158.74	276.49	450.50	9.44	6.84	291.76	5.95
Cotton Apparel	146.40	378.18	919.23	8.70	13.96	772.83	15.77
2. Coir Yarn and Manufactures	19.02	17.26	27.85	1.13	0.42	8.83	0.18
3. Jute Manufactures incl. Yarn	248.31	329.95	341.26	14.76	5.18	92.95	1.90
4. Leather & Leather Manufactures	201.30	337.13	694.83	11.97	10.55	493.53	10.07
5. Footwear	21.20	40.07	48.39	1.26	0.74	27.19	0.55
6. Handicrafts	224.11	935.40	1655.27	13.32	25.14	1431.16	29.20
Pearls & Precious Stones	122.94	601.92	1153.27	7.31	17.52	1030.33	21.02
7. Chemical & Allied Products	84.45	224.80	482.86	5.02	7.33	398.41	8.13
8. Engineering Goods	408.66	815.01	880.25	24.29	13.37	471.59	9.62
9. Iron & Steel (Prime)	68.18	11.68	75.73	4.05	1.15	7.55	0.15
10. Manufactured Goods	1682.12	3643.88	6583.18	100.00	100.00	4901.06	100.00

Source: Based on data provided in Government of India, Ministry of Finance, *Economic Survey: 1986–87*.

An interesting feature emerges from a close examination of the exports of handicrafts. The share of pearls and precious stones as part of handicrafts has been increasing rapidly. From 54.86 per cent in 1975–76 it increased to 64 35 in 1980–81 and further to 69.67 in 1984–85. Its contribution was 17.52 per cent in the total manufactured exports of the country in 1984–85. On the import side, one finds that imports of pearls and precious stones for processing and re-exporting have also been rising rapidly. Imports in relation to exports are generally much higher in recent years as compared to the mid-1970s. While the average imports to exports ratio was 0.60 during the three-year period 1974–77, the corresponding ratio for the period 1983–86 was 0.85.[77] This may be an indication of a leakage in exports earnings or a reflection of the tough international market conditions. The government also expressed its concern over the decreasing net value of exports of pearls and precious stones and attributed it to the saturated international market for small sized diamonds which India specializes in.[78] It may thus be seen that India's exports have largely been confined to low technology goods and primary products. The decline in the share of engineering goods is of significance. The government attributed this to a combination of factors such as excessive protection of domestic industry, lack of quality consciousness, failure to modernize, rising domestic demand, adverse international factors such as slow recovery in the western countries, continued debt problems of developing countries and reduced demand from the OPEC countries.[79] The performance of the chemical industry has also not been satisfactory. Apart from its low share in total exports, its composition also does not present an encouraging picture. Indian exports in this sector are dependent to a large extent on dyeing, tanning and colouring material, medicines and pharmaceutical preparations and toiletries and cleaning preparations.

Viewed from a different perspective, the movement of India's share in world exports is not encouraging as has been shown by Van Dijck in Part I of this volume. In contrast to the pre-1980 period, when India's share was slightly above 0.5 per cent, in the 1980s it varied between 0.4 and 0.5 per cent. Though there was a slight improvement after 1981–82, the trend is not clear. The changes in India's share in world exports of a number of products during 1980–84 are presented in Table 4. It should be mentioned here that the country had a share of more than 1 per cent (1.04) in

TABLE 4
India's Share in World Exports of Selected Commodities, 1980 and 1984
(in percentages)

S. No.	*Commodity Group*	*1980*	*1984*	*Direction of Change*
1.	Meat and Meat Preparation	0.35	0.54	+
2.	Fish, Crustaceans & Molluscs Preparations Thereof	1.97	2.64	+
3.	Cereals and Cereal Preparations	0.48	0.25	–
4.	Vegetables and Fruits	1.08	1.20	+
5.	Sugar, Sugar Preparations and Honey	0.28	0.94	+
6.	Coffee, Tea, Cocoa, Spices and Manufactures Thereof	3.98	2.47	–
7.	Feeding Stuff for Animals	1.59	1.02	–
8.	Tobacco and Tobacco Manufactures	2.38	1.03	–
9.	Oilseed and Oleaginous Fruits	0.32	0.16	–
10.	Metalliferous Ores and Metal Scrap	1.54	1.97	+
11.	Organic Chemicals	0.05	0.07	+
12.	Inorganic Chemicals	0.17	0.14	–
13.	Dyeing, Tanning and Colouring Material	0.82	0.45	–
14.	Medicinal and Pharmaceutical Products	0.79	0.27	–
15.	Essential Oil & Perfume Material Toiletries, Polishing and Cleaning Preparations	1.12	0.41	–
16.	Explosives and Pyrotechnic Products	0.12	0.15	+
17.	Artificial Resins and Plastic Material and Cellulose Esters and Ethers	0.01	0.03	+
18.	Chemical Materials and Products n.e.s.	0.05	0.06	+
19.	Leather, Leather Mfrs., n.e.s. & Dressed Fur Skins	6.79	5.64	–
20.	Textiles Yarn, Fabrics, Made-up Articles n.e.s. and Related Products	2.34	1.71	–
21.	Iron and Steel	0.13	0.13	
22.	Manufactures of Metals n.e.s.	0.60	0.72	+
23.	Power Generating Machinery and Equipment	0.25	0.17	–
24.	Machinery Specialized for Particular Inds	0.11	0.10	–
25.	Metal Working Machinery	0.21	0.09	–
26.	General Industrial Machinery and Equipment n.e.s. and Machine Parts Thereof	0.11	.0.12	+
27.	Office Machinery and ADP Equipment	0.01	0.12	+
28.	Telecommunication and Sound Recording and Reproducing Apparatus and Equipment	0.04	0.02	–

Table 4 (Continued)

S. No.	Commodity Group	1980	1984	Direction of Change
29.	Electrical Machinery, Parts, & Appliances n.e.s.	0.19	0.09	−
30.	Road Vehicles	0.16	0.05	−
31.	Other Transport Equipment	0.08	0.55	+
32.	Articles of Apparel & Clothing Accessories	1.82	1.94	+

Source: Based on information derived from Government of India, *Economic Survey: 1986–87*.

1960 which itself was less than the respective shares in 1958 (1.27 per cent) and in 1948 (2.57 per cent).[80]

As noted earlier, industries that use traditional technology are the main earners of foreign exchange. An additional phenomenon which needs to be underlined is that the small-scale sector has a significant share in exports. Its share in the total exports of the country in 1978–79 was 18.79 per cent (see Table 5), and it increased to 21.96 per cent in 1984–85. Exports from the sector more than doubled within a span of five years. In 1979–80, these exports were to the tune of Rs 1,226 crores. In 1984–85, the contribution of the

TABLE 5

Share of the Small Scale Sector in India's Exports

Year	Small-scale Sector Exports (Rs Crores)	Total Exports (Rs Crores)	Share of Small-scale Sector (%)
1978–79	1076	5726	18.79
1979–80	1226	6459	18.98
1980–81	1519	6704	22.66
1981–82	2029	7798	26.07
1982–83	2095	8803	23.80
1983–84	2350	9771	24.05

Sources: Data on small-scale sector for 1978–79 taken from Government of India, Ministry of Industry, Department of Industrial Development, *Performance Budget*, 1983–84; for 1979–80 to 1984–85 taken from Government of India, Development Commissioner for Small Scale Industries, *Annual Report of the Small Industries Development Organisation, 1985–86*, p. 74; data on total exports based on same source as Table 1.

small-scale sector was Rs 2,579 crores which indicated a 110 per cent increase over 1979–80. These exports do not include the exports of small-scale units effected through export houses and other merchant exporters.[81] The contribution of the small-scale sector to India's exports is quite significant. If exports are less profitable and India's disadvantage lies in fragmented and uneconomic industrial capacities, how can one explain the performance of the small-scale sector on the export front?

The situation becomes more interesting if one considers the role played by the public sector in India's export efforts.[82] The growth and composition of the export earnings of the central public sector undertakings during the period 1977–78 to 1984–85 are presented in Table 6. A striking phenomenon is the increasing share of the sector in total exports. From about 20 per cent in 1977–78, its share more than doubled to 41 per cent by 1983–84, though there was a slight decline in 1984–85. This was due to the faster growth of exports of the public sector as compared to total exports: while its exports have increased by more than four times, total exports of the country have just about doubled during the same period. Was this due to the role of the public sector as a canalizing agency? Available data suggest just the opposite. Canalized exports having remained more or less between Rs 600–700 crores per annum, non-canalized exports seem to account for the growth of public sector exports. In fact, the share of canalized items in exports of the public sector decreased from 61.82 per cent in 1977–78 to 15.81 per cent in 1984–85. Correspondingly, the importance of canalized items declined in the aggregate exports from 12.16 per cent to 6.09 per cent. It may be mentioned here that the expert committees studying the export strategies of the country have generally not been in favour of canalization.[83]

INDUSTRIAL LICENCING, ECONOMIES OF SCALE AND EXPORT PROMOTION

The industrial licencing policy has been viewed by its critics as the cause of a number of shortcomings of the Indian industry.[84] It may be useful at this point to describe the way the licencing policy was implemented, with a view to foresee the possible implications of the changes introduced in the 1980s. For a long time the small and medium scale industrial sectors were exempted from the operation

TABLE 6

Share of the Central Public Sector in India's Exports

Year	*Public Sector Exports*		*Total Exports (Rs Crores)*	*Share of Canalized Exports in*		*Share of Public Sector in Total Exports (%)*
	Canalized (Rs Crores)	*Total (Rs Crores)*		*Public Sector Exports (%)*	*Total Exports (%)*	
1977–78	657.53	1063.57	5407.87	61.82	12.16	19.67
1978–79	723.12	1188.77	5726.07	60.83	12.63	20.76
1979–80	753.82	1139.16	6418.43	66.17	11.74	17.75
1980–81	660.65	1387.68	6710.70	47.61	9.84	20.68
1981–82	611.99	1722.08	7805.90	35.54	7.84	22.06
1982–83	651.57	3404.43	8803.37	19.14	7.40	38.67
1983–84	709.85	4026.74	9770.71	17.63	7.27	41.21
1984–85	715.09	4521.89	11743.68	15.81	6.09	38.50

Source: Based on information derived from Bureau of Public Enterprises, *Public Enterprises Survey*, various issues.

of the industrial licencing system.[85] The approach to regulation of the private industrial sector began to change in the 1970s. This was true in spite of the enactment of the Monopolies and Restrictive Trade Practices Act, 1969 and the Foreign Exchange Regulation Act, 1973. The restrictions envisaged under the licencing system were relaxed significantly in the 1970s.[86]

The MRTPA is viewed as a hindrance to the growth of the large industrial sector. But even leaving aside the fact of avoidance of registration under the Act by companies belonging to large industrial houses which enabled them to enjoy more freedom,[87] the MRTPA did not stand in the way of growth of the large corporate sector. The administration of the Act by the government also did not leave much scope for the MRTP Commission to study each case and advise the government accordingly. No sooner than plugging some of the lacunae in the functioning of the Act in 1984, the asset limit for registration under the Act was raised from Rs 20 crores to Rs 100 crores. Consequently, a number of companies got themselves de-registered. It is even argued that the objective of the MRTPA is not to curb the growth of large industrial houses *per se*.[88] The rapid growth in the assets of the houses/companies registered under the MRTPA should not come as a surprise.[89] Quite apart from this, as a general policy there are no limits on MRTPA or FERA companies to expand into desired areas, if they agree to undertake exports. These companies can also market the products of other non-associated manufacturers, often belonging to the small-scale sector. There is no bar on this practice. Indeed, the policies seem to encourage this.[90] Also, export obligations have been either reduced or abolished in case these manufacturers agree to set up their plants in identified industrially backward areas.[91] These are obviously not in conformity with the export promotion objective.

It may be of interest to estimate the number of companies registered under the MRTPA under clauses relating to product dominance and those registered under FERA. The number of dominant companies under the MRTPA is less than 100.[92] According to the available official information, there are approximately 100 FERA companies (excluding foreign branches and those established in the EPZs) in the country. Out of these only 66 had a subsidiary status as of 31 March 1988, and only 37 were engaged in processing and manufacturing. Most of the companies which had initially attracted the provisions of FERA had diluted their foreign equity to 40 per cent or less, and were eligible to be treated as Indian national companies for purposes of industrial licencing. Any further liberalization would enable the few FERA companies to enter into non-priority, low technology and reserved areas of manufacturing activity, besides encouraging new companies to be established.

Several factors adversely affected the administration of the licencing system. Due to numerous loopholes in the system it was violated with impunity.[93] The unauthorized capacities built up by the industrial units coupled with the various relaxations resulted in the installed capacities not having any direct relationship with the licenced capacities.[94] In practice the unauthorized capacities were 'recognized', 'regularized' and 're-endorsed' through a series of policy announcements. The failure of the licencing system in curbing the growth of the large corporate sector in areas reserved for the small-scale sector is well known.[95]

In the 1980s there were further relaxations in the licencing policy. The exemption limit for industrial licencing was raised from Rs 3 crores to Rs 5 crores. At present, the limit is Rs 50 crores and is subject to locational constraints. The accompanying ceiling on raw material imports was raised from Rs 40 lakhs to Rs 75 lakhs. Significant among the other measures adopted were the broad banding of licences for a number of industries and fixing of a minimum scale of operations in a wide range of industries. The period also witnessed a substantial increase in the number of industries open for MRTPA and FERA companies. Another important policy change was with respect to the opening up of some of the industries reserved for the public sector. Telecommunication equipment is one such industry. There was also systematic and effective de-reservation of industrial products reserved for the small-scale sector.[96]

THE EXPORT PERFORMANCE OF INDIAN COMPANIES

Introduction

The previous sections of this study outlined the evolution of the export policies in India. The general thrust of the policies has been to bring about a shift in the country's export basket i.e. from predominantly primary exports to substantial exports of industrial manufactures. Policy planners have repeatedly emphasized the need to strengthen the industrial sector in such a way so as to enhance the country's export potential. The need for international restructuring has been emphasized not only in India but also at various international fora. The emphasis on expanding industrial exports has led to the impression, in many quarters, that India is probably seeking to pursue export-led growth. While export-led growth may be an exaggeration, it is not disputed that liberal imports and a push towards export marketing are pleaded to improve quality, end monopoly profits, reduce prices and inject a new dynamism in the industrial sector, this can be done only if controls and regulations are relaxed. Thus, export-led growth may not be viewed in terms of size or the relative significance of exports in the national income. The plea is more in terms of qualitative changes. In a large country like India with a foreign trade sector accounting for only a small proportion of the national economy, export-led growth may not be the answer to development. However, it is true that many policy initiatives have been taken with the desire to achieve higher exports. For instance, restrictions on expansion of industrial capacities have been relaxed or even abolished on the plea to harness economies of scale. It has been argued that Indian exports would thus be in a better position to face international competition. Also, the operation of the Indian anti-monopoly legislation has been set aside on the export potential logic.[97] The national sensitivities of the period before independence against the existence or expansion of foreign private capital have been modified to enable the country to earn the much needed foreign exchange. Import policies have been liberalized to help link Indian industry with international sophisticated centres for research and development and to upgrade production technologies.

Another reason for the liberalization policy has been the need to shake up the local industrialists who have been taking advantage of the protected market and have prospered at the cost of the helpless Indian consumer for too long. It has also been said that the controlled regime has made the producers complacent regarding quality, innovation and the genuine demands of a competitive market. In short, export policies have: (*a*) sought to strengthen trends towards large-scale production, (*b*) assigned a larger role to foreign private capital and technology, and (*c*) relaxed administrative controls and restrictions. There is a basic shift in the policy framework. The assumption underlying all-round change is that India's export potential, especially in the industrial sector, would radically improve. The organized and the large private sector along with the TNCs were expected to take the lead in this.

The process of change in the policies was initiated more than a decade ago. The FERA guidelines were notified in December 1973. The industrial licencing exemptions for exports, opening up of the economy to foreign capital and many other measures were initiated during the mid-1970s. In the 1980s the process was taken further. In particular 1985 and 1986 witnessed the publication of three important reports each of which had a direct impact on the process of restructuring of the Indian industrial sector.[98]

Policy makers expect that reduced regulations and increased entry into desired areas would encourage large houses and foreign companies to take advantage of the situation: *first*, to increase their production capacity to economic levels and thus improve their competitive strength in the international markets. *Second*, along with this, the liberal imports of technology would reduce the technological gap with developed countries which would lead to a greater acceptance of Indian exports abroad. Without going into the debate on the influence of protectionism in developed countries on exports from developing countries and in particular on India's own dependence for hard currency earnings, and the possible effects of over- and under-invoicing of imports and exports, one would like to assess the possibilities of success of the current strategy. The focus is on Indian big business and TNCs. This is made amply clear by the Seventh Five-Year Plan document. The rationale for the strategy is provided as follows:

> . . . export selling involves location of buyers and establishment of trading connections over an immensely large area; changes in tariffs or trade regulation in importing countries, intense competitions and shifts in tastes or technology add to the complexities and risks selling in the world market. However, large well-established firms in manufacturing, owing to the experience accumulated and connections developed over decades, possess substantially the type of flexibility and resources required to operate abroad. The success of policy adjustments will therefore depend, among other things, on the responsiveness of large firms, and on their willingness to equip for and invest in a substantial expansion of export operations instead of continuing

to rely mainly on the domestic market. Small firms do not have similar resources at their disposal. In their case an important role could be played by large merchandising houses which would mobilize finance, organize supplies and develop commercial contacts to establish viable export markets.[99]

It has been indicated that the evolution of policies was based on a variety of assumptions and *a priori* reasoning. There remains a need to assess the efficacy of the export policies in terms of achieving the desired results. This question has, in particular, to be addressed to the large private corporate sector, as anti-monopoly legislation, relaxations in industrial licencing and the permission to enter into financial and technical collaborations are more relevant to this sector than to the medium and small-scale enterprises or cottage industries. Indian private industrialists and their representatives often find a place in the committees appointed to study official policies. Occasionally, they might even dominate the constitution of such committees. In the case of official committees appointed to suggest export promotion policies one finds that the private organized sector played an important role.[100] The involvement of the large private sector, one hopes, ensures their cooperation in earning net additional foreign exchange for the country. How this large sector has responded to the governmental efforts at increasing export earnings is thus a matter of crucial concern both for policy makers as well as for students of economics.

An attempt will be made to examine empirically the extent of participation by the large private enterprises in the process of export promotion. At the first instance, one may analyse the rate of growth in exports undertaken by the large companies. The value of exports, however, as a basis to analyse the export efforts may not be a good indicator for two reasons. First, the value of exports conceals the impact of price increases. One would need to undertake an elaborate exercise to obtain deflated prices for each group of exports separately. Second, the export data as such do not show the extent to which the enhanced exports contributed to earning net foreign exchange for the Indian economy. The export performance will be examined in terms of growth rates and also from the viewpoint of net foreign exchange earnings. An attempt will also be made to examine the extent to which the large private corporate sector has become export-oriented *i.e.* the trend in exports as a share of the overall sales turnover by the major constituents of the corporate sector.

In addition to the overall analysis, an attempt will be made to examine trends by grouping companies according to the industry classification. The study also examines the performance of different categories of companies on the basis of the extent of foreign control in enterprises and their association with the top 20 industrial houses of the country.

Data, classification and methodology

Since the objective of the present study is to analyse the performance of the large private corporate sector in response to the export promotion package, only those public limited companies which have more than Rs 1.00 crore risk capital at the end of March 1984 have been included. The period 1975–76 to 1983–84 has been chosen for purpose of the study. The annual data refer to the accounting year of the companies ending any time during the corresponding financial year *i.e.* April to March. Out of the total of 428 public limited companies identified, the number of companies engaged in electricity were nine, shipping eight, and road transport two. Four of the companies were permitted to withhold information on foreign exchange transactions and on their physical functioning by the government. After excluding these 23 companies the coverage is restricted to 405 companies. These companies have been grouped on the basis of the pattern of shareholding and the nature of management control as noted at the end of the period under study.[101] Foreign controlled companies in the list have been divided under the following four sub-groups.[102]

1. Subsidiaries of foreign companies.
2. Companies that retained 40 to 50 per cent foreign equity.
3. Companies with 25–40 per cent foreign equity (subdivided into former FERA companies and others).
4. Companies with 10 to 25 per cent foreign equity.

Categories (1) and (2) cover companies which remained under FERA throughout the period under study. Category (3) comprises the former FERA companies which have diluted their foreign equity to a level that they no longer attract FERA, and those with

25–40 per cent foreign equity at the time FERA was implemented. Many of the former FERA companies were earlier operating in India as subsidiaries.

A note has been made of the companies registered under the MRTPA as at the end of 1983.[103] The house association is determined for the top 20 houses only.[104] Each of these 405 companies has been classified on the basis of the character of its major products.[105] Companies have also been grouped as consumer goods producers and others. Companies which were recognized as export houses by the Government of India are indicated separately.[106]

The group of 405 companies constitutes an important part of the Indian corporate sector. This is reflected by the fact that these companies accounted for nearly 52.28 per cent of the total paid-up capital of non-government public limited companies in India at the end of 1983–84. Their share would be much higher if the comparison had been made with respect to non-financial public limited companies only. The subsidiaries of foreign companies, included in the study, accounted for nearly three-fourths of the assets and sales turnover of the foreign subsidiaries operating in India at the end of March 1984. Out of these 405 companies nearly half (200) were incorporated before 1950. Of the remaining companies 84 were incorporated during 1950–59 and 105 during 1960–69. Only 16 companies were incorporated after 1969. The last one to be registered was in 1973. The relative importance of different groups of companies in terms of their sales during the final year of the study is shown in Table 7. The names of these 405 companies are presented in the Annexure.

In India, the corporate sector is under statutory obligation to provide a variety of information on its functioning, both financial and physical. It is obligatory for each company to report the proportion of the amount of foreign exchange utilized by the company during the year and the amount earned.[107] This study has drawn upon the Annual Reports of companies for data on foreign currency earnings and utilization.[108]

Certain limitations of the data need to be underlined. As a general rule since the data source is the company Annual Reports, the study would have all the inevitable data limitations which are a result of the 'window-dressing' by company managements. In an economy where foreign exchange is a public concern, corporate entities may attempt to project a brighter picture of their foreign

TABLE 7
Distribution of the Companies in the Study, 1983–84

	Category of Companies	*Number of Companies*	*Sales (Rs Crores)*	*Share in Sales (%)*
I	Foreign Controlled Companies (FCCs) (i) to (iv)	181	9224.26	44.32
	(i) Foreign Subsidiaries	36	2294.64	11.02
	(ii) FERA Companies with 40–50 per cent Foreign Equity	27	1010.58	4.86
	(iii) Companies with 25–40 per cent Foreign Equity	91	3867.41	18.58
	(iv) Companies with 10–25 per cent Foreign Equity	27	2051.63	9.86
II	MRTPA Companies (v) + (vi)	244	17699.81	85.05
	(v) MRTPA Companies (Excluding Those Covered Under I)	131	9799.24	47.09
	(vi) MRTPA Companies (Also Covered Under I)	113	7900.57	37.96
III	Registered Under MRTPA or Classified as FCCs (Covered in I or II or Both)	312	19023.50	91.41
IV	FCC Non-MRTPA Companies (Covered Under I But not in II)	68	1327.69	6.36
V	Non-FCC Non-MRTPA Companies (Covered Neither in I nor II)	93	1788.25	8.59
VI	Companies Belonging to 20 Largest Industrial Houses	131	10815.21	51.97
	All Companies	405	20811.75	100.00

Note: Due to the overlapping of groupings the totals of sub-groups do not add up to the grand total.

exchange transactions. Some of the known practices in this regard are:

1. Exclusion of imports obtained through public sector canalizing agencies from the reported import data.
2. Inclusion of foreign exchange, as earnings, in the amounts which were converted into rupees at the foreign exchange counters of hotels or payments in foreign currency for the services rendered.

3. No distinction being made between hard currency and transactions with rupee trade areas.
4. Non-uniformity in treating exports to neighbouring countries such as Nepal and Bhutan.
5. Clubbing of heads to avoid a clear reflection of information on technology payments and other heads.
6. Inclusion of 'deemed exports' and earnings through third parties in total export earnings.
7. Double counting when a company shows earnings through another associate company.
8. Claims to foreign exchange earnings for such exports which are not out of the company's own production but are purchased from the open market and exported.[109]

These limitations create a bias in favour of the large corporate sector and are likely to project a higher export performance and earnings capability. Since these limitations cannot be overcome by individual scholars the data are used as given.

Results of the study

Plan targets

These 405 large private sector companies form an important component of the Indian economic system. The gross exports of these companies rose from Rs 489.25 crores in 1975–76 to Rs 850.40 crores in 1983–84 (see Table 8), indicating an increase of nearly 73.8 per cent in eight years. The corresponding compound growth rate was 7.16 per cent per annum. The Sixth Plan target was to achieve a growth rate of 9.0 per cent per annum (at constant prices) in the country's exports.[110] The two-point comparison does not, however, reflect the true picture since the high point of exports was reached in 1982–83.

The year to year fluctuations in the value of exports have been substantial. If one takes three-point moving averages, the compound growth rate works out to 6.91 per cent during the period. If one examines the year to year changes one finds that while in 1976–77 the export performance was markedly higher (39.26 per cent increase in one year) the next two years witnessed a decline in the level of exports. Such high growth could not be achieved in any

TABLE 8
Growth in Export Earnings of 405 Large Private Companies

Year	*Exports (Current Prices) (Rs Crores)*	*Annual Increase (%)*	*Three-point Moving Average (Rs Crores)*	*Exports (Constant Prices)* (Rs Crores)*
1975–76	489.25	–	–	583.13
1976–77	681.32	39.26	610.98	762.10
1977–78	662.38	−2.78	661.27	660.40
1978–79	640.11	−3.36	662.56	640.11
1979–80	685.20	7.04	702.31	650.09
1980–81	781.61	14.07	801.92	720.38
1981–82	938.94	20.13	889.48	756.60
1982–83	947.90	0.95	912.41	718.11
1983–84	850.40	−10.29	–	563.18

Note: * Calculated with a 1978–79 based unit value index taken from Government of India, Ministry of Finance, *Economic Survey: 1986–87*, Statement No. 6.5, p. S-60.

of the subsequent years. During the 1979–80 to 1982–83 period the growth rate was positive, only to be followed by a 10 per cent decline in the export value in 1983–84. A general hypothesis could be that exports were a direct function of the level of economic growth in the country; or alternatively, there was a four-year cycle. Another influencing factor could be the conditions obtaining in the international market itself. However, at the national level the year 1983–84 was characterized by 10.77 per cent increase in export earnings as compared to 5 per cent growth in the previous year (see Table 1). This indicates that the reasons for the decline in export earnings of the companies under study in 1983–84 may not be the adverse international market conditions.[111] It is important to pursue the exercise so that the real causes of the year to year fluctuations can be identified. The export figures are at current prices. There is a need to adjust the value of exports by an appropriate deflator. As a general observation, by using the unit value index of exports one finds that the growth rate of exports has been quite low.[112] In particular, if one compares the initial and final years alone, there appears to be a fall in the export earnings at the end of the period. A comparison of the average exports for the initial and final three-year periods shows that the overall increase was only 1.6 per cent; the average value of exports during 1975–78 was Rs. 668.54 crores, and Rs. 679.30 crores during 1981–84. Leaving aside the Plan expectations, the performance of the large corporate sector appears to be rather disappointing.

Exports industry-wise

As seen in Table 8, the export earnings of the companies under study show fluctuations from year to year. To reduce the effects of these random fluctuations, the export data were recalculated using the three-point moving average method. The following industry-wise analysis is based on the re-computed data. As a result of this exercise, 1976–77—the middle year of 1975–76, 1976–77 and 1977–78—is the starting year for purpose of this analysis and 1982–83—the middle year of 1981–82, 1982–83 and 1983–84—the final year of the analysis. The industry-wise distribution of export earnings of 405 companies is shown in Table 9. These companies covered a wide range of industries. A few of them (24) were engaged in non-manufacturing activities like trading, hotels and construction. Of the manufacturing industries, the exports of engineering industries were the highest in 1976–77. These industries contributed Rs 193.81 crores out of the total export earnings of Rs 610.98 crores (31.72 per cent). Textiles, of all varieties, contributed Rs 126.43 crores (20.69 per cent). Chemicals and chemical products followed with a share of 12.58 per cent in the total exports. Cigarettes and tobacco products also had a significant share of 5.62 per cent.

The non-manufacturing sector contributed nearly one-fifth of the total exports of the companies under study. Of the non-manufacturing activities, trading contributed the maximum to export earnings. The share of other activities was quite low. There may be a case for including the exports of trading companies with those of manufacturing companies as most of their exports would be of manufactured products. However, due to the possibility of: (*a*) the manufacturing companies exporting non-manufactured commodities procured from others, and (*b*) the output of some of the manufacturing companies covered in the study being exported by these trading companies, the exports of trading companies are treated outside the group of manufactured products. An important contributor to foreign exchange earnings in the non-manufacturing

	Category of Companies	Number of Companies	Exports* (Rs Crores)			Share (%)		Export Increase (Rs Crores)		Export Increase (%)
			1976–77	1979–80	1982–83	1976–77	1982–83	1976–77 to 1982–83	1979–80 to 1982–83	1976–77 to 1982–83
I	Engineering Industries	146	193.81	223.24	300.31	31.72	32.91	106.50	77.07	54.95
	Automobiles & Components	26	60.13	94.13	123.08	9.84	13.49	62.95	28.96	104.69
	Electrical m/c Apparatus etc.†	40	49.83	62.11	105.38	8.16	11.55	55.56	43.27	111.50
	Non-elect. m/c.	46	30.53	36.75	42.19	5.00	4.62	11.66	5.44	38.19
	Metals, Metal Pdts etc.	34	53.32	30.25	29.65	8.73	3.25	−23.67	−0.60	−44.39
II	Chemicals & Chemical Pdts	103	76.84	110.49	183.98	12.58	20.16	107.14	73.49	139.44
	Other Chmls, Toiletries, Paints	20	27.13	45.25	90.39	4.44	9.91	63.26	45.14	233.13
	Drugs & Pharmaceuticals	20	10.78	15.40	28.67	1.77	3.14	17.88	13.26	165.80
	Automobile Tyres & Rubber Pdts	7	12.32	12.09	18.49	2.02	2.03	6.17	6.40	50.05
	Manmade Fibres	17	5.79	8.52	16.00	0.95	1.75	10.21	7.48	176.32
III	Textiles, All Varieties	55	126.43	159.31	155.09	20.69	17.00	28.66	−4.21	22.67
IV	Cigarettes & Other Tobacco Pdts	4	34.31	36.02	47.03	5.62	5.15	12.72	11.02	37.08
V	Paper & Paper Pdts	14	2.36	3.44	9.34	0.39	1.02	6.98	5.90	296.22
VI	Sugar & Vanaspati	21	10.67	7.49	6.04	1.75	0.66	−4.63	−1.45	−43.36
VII	Cement, Asbestos Cement & Pdts	14	28.74	7.37	5.24	4.70	0.57	−23.50	−2.13	−81.78
VIII	Miscellaneous Mfg	24	14.01	16.95	15.75	2.29	1.73	1.73	−1.20	12.35
	Total Manufacturing (I–VIII)	381	487.17	564.29	722.78	79.74	79.22	235.61	158.49	48.36
IX	Trading	12	91.55	89.36	104.73	14.98	11.48	13.18	15.37	14.40
X	Construction & Engg Contracts	6	7.80	15.25	45.87	1.28	5.03	38.07	30.61	488.39
XI	Hotels	3	14.56	22.98	29.96	2.38	3.28	15.40	6.98	105.73
XII	Tea	3	9.91	10.43	9.09	1.62	1.00	−0.82	−1.34	−8.25
	Non-manufacturing (IX–XII)	24	123.81	138.01	189.64	20.26	20.78	65.83	51.63	53.17
	Total	405	610.98	702.31	912.43	100.00	100.00	301.44	210.12	49.34

Notes: * Export values in these three columns are three-year averages with the years mentioned as the middle years.
† m/c Machinery and components.

group is the hotel industry. Earnings from the hotel industry could, however, be equated more with earnings from tourism rather than being treated as earnings of the individual companies. Tea, one of the important earners of foreign exchange for the country, is not well represented in the study. Against a 5 per cent share in the country's exports, its share in the total exports under consideration was about 1.62 per cent only.

During the period 1976–84 a variety of incentives were offered to promote exports. This probably affected the composition of the export basket; specially that of the large private corporate sector. In the case of 405 companies under study one finds that the relative shares of manufacturing and non-manufacturing sectors did not undergo any appreciable change during the period. They broadly retained the 4:1 ratio. The export basket of these companies, however, differs from the national pattern of exports. At the national level the average share of manufactured exports was slightly higher than 50 per cent during 1981–84. The share of the engineering sector was a little less than 10 per cent. The results indicate that as compared to national exports, exports of the large private sector were concentrated more in the sectors of engineering and chemical industries and related products. During 1981–84 these industries had a combined share of 53.07 per cent. The textiles industry also occupied an important place.

There were significant changes in the manufacturing and non-manufacturing sectors. Two changes were particularly striking: (*a*) the share of textiles industry declined from 20.69 per cent to 17.00 per cent; and (*b*) the share of chemicals and chemical products increased from 12.58 per cent to 20.16 per cent. The share of the engineering industry stagnated but different sub-groups of the industry experienced diverging movements. While the shares of automobiles and components, and electrical machinery and apparatus increased, the share of metals and metal products declined sharply from 8.73 to 3.25 per cent of the total exports. Indeed, their exports registered negative growth between 1976–77 to 1982–83 and were reduced to a little more than half of the initial value.

The major share of the export increase in the chemical industry was largely due to companies predominantly engaged in consumer products. Their share in the total exports of the industry was nearly half in 1982–83. This is also supported by the fact that the exports of the category of 'other chemicals and chemical products group' increased by more than 233 per cent during the period under investigation. Drugs and pharmaceutical preparations also registered a high growth rate. Of the non-manufacturing companies those engaged in construction and engineering contracts showed significant improvement. At the aggregate level, export earnings of non-manufacturing companies increased slightly faster than those of manufacturing companies.

Concentration in export earnings and role of export houses

It can be stated in general that sub-sectors which registered high rates of growth also had a sizeable concentration in export earnings. In other words, a few companies in each of such groups accounted for a substantial share of export earnings. This appears to be mainly due to the fact that these companies were taking credit for the export of goods manufactured by others. An attempt has been made to identify the companies covered under the study on the basis of their having been recognized as export houses by the Government of India.[113] These houses accounted for as much as 61.08 per cent of the total export earnings of the companies during 1981–84, as shown in Table 10. Their contribution to the increased export earnings was 84.91 per cent. In the case of the manufacturing sector it was slightly higher at 88.18 per cent. As a result, the contribution of export houses to the exports of companies classified under the manufacturing sector rose from 41.47 per cent (1975–78) to 56.69 per cent (1981–84). It may be seen that in different industrial groups and sub-groups these houses enjoyed varying levels of importance. A share of over 100 per cent in the increase of exports of a group suggests that the share of other companies declined and the share of export houses increased. The role played by the export houses calls for a closer examination of the concept of export house status as it is being awarded to individual companies.

In the Indian context, an additional factor comes into play. The export earnings reported by the companies need not always represent earnings from actual exports to other countries. Certain sales are 'deemed exports' and are eligible for the concessions and facilities available for the regular exports though on a slightly lower scale. 'Deemed exports' not only include those earnings

TABLE 10

Role of Recognized Export Houses in the Exports of 405 Companies

	Industry Group	*Exports* (Rs Crores)*		*Exports of EH (Rs Crores)*		*Share (%) of EH in Exports*		*Share (%) of EH in Export Growth*
		1975–78	*1981–84*	*1975–78*	*1981–84*	*1975–78*	*1981–84*	
I	Engineering Industries	193.82	300.30	70.26	150.41	36.25	50.09	75.28
	Automobiles & Components	60.13	123.08	15.23	44.00	25.32	35.74	45.70
	Electrical m/c Apparatus etc.	49.83	105.38	32.96	81.39	66.16	77.23	87.17
	Non-elect. m/c.	30.53	42.19	10.02	12.12	32.80	28.73	18.08
	Metals, Metal Pdts etc.	53.32	29.64	12.05	12.90	22.60	43.54	–
II	Chemicals & Chemical Pdts	76.84	183.98	43.71	123.04	56.89	66.88	74.04
	Other Chmls, Toiletries, Paints	27.13	90.39	17.46	57.81	64.33	63.95	63.79
	Drugs & Pharmaceuticals	10.78	28.67	4.98	16.74	46.20	58.41	65.77
	Automobile Tyres & Rubber Pdts	12.32	18.49	10.33	17.31	83.87	93.64	113.16
	Manmade Fibres	5.79	16.00	2.00	14.35	34.58	89.67	120.91
III	Textiles, All Varieties	126.43	155.09	42.88	80.78	33.91	52.09	132.26
IV	Cigarettes & Other Tobacco Pdts	34.31	47.03	31.43	43.92	91.60	93.38	98.20
V	Paper & Paper Pdts	2.36	9.34	0.00	0.00	0.00	0.00	0.00
VI	Sugar & Vanaspati	10.67	6.04	4.21	4.36	39.50	73.74	–
VII	Cement & Asbestos Cement & Pdts	28.74	5.24	4.79	0.19	16.68	3.71	19.57
VIII	Miscellaneous Mfg	14.01	15.75	4.73	6.96	33.78	44.23	128.88
	Total Manufacturing (I to VIII)	487.18	722.77	202.02	409.77	41.47	56.69	88.18
IX	Trading	91.55	104.73	77.07	97.25	84.19	92.86	153.06
X	Construction & Engg Contracts	7.80	45.87	7.68	20.52	98.48	44.73	33.73
XI	Hotels	14.56	29.96	14.56	29.73	100.00	99.25	98.53
XII	Tea	9.91	9.09	0.00	0.00	0.00	0.00	0.00
	Non-manufacturing (IX to XII)	123.81	189.64	99.31	147.50	80.21	77.78	73.20
	Total	610.98	912.41	301.33	557.27	49.32	61.08	84.91

Notes: * Average values of exports during the periods mentioned.
EH Export Houses.

from supplies against global tenders to the IBRD/IDA aided projects in the country and to 100 per cent EOUs but also to holders of advance licences for the supply of intermediate products.[114] The holders of advance licences are expected to sell the resultant output in the export markets or to other advance licence holders. The phenomenon of 'deemed exports' is more applicable to engineering and chemical industries than to other industries. Another important practice which is also considered to be 'exports', for the purpose of availing of export benefits, is the supply of scooters against foreign exchange remittances. The sale is made within the country to Indian consumers against payment in foreign exchange remitted to India by non-resident Indians. This cannot be equated with earnings through exports as it is basically an incentive for non-resident Indians to remit their earnings to the country, the incentive being the allotment of a two-wheeler which carries a premium in the secondary market.[115] Whenever there was a clear mention to this effect—for instance, in the case of sales against remittances by non-resident Indians—such sales were not taken as export earnings for the purpose of this study.

Categories of exporters and their export levels

The study covers a large number of companies registered under the MRTPA and those with substantial foreign equity. Besides offering specific export incentives that have been discussed earlier, government policy also aims at making these companies more export-oriented by imposing export obligations while permitting expansion. Companies with substantial foreign equity are obliged to export part of their production. This, the policy assumes, would make foreign-linked companies seek export markets. The relative share of different categories of companies in exports will be discussed later.

The most important category of companies, in terms of their share in the total exports of the companies under study, was that of companies which were either registered under the MRTPA or those falling under the purview of the FERA. Their share in the total exports was 93.56 per cent during the initial three years (Table 11). This is higher than their share in the total sales (87.48 per cent) of all the 405 companies. Since most of the companies under study fall in either of the two categories—MRTPA registered

TABLE 11

Category-wise Export Earnings of 405 Companies

	Category of Companies	*Number of Companies*	*Exports* (Rs Crores)* 1975–78	1978–81	1981–84	*Share (%)* 1975–78	1981–84	*Export Growth# (Rs Crores)*	*Share in Export Growth (%)*	*Export Growth (%)*
I.	MRTPA Cos or FCCs	312	590.36	681.78	887.83	96.63	97.31	297.47	98.69	50.39
II.	MRTPA or FERA Cos	267	571.62	659.11	852.94	93.56	93.48	281.32	93.33	49.21
III.	MRTPA Cos	244	556.96	643.95	827.48	91.16	90.69	270.52	89.75	48.57
	FCCs	113	243.68	302.86	415.86	39.88	45.58	172.18	57.12	70.66
	Non-FCCs	131	313.28	341.10	411.62	51.27	45.11	98.34	32.63	31.39
	FERA Cos	40	74.23	102.37	163.34	12.15	17.90	89.11	29.56	120.05
	Non-FERA Cos	204	482.73	541.59	664.14	79.01	72.79	181.41	60.18	37.58
IV.	FERA Cos	63	88.89	117.53	188.79	14.55	20.69	99.91	33.14	112.40
	Non-MRTPA Cos	23	14.66	15.16	25.46	2.40	20.79	10.80	3.58	73.66
V.	FCCs	181	277.09	340.69	476.21	45.35	52.19	199.12	66.06	71.86
	Former FERA Cos	49	80.76	84.72	112.77	13.22	12.36	32.01	10.62	39.64
	Cos with 40–50% FE†	27	20.60	25.31	41.21	3.37	4.52	20.61	6.84	100.02
	Foreign Subsidiaries	36	68.29	92.21	147.59	11.18	16.18	79.30	26.31	116.13
	Other Cos with 25–40% FE	42	27.97	32.18	43.63	4.58	4.78	15.66	5.20	56.00
	Other Cos with 10–25% FE	27	79.48	106.25	131.02	13.01	14.36	51.54	17.10	64.85
	Non-MRTPA Cos	68	33.41	37.83	60.35	5.47	6.61	26.94	8.94	80.65
VI.	Non-FCCs & Non-MRTPA Cos	93	20.62	20.53	24.58	3.37	2.69	3.96	1.31	19.22
	All Companies**	405	610.98	702.31	912.41	100.00	100.00	301.43	100.00	49.33

Notes: * Average annual values of exports during the periods mentioned.

† FE Foreign equity.

This and the subsequent columns refer to growth in average annual exports between 1975–78 and 1981–84.

** Due to overlapping of groups, the sub-totals do not add up to the grand total.

or foreign controlled—this is not a significant conclusion. Companies registered under the MRTPA accounted for 91.16 per cent of the exports in the initial three years. These companies can further be subdivided into those that continued to be regulated under FERA and non-FERA companies. Non-FERA companies contributed 79.01 per cent of the total exports as compared to a share of 70.84 per cent in the net sales During the earlier period, the share in exports was higher than the corresponding share in sales, in the case of companies which were formerly under FERA and companies with 10–25 per cent foreign equity.

During the later three years of the study also, companies registered either under the MRTPA or falling under the purview of the FERA retained their share of over 93 per cent. Such stability was also observed in the case of MRTPA registered companies both in terms of exports and sales. However, MRTPA companies which attracted the provisions of FERA also improved their position in terms of their share in exports. While practically retaining their share in sales, they contributed a higher proportion of exports (17.90 per cent as compared to 12.15 per cent). Due to this better performance in this respect, the overall share of foreign controlled companies in exports increased from 45.35 per cent to 52.19 per cent. Much of the observed increase seems to be due to the better performance of companies which continued to retain the foreign subsidiary status throughout the period. In contrast, the share of other FERA companies increased only marginally. Once again, companies with 10–25 per cent foreign equity fared better. The shares of non-MRTPA-*cum*-non-FCC companies declined both in terms of exports as well as sales. The increased exports of the foreign subsidiaries were mainly accounted for by companies classified under chemical and engineering industries. Within the chemical industries as much as Rs 50 crores was accounted by the exports of miscellaneous chemicals including cosmetics, toilet preparations, paints etc. In the case of engineering industries, companies with 10–25 per cent foreign equity accounted for over 90 per cent of the increase in exports.

Net foreign exchange earnings of 405 companies

We have observed earlier that the export earnings of the companies under study increased over time though there was no steady trend.

A number of companies reported foreign exchange earnings on other accounts also. These included commissions, royalties and dividend repatriations. On the other hand, the operations of these companies resulted in a foreign exchange outgo following a somewhat similar pattern. The main heads of foreign currency expenditure were imports of raw materials, components, spares and capital goods. Foreign exchange was also used for travel abroad, or for expenses related to the import of technology (royalties, technical fees etc.). A certain amount of foreign exchange was remitted abroad by way of dividend payments to foreign shareholders. What has been the net contribution to the economy in terms of foreign exchange transactions of these companies? The foreign exchange transactions of these companies in each of the nine years under study are presented in Table 12. It can be seen that the movement of total foreign exchange earnings is similar to that of export earnings. This can be explained by the fact that exports constituted the single most important item of foreign exchange earnings for these companies. On the other hand, their foreign

TABLE 12
Foreign Exchange Earnings and Expenditure Pattern of 405 Companies

Year	*Total Foreign Exchange (Rs Crores)*		*Net Earnings (Rs Crores)*	*Earnings/ Expenditure (Ratio)*
	Earnings	*Expenditure*		
1975–76	512.30	419.25	93.05	1.22
1976–77	717.24	472.73	244.51	1.52
1977–78	705.93	622.62	83.31	1.13
1978–79	680.63	748.65	−68.02	0.91
1979–80	744.38	973.51	−229.13	0.76
1980–81	848.92	1093.32	−244.40	0.78
1981–82	1031.27	1378.27	−347.00	0.75
1982–83	1105.42	1537.89	−432.47	0.72
1983–84	998.02	1459.33	−461.30	0.68

exchange expenditure grew steadily, except during the final year of the study *i.e.* 1983–84. Compared to the growth in earnings, the increase in expenditures was more rapid. If one takes the initial and final years the percentage increase in earnings was 94.8 while the corresponding increase in expenditure was 248.1 per cent. As a result, the net earnings of these companies decreased from Rs 93.05 crores to a net outgo of Rs 461.30 crores. The decrease in net earnings was nearly continuous after 1976–77. The fall was indeed precipitous in 1979–80. From a deficit of Rs 68.02 crores in 1978–79, the net outflow of foreign exchange increased in one year to Rs 229.13 crores by the next year. By the end of the period, the size of the deficit more than doubled (over the 1979–80 level) to Rs 461.30 crores.

The continuous decline in the net earning capability of the companies could be due to the variations in international prices whereby India had to pay higher prices for its imports while the unit value realization of her exports did not rise as fast. To check for this possibility, the data on India's terms of trade were examined.[116] The movement of net terms of trade was not uniform during the period under study. There were two peaks: in 1977–78 and 1983–84, and the lowest point was reached in 1980–81. However, re-computed indices of India's unit values of exports and imports, with 1975–76 as the base year, show that except in 1980–81, the index for exports remained higher than that of imports during the period 1975–76 to 1983–84. This may indicate a further weakening of the net earnings position of the companies under study. The applicability of these indices to our data is limited. The main problem is in the composition of imports and exports at the national level. Moreover, from the point of view of the economy, the net impact of the operations of the companies would be in terms of their year to year operations. In the light of this, it is not necessary to adjust these figures for relative movements of export and import prices. It is thus clear that from a position of net earners of foreign exchange, the large private sector companies turned out to be net losers over time, particularly since the beginning of the 1980s. The next question to be answered is to what extent there are differences among the groups of companies with respect to their net foreign exchange contribution to the economy.

Contributions of different categories of exporters to net foreign exchange earnings

The net foreign exchange earnings of different groups of companies are presented in Table 13. It can be seen that no single group was able to earn net foreign exchange in 1981–84. This was true for both MRTPA companies and FCCs. While at the major group level MRTPA companies and FCCs were earning net foreign exchange during 1975–78, FERA companies and those with 25–40

TABLE 13

Category-wise Net Earnings of Foreign Exchange (in Rs crores)

	Category of Companies	*No. of Cos*	*Net Foreign Exchange Earnings**			*Earnings/Expenditure†*		
			1975–78	*1978–81*	*1981–84*	*1975–78*	*1978–81*	*1981–84*
I.	MRTPA or FCCs	312	162.18	−132.62	−334.01	1.35	0.85	0.75
II.	MRTPA or FERA Cos	267	165.05	−109.22	−298.46	1.38	0.86	0.76
III.	MRTPA Cos	244	163.84	−97.18	−286.72	1.39	0.88	0.76
	FCCs	113	22.22	−62.09	−123.30	1.10	0.84	0.79
	Non-FCCs	131	141.62	−35.09	−163.42	1.77	0.91	0.74
	FERA Cos	40	−24.59	−55.67	−47.80	0.75	0.66	0.79
	Non-FERA Cos	204	188.43	−41.51	−238.92	1.59	0.93	0.76
IV.	FERA Cos	63	−23.38	−67.71	−59.54	0.80	0.64	0.77
	Non-MRTPA Cos	23	1.21	−12.04	−11.74	1.08	0.57	0.69
V.	Foreign Controlled Cos	181	20.56	−97.53	−170.59	1.08	0.79	0.76
	Former FERA Cos	49	35.12	7.22	−42.51	1.75	1.09	0.75
	Cos with 40–50% FE‡	27	−16.70	−33.95	−51.17	0.57	0.44	0.46
	Foreign Subsidiaries	36	−6.68	−33.76	−8.37	0.91	0.74	0.95
	Other Cos with 25–40% FE‡	42	−12.19	−47.43	−62.58	0.76	0.43	0.47
	Other Cos with 10–25% FE‡	27	21.01	10.39	−5.97	1.34	1.10	0.96
	Non-MRTPA Cos	68	−1.66	−35.44	−47.30	0.96	0.57	0.61
VI.	Non-FCCs & Non-MRTPA	93	−21.88	−47.90	−79.58	0.53	0.37	0.37
	All Companies#	405	140.29	−180.52	−413.59	1.28	0.81	0.72

Notes: * Average annual net foreign exchange earnings during the period mentioned.
† Average ratio for the period mentioned.
‡ FE Foreign equity.
# Due to overlapping of groups, the sub-totals do not add up to the grand total.

per cent foreign equity were net losers even then. Non-FCCs-*cum*-non-MRTPA companies were also net losers during this period. In spite of contributing significantly to increased export earnings, foreign subsidiaries remained net losers of foreign exchange.[117] Even in the case of companies with 10–25 per cent foreign equity, which is another important group of companies in terms of increased export earnings, total expenditure of foreign exchange outgrew total earnings. Viewed from a slightly different perspective, one finds that the earnings to expenditure ratio during 1975–78 was the highest at more than 1.7 for non-FCC-*cum*-MRTPA companies and companies which were formerly under FERA. However, this ratio declined by more than half to about 0.75 during the final three years. The declining earning to expenditure ratio was seen in the case of nearly all the groups, the only exceptions being FERA companies registered under the MRTPA and foreign subsidiaries. However, the increase they achieved was quite small.

Out of the 405 companies in the study, 131 belong to the 20 largest industrial houses in the country. The year-wise foreign exchange transactions of these companies are presented in Table 14. An examination of the figures in the initial and final years shows that the companies belonging to the top 20 houses contributed about 54.5 per cent to the total exports of the companies under study. The figures also reveal the declining net earning capability observed at the aggregate level. It is obvious that if the companies classified under trading (Tata Exports Ltd exports vehicles manufactured by TELCO) are separated to avoid double counting, and the items traded by these companies are excluded from the calculations of the net foreign exchange earnings, the results would even be more depressing for the large private sector. This is partly attempted by excluding the net earnings of export and trading houses. The result is an increase in the net loss of foreign exchange by more than Rs 100 crores.[118] The net earnings of export houses also stagnated and during the final years there was a declining trend. Though some of the foreign subsidiaries are part of the top 20 houses, the behaviour of foreign subsidiaries also calls for a separate examination. Under FERA, majority equity by a foreign shareholder is allowed only if the company is operating in industries requiring sophisticated technology, is export-oriented, or both. On both accounts they are expected to take a lead in the export sector: if allowed on the basis of the export capabilities,

TABLE 14
Net Foreign Exchange Earnings of 131 Companies Belonging to the Top 20 Industrial Houses (in Rs crores)

Year	*Net Earnings Reported by 23 EH and TH**	*Net Earnings of 108 Other Companies*	*Total Net Earnings*
1975–76	103.11	−16.20	86.91
1976–77	145.68	39.58	185.26
1977–78	130.67	−15.32	115.35
1978–79	123.13	−75.96	47.17
1979–80	135.98	−162.33	−26.35
1980–81	137.41	−160.28	−22.87
1981–82	150.08	−252.59	−102.51
1982–83	111.44	−289.15	−177.71
1983–84	114.72	−320.86	−206.14

Notes: * EH Export Houses.
TH Trading Houses.

they should show higher export propensity; if allowed on the basis of sophisticated technology, they should fare better in the international market on the strength of technology.

It has been observed earlier that the net foreign exchange earning capability of foreign subsidiaries declined over time. What have been the main contributing factors to this decline? The contribution of foreign subsidiaries to net foreign exchange earnings would have been much lower but for the fact that some of them have converted themselves into export houses (see Table 15). Export and trading houses played a significant role in the export performance of the 20 largest monopoly houses, and also in the case of foreign subsidiaries. The exclusion of these companies results in a substantial increase in the net outgo of foreign exchange. The six export/trading houses were: (*a*) Hindustan Lever Ltd; (*b*) Siemens India Ltd; (*c*) Ashok Leyland Ltd; (*d*) Chloride India Ltd; (*e*) Union Carbide India Ltd; and (*f*) Sandoz India Ltd.

It may be interesting to examine the pattern of utilization of foreign exchange by foreign subsidiaries. A comparison with companies which had since opted out of the FERA category may throw light on the impact of FERA on the pattern of foreign exchange utilization of these companies. Data on various heads under which subsidiaries and companies which were initially covered

TABLE 15

Role of Export Houses in the Net Foreign Exchange Earnings by Foreign Subsidiaries (in Rs crores)

Year	*Six Export/ Trading Houses*	*30 Other Subsidiaries*	*Total of 36 Foreign Subsidiaries*
1975–76	6.20	−18.40	−12.20
1976–77	12.66	−3.47	9.18
1977–78	6.14	−23.14	−17.00
1978–79	9.11	−30.31	−21.21
1979–80	2.91	−51.60	−48.69
1980–81	11.84	−43.22	−31.38
1981–82	23.77	−40.36	−16.59
1982–83	32.58	−38.67	−6.09
1983–84	38.53	−40.96	−2.43

under FERA were incurring expenditure in foreign exchange are presented in Table 16. The utilization of foreign exchange by the former FERA companies increased much faster than that by foreign subsidiaries: 303.6 per cent for the ex-FERA companies against only 139.1 per cent for foreign subsidiaries. A large part of the increase in the expenditures by ex-FERA companies can be explained by increased imports of raw materials. In relative terms, imports of capital goods increased faster in the case of foreign subsidiaries. An interesting point that emerges from an examination of the table is that dividend remittances by the former FERA companies increased by more than five times during the period under study.[119] Dividend remittances of foreign subsidiaries nearly doubled during the period. One of the reasons for this could be that ex-FERA companies expanded rapidly into more profitable activities during the post-FERA phase.

Changes in export orientation

The third exercise is based on the assumption that if the exports to sales ratios of the companies showed a rising trend, the Indian corporate sector could be considered as orienting itself towards export marketing. This ratio is significant as one ignores the nature of industry and places greater emphasis on the organizational capabilities of the companies in general. Given the policy package for export promotion, one should expect that with the withdrawal

TABLE 16

Changes in the Pattern of Foreign Exchange Utilization by Ex-FERA Companies and Foreign Subsidiaries (in Rs crores)

Utilization	*Ex-FERA Companies (49)*				*Foreign Subsidiaries (36)*			
	1975–76	*1983–84*	*1975–76*	*1983–84*	*1975–76*	*1983–84*	*1975–76*	*1983–84*
Raw Materials	27.30	123.91	59.88	67.34	48.01	96.75	73.62	62.04
Capital Goods	4.56	11.80	10.01	6.41	4.15	21.96	6.36	14.09
Stores	2.57	19.60	5.64	10.65	2.47	11.34	3.79	7.27
Other Imports	0.77	0.74	1.70	0.40	0.04	0.12	0.06	0.07
Royalty	0.19	0.46	0.42	0.25	0.35	0.41	0.54	0.27
Technical Fee	1.73	1.47	3.79	0.80	1.44	0.70	2.21	0.45
Interest	0.44	0.75	0.97	0.41	0.65	2.38	0.99	1.53
Travel	0.10	0.42	0.22	0.23	0.09	0.92	0.13	0.59
Other Expenses	4.47	2.97	9.80	1.62	2.08	3.59	3.19	2.30
Dividends	3.46	21.89	7.58	11.89	5.94	17.76	9.10	11.39
Total	45.60	184.01	100.00	100.00	65.21	155.94	100.00	100.00

Note: Number of companies within parentheses.

of restrictions on industrial capacity expansion to harness economies of scale, the exports to sales turnover ratio for the Indian large private sector would show a positive trend. This, however, does not appear to be the case. The exports to sales ratio registered a steady decline during 1975–76 to 1983–84 period as shown in Table 17.

TABLE 17
Changes in the Export Propensity of 405 Companies

Year	*Current Prices (Rs Crores)*		*E/S (%)*	*Constant Prices (Rs Crores)*		*E/S*(%)*
	Exports	*Sales*		*Exports*	*Sales*	
1975–76	489.25	7806.16	6.27	583.14	8184.61	7.12
1976–77	681.32	8863.64	7.69	762.11	9081.18	8.39
1977–78	662.38	9559.53	6.93	660.40	9575.54	6.90
1978–79	640.11	10670.71	6.00	640.11	10670.71	6.00
1979–80	685.20	12397.45	5.53	650.09	10312.05	6.30
1980–81	781.61	14540.39	5.38	720.38	10143.80	7.10
1981–82	938.94	17625.84	5.33	756.60	11691.94	6.47
1982–83	947.90	19238.54	4.93	718.11	12691.36	5.66
1983–84	850.40	20811.75	4.09	563.18	12629.17	4.46

Notes: * E/S exports to sales.
Constant prices of exports are obtained by using the unit value index for exports (base 1978–79 = 100). Index taken from Government of India, Ministry of Finance, *Economic Survey, 1986–87*, Statement 6.5, p. S-60; constant prices of sales are obtained using the wholesale price index for manufactured products (base 1970–71 = 100). The series was recalculated taking 1978–79 = 100. Index taken from *Economic Survey, 1986–87*, Statement 5.4, p. S-53.

It may be that the higher rate of growth of sales in the domestic market and the decline of the exports to sales ratio was due to a relative increase of the domestic price over the international price. To examine the impact of the price increase, exports and the sales series were re-computed using the unit value index of exports and the wholesale price index for manufactured products respectively. It can be seen from Table 17 that measured in constant prices the sales value did not uniformly move upward. However, barring the two years 1979–80 and 1980–81, when the exports to sales ratio showed signs of improvement, it can generally be stated that exports constituted a declining portion of the total sales of the large Indian companies. This trend has been more prominent since 1980–81.

This exercise shows an unmistakable trend of increasing dependence of the large private sector companies on the domestic market. This may also reflect the incapacity, or unwillingness of this sector to penetrate overseas markets. The other view, however, would be that the package of incentives and subsidies presently offered was not adequate to motivate them to make a larger contribution to India's exports. In that case there are two alternatives: (*a*) not to expect this sector to be export-oriented and, therefore, to withdraw all incentives, subsidies and concessions to this sector; (*b*) if the large companies are awarded facilities for expanding the production base, they should be under an obligation to earn twice of what they utilize, out of their own exports. The export house function should be an activity entirely separate from the manufacturing activity. Whenever export obligations are imposed, these should be in terms of goods that have been manufactured, not in terms of earnings through exports of goods produced by others i.e. by trading activities. The large increase in internal sales as compared to exports may also be an indication of the fact that Indian companies took advantage of the relaxations in regulations under the plea of export promotion, and expanded rapidly to exploit the more profitable domestic market. As long as the internal market was more rewarding, one cannot expect the private corporate bodies to undertake exports. An alternative strategy could be to make internal markets less attractive to them through fiscal measures.

The industrial expansion over the past few years, one would have expected, gave the large Indian manufacturers an opportunity to derive the benefits of economies of scale and improve their competitiveness in the overseas markets. The available evidence does not, however, support this. The total assets under the control of these 405 companies increased from Rs 6,862.09 crores in 1975–76 to Rs 20,056.56 crores in 1983–84. The increase in the assets reflects the trends in their productive capacity. The build-up of assets was particularly marked after 1980–81. However, an increase in sales or assets need not necessarily be due to the harnessing of the benefits of the scale economies by these companies. The increase in assets could be due to an expansion into unrelated areas while the original lines of manufacture remained stagnant. Though such expansion offers the advantages of large-scale operations, such as those in marketing and administration, it does not lead to economies of large-scale production. One rationale advanced for the re-endorsement of industrial capacities was that large amounts of capacities were remaining unutilized due to capacity restrictions. However, since production in excess of licenced capacities being so common in the Indian industry, a mere re-endorsement would not result in higher productivity and consequent reduction in costs. The behaviour of the large private sector seems to suggest such an explanation. There appears to be a need to study the expansion pattern of India's large private sector in the recent past.

The reduction in the exports to sales ratio could be either because there was a general decline in the export propensity of these companies or due to a reduction or even withdrawal of certain companies from the export market. To check this hypothesis, the number of exporting companies in each year under study was examined. It is clear from Table 18 that the number of exporting companies varied from year to year. While the peak was reached in 1977–78 when 315 out of the 405 companies reported export earnings, the number declined to 271 in the final year of the study. In spite of the increasing importance attached to export promotion, the number of exporters declined over time. On the other hand, there was no significant change in the number of companies effecting imports. The phenomenon of a decrease in the number of exporting companies is even more significant than the decline in the exports to sales ratio. This suggests a withdrawal of companies from export trade. There were 60 companies that exported in 1977–78 but did not report any export earnings during 1983–84. Out of these 60 companies only 18 did not register themselves under the MRTPA or did not fall into any of the FCC categories. Only 214 companies — 52.8 per cent — reported export earnings in all the years under study.

The data suggest that a downward trend in the exports to sales ratio was not only due to the declining number of exporters but also because of a general decline in the export efforts of the companies. This phenomenon is evidenced by the fact that an increasing number of companies moved into the lower ranges of the ratio. It is clear from Table 19 that 108 companies were not exporting during 1975–76. Their number increased to 134 by

TABLE 18
Annual Changes in the Number of Exporting and Importing Companies

Year	*Number of Companies*	
	Exporting	*Importing*
1975–76	297	379
1976–77	310	383
1977–78	315	385
1978–79	300	384
1979–80	298	387
1980–81	296	386
1981–82	285	386
1982–83	284	385
1983–84	271	383

TABLE 19
Distribution of Companies According to the Exports to Sales Ratio (E/S)

*E/S (%)**	*Number of Companies*		
	1975–76	*1979–80*	*1983–84*
0	108	107	134
0–1	77	75	91
1–5	95	121	99
5–10	65	51	48
10–20	35	37	23
20–25	10	4	3
25 and above	15	10	7
All Companies	405	405	405

Note: * E/S Exports to sales.

1983–84. The number of companies in the ranges above 5 per cent decreased over time. In 1975–76, there were 60 companies whose exports constituted 10 per cent or more of their total sales. The number almost halved in 1983–84 to 33. Such a decrease is also discernible in the 5–10 per cent range.

It can be seen from Table 20 that the declining exports to sales ratio observed at the aggregate level was common to all the categories of companies with the exception of foreign subsidiaries and MRTPA registered FERA companies (the two groups have a

TABLE 20

Variation in Export Propensity of 405 Companies (in Rs. Crores)

	Category of Companies	No. of Cos	Average Annual Exports			Average Annual Sales			E/S (%)*		
			1975–78	1978–81	1981–84	1975–78	1978–81	1981–84	1975–78	1978–81	1981–84
I.	MRTPA or FCCs	312	590.36	681.78	887.83	7988.96	11499.44	17594.90	7.39	5.93	5.05
II.	MRTPA Cos or FERA	267	571.62	659.11	852.94	7640.44	10965.98	16781.54	7.47	6.01	5.08
III.	MRTPA Cos	244	556.96	643.95	827.48	7461.74	10706.45	16381.63	7.46	6.01	5.05
	FCCs	113	243.68	302.86	415.86	3417.30	4875.18	7420.06	7.13	6.21	5.60
	Non-FCCs	131	313.28	341.10	411.62	4044.43	5831.27	8961.57	7.75	5.85	4.59
	FERA Cos	40	74.23	102.37	163.34	1268.00	1824.22	2695.29	5.85	5.61	6.06
	Non-FERA Cos	204	482.73	541.59	664.14	6193.74	8882.24	13686.34	7.79	6.10	4.85
IV.	FERA Cos	63	88.89	117.53	188.79	1454.70	2083.74	3095.21	6.11	5.64	6.10
	Non-MRTPA Cos	23	14.66	15.16	25.46	186.70	259.53	399.91	7.85	5.84	6.37
V.	Foreign Controlled Cos	181	277.09	340.69	476.21	3944.52	5668.17	8633.34	7.02	6.01	5.52
	Ex-FERA Cos	49	80.76	84.72	112.77	1049.19	1383.28	2086.55	7.70	6.12	5.40
	Cos with 40–50% FE†	27	20.60	25.31	41.21	419.59	568.55	904.55	4.91	4.45	4.56
	Foreign Subsidiaries	36	68.29	92.21	147.59	1035.11	1515.19	2190.66	6.60	6.09	6.74
	Other Cos with 25–40% FE†	42	27.97	32.18	43.63	688.69	1001.78	1524.88	4.06	3.21	2.86
	Other Cos with 10–25% FE†	27	79.48	106.25	131.02	751.94	1199.37	1926.71	10.57	8.86	6.80
	Non-MRTPA Cos	68	33.41	37.83	60.35	527.22	792.98	1213.27	6.34	4.77	4.97
VI.	Non-FCCs & Non-MRTPA Cos	93	20.62	20.53	24.58	754.15	1036.74	1630.47	2.73	1.98	1.51
	All Companies	405	610.98	702.31	912.41	8743.11	12536.18	19225.37	6.99	5.60	4.75

Notes: Due to the overlapping of groups, the sub-totals do not add up to the grand total.
* E/S Exports to sales. † FE Foreign equity.

number of companies in common). In the case of companies with 10–25 per cent foreign equity, the decline was quite significant. More than 10 per cent of their sales was accounted by exports during the initial three years. Though they remained the most export-oriented group of companies during the final three years the corresponding share of exports declined to less than 7 per cent. The steady ratio achieved by foreign subsidiaries may be indicative of their attempt to maintain a certain export level which enabled them to enjoy their subsidiary status. The top 20 houses also showed a declining export orientation. After 1976–77 the decline in export propensity was almost continuous. The level of 4.29 per cent in 1983–84 was less than half of what it was in 1976–77 (see Table 21).

TABLE 21

Export Orientation of 131 Companies Belonging to the Top 20 Industrial Houses

Year	*Exports (Rs Crores)*	*Sales (Rs Crores)*	*E/S (%)**
1975–76	266.31	3776.23	7.05
1976–77	378.11	4273.00	8.85
1977–78	368.81	4634.05	7.96
1978–79	355.54	5219.57	6.81
1979–80	382.00	6027.74	6.34
1980–81	435.88	7127.05	6.12
1981–82	562.58	8911.61	6.31
1982–83	548.55	9817.93	5.59
1983–84	463.66	10815.21	4.29

Note: * E/S Exports to sales.

No matter how one views the data, it appears that barring a few exceptions where there was a marginal increase in the ratio, none of the groups of companies became more export-oriented during the period under study.[120]

At this point it may be useful to refer to the net contribution of the 'private limited companies' in terms of their foreign exchange earnings. On an average public limited companies represent the larger sector and private limited companies represent organized small units. An examination of the data for 1,004 large and medium private limited companies shows that they continued to be net earners of foreign exchange during 1980–83 (see Table 22). Though

TABLE 22
Foreign Exchange Transactions of 1004 Large and Medium Private Limited Companies (in Rs crores)

	1980–81	*1981–82*	*1982–83*
Exports	256.07	314.13	339.26
Sales	2485.94	2889.95	3182.23
Earnings of Foreign Exchange	328.28	421.14	499.25
Expenditure of Foreign Exchange	158.58	230.62	288.85
Net Earnings of Foreign Exchange	169.70	190.52	210.67
E/S (%)*	10.30	10.87	10.66
Earnings to Expenditure Ratio	2.07	1.83	1.73

Note: * E/S Exports to sales.
Source: Based on the data provided by Reserve Bank of India, Finances of medium and large private limited companies, 1982–83, in *Reserve Bank of India Bulletin*, Vol. XXXIX, July 1985.

the earnings to expenditure ratio for the group of smaller companies also showed a declining trend, their exports to sales ratio was above 10 per cent. It is equally noteworthy that their dependence on external sources for technology or equity was quite low. This is reflected by the fact that dividends, royalties, technical fees and professional and consultation fees paid in foreign exchange amounted to Rs 93 lakhs in 1982–83 i.e. less than 0.44 per cent of the total foreign exchange utilized by these companies during the year.

It is an interesting coincidence that in the first year of the study the recommendations of the Sondhi Committee were implemented. Instead of contributing to the foreign exchange earning capability of the country, the operations of the large private sector companies led to a worsening of the net earnings situation in the 1980s. This is in line with the national level experience of increasing trade deficit since the beginning of the 1980s. In contrast, it appears that private limited companies which are generally much smaller in size in terms of assets and turnover, are the major earners of net foreign exchange for the country.

Recent evidence shows the continuation of the foregoing trends. The RBI study of 1,942 non-financial, non-government public limited companies reveals that utilization of foreign exchange in excess of foreign exchange earnings increased from Rs 307.41 crores in 1984–85 to Rs 1,653.80 crores in 1986–87. The operations of manufacturing companies among this category of companies followed a similar pattern. Excess utilization in their case was to the tune of Rs 691.15 crores in 1984–85 which increased to Rs 1,382.33 crores in 1985–86 and further to Rs 1,830.00 crores in the subsequent year. The exports to sales ratio also registered a continuous decline from 4.52 per cent to 3.84 per cent. The corresponding percentages for manufacturing companies are 4.02 and 3.49 respectively.[121]

Another study conducted by the Industrial Development Bank of India covers 401 non-government companies assisted by the Bank. On the basis of the Annual Reports of these companies it was found that only 173 were engaged in export activities. Even in the case of these 173 companies, the exports to sales ratio was 3.8 per cent in 1987–88 which itself was lower than that in the previous year. These companies accounted for about 39 per cent of the paid-up capital of non-government public limited companies at the end of March 1984. Evidently, the exports to sales ratio for all these 401 companies put together would be much smaller. Another significant finding was that the companies under study were net spenders of foreign exchange: the deficit for 1987–88 was Rs 1,438.7 crores.[122]

Major exporters

For some time now individual companies have been granted the status of export and trading houses. In the presentation of the results of the companies, these trading activities are not shown separately but are clubbed with other operations. This enables companies that are net losers of foreign exchange in their own manufacturing operations to project a brighter picture, often as net earners of foreign exchange. Export houses appear to have played a significant role in the increased export earnings of the companies under study. Their importance in industries that registered substantial increases in the level of exports has also been noticed. The role of export houses in some of the industrial groups raises serious doubts as to the composition of exports of companies included in them. This is due to the fact that the industries have been grouped on the basis of the companies' major line of production, not their main export item. It has also been pointed out that the reported export earnings may include earnings from 'deemed exports'. A detailed product-wise break-up coupled with information on items traded and 'deemed exports' would have enabled an analysis on the basis of *actual earnings* of foreign exchange by these companies from out of their own production. Unfortunately, such information is not provided by these companies on a uniform basis.

With the limited information available from the Annual Reports of the companies an attempt has been made to identify the main export products and markets and the extent of incentives received by some of the important exporters and export houses covered in the study. Hopefully this will lead to some tentative answers to questions such as: what part of the engineering and chemical exports was destined for the markets of advanced countries where they have to face stiffer competition, and where does the country obtain most of its technology from? Did the import of technology enable the companies to face international competition? Also, to what extent these exports were destined for rupee trade areas and for other developing countries? Finally, how much of these exports were from the companies' own production and what part of it was realized through supplies from the small-scale sector and other manufacturers? These questions are relevant when assessing the real strength of the companies in the international market.

It is interesting to note that nearly three-fourths of the exports in the other chemicals, toiletries, paints in 1982–83 were accounted for by just two out of the total of 20 companies. Their exports of Rs 65.64 crores constituted 72.62 per cent of this industry group. These were Hindustan Lever Ltd (57.48 per cent) and Hindustan Ciba-Geigy Ltd (15.14 per cent). Incidentally, Hindustan Lever Ltd is a recognized trading house thereby implying that products of the small-scale sector constitute at least 10 per cent of its exports.[123] It is equally important to note that the fact of the company having been recognized as a trading house also implies that the export basket of the company is a diversified one. This becomes clear from the items traded by the company for export purposes. The company's exports include not only cosmetics and toilet preparations but also processed sal and castor, marine products, garments, footwear, carpets and some engineering items. In 1986 it even began to export a superior quality of rice (*Baśmati*) to the Middle East.[124] From the reports of the Directors of the company for several years and the company's in-house journal *Hamara*, it is evident that the rupee trade areas are the main importers of the company's products. During 1986, the company concluded an export order for Rs 1.20 crores worth of 'Elizabeth Arden' cosmetics with the socialist countries. It was claimed that the company was the 'Indian licencee for many world famous cosmetics brands, among them Coty, Goya, and Yardley range of products. Elizabeth Arden—USA is now joining this distinguished list'.[125] It may also be mentioned that the reported export figures of the company include exports to India's neighbours Nepal and Bhutan. It may be noted that Hindustan Lever Ltd made sustained efforts at retaining the majority share by Unilever Ltd in the company. Increased export turnover and transferring of food business to Lipton India Ltd, another Unilever associate in India, are part of this strategy. During the past few years the company not only took over Stepan Chemicals Ltd, as a subsidiary, but also expanded its operations by taking over on lease garment manufacturing units and a rice milling factory. Hindustan Ciba-Geigy, the second largest exporter of the group, exported tooth-paste and other items to the former USSR.

Similarly, in the case of pharmaceutical products, the top two exporters accounted for more than half (55.5 per cent) of the total exports of the group. Hoechst India Ltd, the largest exporter, accounted for as much as 41.65 per cent of the total exports of the group in 1982–83. The company was recognized as an export house in 1981. It may be noted that the bulk of the exports of the company were to the rupee trade areas. For instance, out of Rs 10.22 crores worth of exports of the company during 1981, exports to one of the rupee trade countries accounted for as much as Rs 9.41 crores or 92.07 per cent.[126] The company's dependence on the rupee trade areas seems to have further increased. Exports to rupee trade areas accounted for Rs 22.60 crores out of its total exports of Rs 22.80 crores (99.12 per cent) during 1985.[127] The company's subsidiary, Roussel Pharmaceuticals (India) Ltd, has also been heavily dependent on the former USSR market for exports. To boost its exports Hoechst India has been receiving large amounts of duty drawback and export subsidies. While its receipts on this account were Rs 4.27 crores in 1981, they increased to Rs 6.95 crores in 1985.[128] The other company in the pharmaceuticals group namely Glaxo Laboratories also appears to have been dependent on the rupee trade areas for its exports. For instance, the company reported that 'exports to regions other than USSR increased from 10 per cent of total exports of the Company in 1981–82 to 25 per cent in 1982–83.'[129] This suggests that during the year ending June 1983, exports to the former USSR accounted for 75 per cent of the company's exports, though the company was trying to diversify its markets. In addition to its exports to the erstwhile USSR, the company also exported its products to Japan, Ireland, Australia, parts of Southeast Asia and Africa and the Gulf countries. 'Complan' (a health drink) and 'Farex' (baby food) were exported to Sri Lanka and Bangladesh and Nycil' (prickly heat powder) to Nigeria.[130] Both Hoechst and Glaxo have been availing of the services of non-associated formulators in the small-scale sector for getting a number of their products manufactured.

In the case of electrical machinery, components and appliances industry, the top five exporters who accounted for 53.3 per cent of the total exports of the group, were all export houses. The topmost amongst them was Siemens India Ltd. A study of the company's Annual Reports shows that the company has been dependent on projects of the World Bank and IDA as well as the markets of the former USSR and developing countries for its export earnings. For instance, during 1986 the company reported that cables, miniature circuit-breakers and medical equipment mainly contributed to its export earnings. Cables were wholly purchased by the company from other parties and medical equipment was exported to the former USSR. The former USSR was also one of its main markets for cables. The importance of the former USSR is illustrated by the fact that the company attributed the decrease in its exports during 1982–83 to the '(s)izeable drop in our export of cables to Russia under the bilateral trade agreement.'[131] A little earlier, the company had informed that electrification of projects on a turnkey basis had been undertaken in the 'Persian Gulf, Africa, South East Asia, etc.'.[132] At that time the company was executing projects in Muscat, Salalah, Iraq and Tanzania. The company made its policy clear when it stated that the thrust of its project business in '(s)everal Asian and African countries, will continue'.[133] Projects under the IDA credit accounted for over 30 per cent of its export earnings in 1982 and 1983. It is difficult to comment on the other products which constituted the bulk of its traded items since their break-up is not available. It is likely that these products were purchased from small-scale units as the company informed in one of its reports to the shareholders that it had extended its export infrastructure to small-scale manufacturers and that as a recognized export house it was instrumental in developing their exports.[134] Continuity of the above trends is further reflected in the company's report, for the year 1986–87. According to the company,

> The performance on the export front has been very encouraging. We have received further major orders from Russia and Indonesia, while we have been able to break fresh ground in the Australian market for our switchgears. Our exports, including the deemed exports under the IDA credit, increased by 45 per cent to Rs. 360 million from last year's level of Rs. 247 million. We exported medical equipment valued at Rs. 66 million and cables worth Rs. 71 million to Russia. The deemed exports executed during the year also increased sizeably from Rs. 76 million last year to Rs. 126 million in the current year.[135]

It will not be out of place to mention that under FERA the company was made to give up distribution of the products of Cable Corporation of India Ltd and Bharat Bijlee Ltd so as to allow it to retain 51 per cent of foreign equity.[136]

Another company in the electrical industry group which was also recognized as an export house is Union Carbide India Ltd. The company had set up a marine product processing unit way back in 1970. The sales of marine products accounted for 64 per cent of the total exports of the company during 1984. It is somewhat strange that the company decided to dispose of its marine products division as it had become 'uneconomical'.[137] The importance of the rupee trade areas is evident from the company's explanation that the decrease in exports over the previous year (1984 over 1983) was 'due to reduced off-take of batteries by Russia and reduction in exports of shrimps'.[138] The company has been gradually shifting to exports of purchased products such as leather goods, engineering components, reactive dyes and intermediates.[139] Industrial Cables (India) Ltd in the electrical machinery industry group is also a recognized export house. Its dependence on the markets of the socialist bloc is reflected in its statement that '(t)he position (of the cable industry) has been further aggravated owing to cut back of import of cables by Soviet Union, owing to their adverse balance in trade with India.'[140] It is specifically stated that its performance during 1983–84 largely depended upon the financial position of the 'Electricity Boards, and orders from USSR and other export markets'. It is interesting to note that there was a slump in the company's export earnings during the year from Rs 14.28 crores to just Rs 5.07 crores. Earlier, the company informed its shareholders that its cables and wires were well accepted in 'West Asia, Africa, East European countries including Singapore, Pakistan, Kuwait, Dubai, Iraq, Mauritius, Bahrain, Argentina and USSR.'[141]

Another interesting case in the group is that of Peico Electronics and Electricals Ltd (formerly Philips India Ltd), also a recognized export house. Radios and lamps have been the predominant export items of the company. In 1985, it is reported to have exported 2,00,000 radios. Other exports of the company include multimeters, electrodes and cassette recorders, microphones and public address systems.[142] An important feature of the company's operations in India is its close association with the small-scale sector. The company has subcontracting arrangements for many of its products sold within and outside India. The items traded include radio sets, tape recorders, record players, lamps, fittings, dry cells, welding electrodes and equipment and several other items. Traded items accounted for more than one-third of the total sales of the company. It has also started exporting marine products. For instance, in 1984 Peico Electronics exported marine products worth Rs 2.94 crores which accounted for over 39 per cent of its total exports during the year. The corresponding figures for 1987 were Rs 3.89 crores and 35.8 per cent respectively. Peico Electronics has been registered with the Marine Products Exports Development Authority. While describing its export performance in 1987 the company stated:

> Exports of the company have reached the level of Rs. 108.9 million—a notable aspect for 1987 being the success in exports of computer software. During the year the company made impressive entries into some new markets in Asia, Africa and Eastern Europe with its consumer electronics products.[143]

Incidentally, the company floated a subsidiary—Unique Dataware

Systems and Consultants Pvt. Ltd—in 1983. The software packages developed by the subsidiary were exported by Peico Electronics.[144]

The largest exporter in the automotive tyres industry, Dunlop India Ltd, was recognized as an export house in 1982. The chairman of the company explained in his review of activities that the increase in the company's sales was made possible through third party exports and the company's own products which resulted in the company's recognition as an export house.[145] It is interesting to note that during 1982 the company reported Rs 5.02 crores worth of sales of marine products. Assuming that all these were realized through exports, it appears that marine products accounted for 57.93 per cent of the total exports of the company during the year. As per the latest report (1988–89), the company sold Rs 12.19 crores worth of marine products during the period April 1988 to March 1989, its total exports for the year being Rs 22.53 crores. The company also informed that '(s)ubstantial orders were received from Afghanistan, Africa and USSR'. Regarding the USA market it reported that 'appropriate product lines' were being developed.[146] Interestingly enough, the second largest exporter in the group, MRF Ltd, also deals in marine products. Its exports of Rs 2.11 crores worth of marine products in 1980–81 would have accounted for more than 60 per cent of the total exports of the company during the year if the entire quantity of marine products that it purchased from the market were exported. Going by the same assumption, its sales of marine products worth Rs 44.64 crores during the 18 month period ending March 1989 would have accounted for over 72 per cent of the total export earnings. MRF Ltd, a recognized export house, is also registered with the Marine Products Export Development Authority.[147] Going by the published data, the company lost on the sale of marine products (against a purchase value of Rs 470.62 lakhs of 795 tonnes of marine products, the sale realization was only Rs 461.05 lakhs for the same quantity). It was a recipient of the Capexil Award 'for becoming the first Indian company to export tyres to the USA'. It should be noted that the company's former and present collaborators, Mansfield and B.F. Goodrich belong to the USA. The company had appointed sole selling agents for its exports to Egypt, Pakistan and Bangladesh. The rupee trade area has been an important market as, according to the company, it was the largest supplier of tyres in

1980 to the socialist world. Other important markets for the company included Mauritius, Afghanistan, Iraq and Burma.

Other important cases of export houses include ITC Ltd, classified under the cigarettes industry; its exports include marine products and carpets. Both Century Spinning & Manufacturing Co. Ltd and Madura Coats Ltd, the highest ranking exporters among the textile companies covered in the study, are export houses. Bombay Dyeing and Manufacturing Company's export earnings were almost entirely derived from 'local sales for exports'. The case of Reliance Industries Ltd, also an export house, is particularly interesting. The company seems to have derived a very high proportion of its export revenue from the sale of marine products. In 1982, it reported exports worth Rs 18.40 crores while the sales of marine products were reported to be Rs 16.67 crores (90.60 per cent). In the other years also, the sale of marine products constituted quite a significant proportion of its exports.[148] It is of significance that the purchase and sales values of 3,103 tonnes of marine products traded by the company during 1982 were reported to be equal. The company received an award from the government of Gujarat for best export performance during the year 1981–82. From the company's Annual Report it becomes evident that it was under an obligation to export, the obligation having been placed on it for importing machinery and other capital goods. What items are to be exported, is probably not the official concern.

We have observed earlier that automobile manufactures and components accounted for a significant increase in the export earnings. More than 60 per cent of the exports of the industry were accounted for by two companies — Tata Engineering and Locomotive Co. Ltd (39.75 per cent) and Mahindra and Mahindra Ltd (21.02 per cent). Tata Engineering and Locomotive Co. Ltd (TELCO) received substantial amounts of export incentives during the period under study. During the three years 1981–82, 1982–83 and 1983–84, such incentives amounted to Rs 33.40 crores while exports in the corresponding period amounted to Rs 147.08 crores. The net earnings of the company after taking note of other earnings and adjusting for expenditure in foreign exchange on account of imports, dividends etc. worked out to only Rs 7.92 crores.[149] It is interesting that the company has been pleading for according exports the 'highest priority' matched by a 'stable and equitable policy of incentives and rewards'. African and Gulf countries seem to be the main markets for the company's exports. In its Annual Report for the year 1985–86, the company clearly stated that '(d)epressed oil prices seriously affected the oil economies of the Middle East, depriving us of some of our principal markets'.[150] Though separate details are not available, the company's export earnings included exports 'through Export House and local sales eligible for export incentives'.[151] It may be noted that Tata Exports Ltd, a company belonging to Tata house, is a recognized trading house. Among the many different items exported by Tata Exports Ltd, such as leather goods, cosmetics, garments, carpets, diamonds and marine products are Tata commercial vehicles. From this it can be understood that the export house referred to by TELCO was Tata Exports Ltd. It is pertinent to narrate the case of Tata Iron and Steel Co. Ltd (TISCO), the largest private sector company in the country, which has recently been recognized as an export house. The company is also a part of Tata house. Going by the list of products exported by the company and their suppliers, it appears that the company has been dependent on its subsidiaries and associate companies, apart from several commodities purchased from others. Including deemed exports the export earnings of the company for the year 1988–89 amounted to Rs 93 crores. Chrome ore exports contributed 37.6 per cent of the total export earnings. The company also exports shrimps and coffee.[152] It is interesting to note that the company has decided to set up a joint sector venture with the equity participation of Acquatic Farms Ltd, USA. The case of TISCO clearly demonstrates the extent of double counting involved in adding up individual company exports. This also illustrates how a house can maximize its advantage by converting more than one of its companies into an export house.[153]

Mahindra and Mahindra Ltd is also a recognized export house. The company's main products are jeeps, light commercial vehicles and tractors. 'Deemed exports' form an important part of foreign exchange earnings of the company. For instance, while in 1983–84 vehicle exports stood at 1914 units, 955 units were sold under the category of 'deemed exports' for which the company is reported to have received payment in foreign exchange.[154] Iran was the major importer of the company's vehicles. Other important countries were Mauritius and Zimbabwe. During the same year, merchant exports on behalf of other manufacturers were of the order of Rs 3.26 crores against the total exports of Rs 20.84 crores. These were mainly the products of the small-scale sector which include diesel engines, leather goods, fasteners, hand tools, sewing machines etc. Of late, fruits, marine products and handicrafts and garments have also been added to the items traded by the company.

Greaves Cotton and Co. Ltd, a company belonging to the Thapar house, is also a recognized export house. The company's case is being cited for reasons somewhat different from the above.[155] The company had set up several branches abroad including one in the United Kingdom. The UK branch is presumably part of its infrastructure developed for export purposes; part of the export sales has been attributed to the sales of foreign branches. The company has shown expenditure in foreign exchange to the tune of Rs 5 – Rs 7 crores annually on '(o)ther matters (including foreign branch)'.[156] Total expenses shown under this head during the period 1978–86 amounted to Rs 63.53 crores. This is in addition to the capital expenditure on the branch reported regularly. How much of this expenditure was incurred on the foreign branch and what part of it was incurred on other matters? Does the branch take up trading activities on its own abroad which may be one of the reasons for such high expenditure? These particulars are not available in the company's Annual Reports. Its annual accounts also do not give a clue as to the physical assets, stocks and turnover of the UK branch. The fact that a number of persons are employed in the UK branch becomes evident from the list of employees who earn Rs 3,000 and above per month. The company's erstwhile subsidiary, Greaves International Ltd, had an office in Paris. While the auditors of the parent company report that the audited accounts of Greaves Cotton's UK branch have been incorporated into its accounts, the subsidiary's auditors were not referring to the operation of its Paris branch. The cases of Greaves Cotton and its subsidiary illustrate the problems involved in monitoring the foreign branches of Indian companies.

The above account leads to a few important conclusions. First, exercises to obtain an understanding of the changing 'export basket' cannot be undertaken on the basis of a company as a reporting unit. Peico may be a well-known TNC in the area of electricals, but its exports, as stated in the Annual Reports, do not reflect exports of 'electrical machinery'. Exports by the Indian tyre companies do not indicate that India has emerged as an important exporter of automotive tyres.[157] The major exporters of the main industry groups have been discussed to demonstrate that general impressions can be very misleading, Second, on the face of it, performance in terms of export promotion has been good, especially by the largest TNCs operating in India. A closer examination reveals that their exports have been essentially directed to the 'rupee trade areas' and did not contribute to India's capabilities to earn hard currency, which was utilized by these companies for their enhanced level of imports. Third, the level of exports did not reflect the enhanced capabilities of these companies to face open international competition.

The rise in exports was more a result of bilateral agreements and 'captive buyers' than due to costs reduction or higher quality as visualized in the 'package of liberalization'. Finally, the nature of their export markets did not reflect the 'strength of the TNC exporters' in their home countries—an argument repeatedly underlined in the export promotion debates.

CONCLUSIONS

The review of the evolution of export policies suggests that a variety of export measures have been adopted by the government without adequate appreciation of the objective conditions or a systematic and scientific review being attempted at any one time. One also gets the impression that the general approach of the committees was to respond to government's thinking and to provide justification for policies already thought of. Very little thinking has gone into providing alternative strategies and policy measures. For instance, the dissenting experts on the first Tandon Committee (1980) voiced many apprehensions regarding the recommendations of the majority. But their note of dissent did not have any impact on the policy makers' subsequent decisions. The role of the experts on the committee obviously did not suit the views of the government.

Export has been a favourite subject for inquiry. Yet no serious attempt has ever been made to assess the costs of the policies to society.[158] Increased incentives and further relaxations were offered, especially for the larger undertakings, which were either MRTPA or FERA companies. India is credited with a reasonably efficient administrative system which obtains a good deal of economic intelligence. The country has evolved an extensive reporting system. Given all this, it is somewhat surprising that the committees did not take full advantage of the reporting system on trade data. For instance, the first EPZ was established in 1965. What has been the net contribution of the EPZs in promoting Indian exports and in helping India to earn net foreign exchange? Similarly, has the policy contributed to India's export potential? This could be easily verified. However, the establishment of EPZs and 100 per cent EOUs was pursued without attempting to gain an understanding of the implications.

The need for upgrading technology was stressed repeatedly. In spite of the government maintaining a position of non-acceptance of restrictions on exports in foreign collaboration agreements, the prevalence of such restrictions is only too well known.[159] The clauses in official approvals reveal the helplessness of the government in forcing exports. This, however, did not find any mention in either the discussion or in the recommendations of the committees. Ironically, the very strength on which foreign technical collaborations and joint ventures have been encouraged has the built-in danger of transfer pricing.

Indian exports still constitute, to a large extent, low technology and traditional items. Engineering and chemical industries, in whose case the arguments of technological obsolescence and economies of scale are more relevant and the development of which is the aim of the industrial policy, have not made much headway in exports. The decline in engineering exports in the 1980s is particularly significant. In this context, it would probably not be surprising to find many of the 'thrust sectors', selected for providing special emphasis with a view to increasing India's exports, include an overwhelming majority of items which do not require sophisticated technology.[160] One even finds wheat, handicrafts, fruits and vegetables among the items so selected. This should be viewed along with the increasing importance attached to export and trading houses, which were expected to deal in these items. These houses have been extended the facilities to retain a part of their export earnings abroad and to set up offices and warehouses abroad; they have been offered blanket foreign exchange permits for travel abroad etc. In a sense, the 'free trade regime' advocated by the First Tandon Committee has been created for export and trading houses.

While concentrating on export earnings, the committees did not discuss the possible steps for reducing the leakages of foreign exchange through over-invoicing of imports and under-invoicing of exports. The recent period has witnessed the disclosures of a number of cases of unauthorized foreign exchange dealings by well known companies. Even the first Export Promotion Committee of A.D. Gorwala in 1949 felt it necessary to mention this practice and had specifically prescribed a procedure for dealing with such cases. The Gorwala Committee had estimated that 5 to 15 per cent of the foreign exchange earned was being retained abroad by Indian nationals. The committee called for exemplary punishment when such a case was detected. In contrast to such a stance, exporters are now permitted to retain a certain proportion of their foreign exchange earnings to develop overseas markets. Similarly, permissions to set up branches and offices abroad have their own negative implications. It may be recalled that one of the objectives of FERA, 1973 was to make foreign branches operating in India to transfer their operations to companies incorporated in India for the purpose. This was expected to plug leakage of foreign exchange being effected in the form of 'head office expenses'. The policy to permit opening of branches abroad would open yet another avenue for retaining foreign exchange. There are no indications of the measures that would be taken to minimize such possibilities.[161]

An attempt has been made in the foregoing to assess the response of the large private corporate sector to the liberal policy mix and the package of incentives offered for the promotion of exports. The relevance of such an analysis is found in the recent policy thrust which places special reliance on the large sector to take a lead in export efforts. It has also been noted that the liberalization of economic policies, the stated objective of which was to increase international competitiveness which is necessary for promoting exports, was initiated during the 1970s itself. Apart from an increase in the volume of exports, the success of the policies is also reflected in increased export orientation. It is obvious that the main objective underlying export promotion is to earn net foreign exchange in order to finance essential imports. An analysis of export performance has particular significance for the behaviour of TNCs. The point for consideration is whether TNCs treat India as a manufacturing base to cater to other markets because of the advantages offered by India in terms of cheap labour.

The analysis of the data on the large private corporate sector has shown that growth in exports has been below the expectations. In terms of constant prices, the rise in the level of exports has been marginal.

From a position of net earners of foreign exchange, large companies started utilizing more foreign exchange than what they earned. By the end of the period, large companies accounted for a deficit of Rs 400 crores. The implications of the trends are disturbing. Irrespective of the grouping of the companies, the net foreign exchange earning capacity became negative by the end of the period. This was equally true for companies belonging to the top 20 industrial houses as it was for foreign majority companies (subsidiaries). Recent evidence further supports this conclusion as foreign exchange earnings of large private companies have been accompanied by larger amounts of foreign exchange expenditure. The decline in export orientation as measured by the ratio of exports to net sales has been gradual and continuous, and reflected the growing dependence on the domestic market. The declining ratio of exports to sales seems to have affected all ranges of the ratio as evidenced from the decreasing number of companies in the higher ranges of the ratio. Even companies belonging to the top 20 houses showed a declining export orientation in as much as the ratio reduced in 1983–84 to half of what it was in 1976–77. At the aggregate level, private limited companies, which have generally lower scales of operations, showed better performance both in terms of net earning of foreign exchange as well as the exports to sales ratio. Instead of expanding into export markets, a number of large companies began to withdraw from overseas markets. The number of exporting companies declined from a peak of 315 in 1977–78 to 271. The much blamed industrial policy has been accommodative enough not to impose restrictions on export production. This has been the case for a long time. But the large sector preferred to take shelter behind the seemingly harsh licencing regime.

Though the industry-wise analysis has shown that certain chemical product groups and engineering items performed better in terms of exports, not much significance could be attached to it because of the export house activity getting mixed up with own exports by the manufacturers.

An examination of the pattern of exports of some of the important exporters — export houses and others — revealed that the phenomena of export houses coupled with unrelated diversification was largely responsible for the divergence between the production basket and the composition of export items of individual companies. This makes the industrial classification meaningless. The export trading house scheme propelled these companies into areas which are unrelated to their main line of activity, the favourite items being marine products, leather and its products, and garments. Being merchant exporters they retain the option to withdraw from exporting these items at the first sign of adversity. In spite of the permissive approach of the government the export/trading house scheme has been unable to expand further.

Some other observations worth mentioning are as follows. TNCs in India have been more interested in the domestic market than in making India a base for farming out part of their production. Their exports were primarily a result of the need to retain the majority stake of the foreign shareholders. Indian policies have worked well to their advantage. Whether it was moving into low priority industries or marketing of other unassociated manufactures, mostly in the small-scale sector, the policies seem to have facilitated the expansion of TNCs. Socialist countries with which India's trade is conducted in rupee terms have become the main export markets for TNCs. Dependence of TNCs on the socialist countries is also a matter of concern. In view of the rapidly changing international political situation would the Indian affiliates be directed by their parent companies to cater to this market for long?

There is no substantial evidence to suggest that exports of TNCs were predominantly non-traditional, technology intensive manufactured items to advanced capitalist countries from where they import most of their requirements of technology, materials and capital goods. As a result, in hard currency terms, their net earnings are far lower than what our analysis indicates. Given the fact that equity participation is allowed liberally in the case of export ventures and India has been canvassing vigorously to attract foreign investment if foreign direct investment still does not flow in as anticipated, the most plausible interpretation could be that the major attraction for TNCs is India's domestic market and not exports. Otherwise, EPZs would have been beehives of transnational production. Taking into consideration the keen competition among developing countries for attracting foreign investment it could be argued that TNCs could be brought to India on their own terms which may prove expensive in the long run.

The large Indian companies have been heavy importers of technology. For instance, the 405 companies under study, entered into more than 2,000 foreign collaboration agreements until the middle of 1986. Subsidiaries of foreign companies are expected to update their technology regularly from their parent companies. Against this background it may be difficult to sustain the argument that technology was a significant handicap for the failure of India's large sector in making an impact in the exports of manufactured products.

It is the global strategy, as conceived by the suppliers of technology, which determines where to produce and where to sell. Making technological upgradation through import of technology as a focal point for increasing India's competitiveness in the international market is likely to lead to a dependence syndrome instead of contributing to her exports. This does not, however, mean that technological improvements do not play a role in creating export capabilities. It is the method of acquisition which could determine whether the resulting production would be confined to domestic markets or directed to export markets as well.

Giving more and more incentives is obviously not the solution for better export performance. Nor the weakening of the planning process in the name of export promotion helps in the long run. Export and trading house schemes highlight the way in which the initial and basic objectives of economic policy have been set aside. If one permits exports to have an important role, as indeed has been the case, it should not come as a surprise that it is the trader-exporter who decides what to sell and where to sell; where to import from and at what price. This opens up a number of possibilities of foreign exchange outgo from the country. The practice of transfer pricing is bound to become a matter of serious concern for India.

POSTSCRIPT

Introduction

Since the preparation of the manuscript of this book in February 1990, the Indian economic policy environment has witnessed unprecedented transformation, more so with the new government coming into power in 1991. This period also witnessed political instability and the BOP crisis arising out of the Gulf conflict. Further, the break-up of the Soviet Union and radical developments in the socialist world have significant implications for Indian economic policy thinking. The last four years saw four governments—the changes taking place in December 1989, November 1990 and June 1991. Each one of the elected governments preferred to introduce its own trade policy. The 1988 policy was replaced in 1990; and the 1990 policy was substituted in April 1992. While the process of withdrawal of regulations initiated in the mid-1970s reached a different phase first in 1980 and later in 1985, the policy measures introduced over the last 15 months represent an attempt to break with the past. The changes cover a broad spectrum ranging from industrial licencing policy, anti-monopoly legislation, public sector, technology and capital imports, foreign trade, exchange control, capital issue control to taxation structure. The process of change is still continuing.

This note examines whether the trends observed in the main study which covered the pre-1989 period are still continuing or have been reversed. The export performance of 405 large private sector companies for the period 1975–76 to 1983–84 was examined in the main study. The study highlighted certain characteristics of the large Indian exporters. The company level published data has serious limitations to permit a fuller understanding of the corporate strategies for exports. At the same time, it is a fact that broad trends of exports and imports by the large corporate sector did show the extent of direct burden placed on the economy.

The issues examined in the study continue to be relevant today as India strives to increase her export earnings and reduce pressure on balance-of-payments. In fact, it is increasingly imperative that India's exports grow faster than her imports and thereby the adverse trade balance could at least be contained, if not reversed. The experience of the 1980s shows that while Indian exports increased at a rapid pace, they were accompanied by a higher level of imports. The outcome was a continued negative trade balance. The 'quantum jump' in exports which was the aim of the first Tandon Committee seems to have been achieved, though the jump has been higher in the case of imports. External debt and trade deficits grew simultaneously—the accumulated deficit since the mid-1980s almost equals the debt in rupee terms at the end of

1990–91. India's foreign debt increased from US $18 billion in 1980 to US $70 billion in 1992 (Table 23). The debt GNP ratio has also increased substantially. Debt service ratio stood at 28.8 per cent during 1989. In 1992 it was estimated to be more than 30 per cent.

TABLE 23

India's External Debt and Debt Servicing Costs (in millions of dollars)

Year	*Outstanding Debt*	*Debt as % of GNP*	*Debt Service*	*Debt Service as % of Exports of Goods & Services*
1975	12,470	14.5	861	15.3
1980	18,182	10.5	1,394	11.3
1986	47,150	20.7	4,560	32.6
1987	55,786	22.0	5,077	32.3
1988	59,534	22.1	5,693	32.1
1989	63,467	24.2	5,820	28.8
1992 (End March)	70,000			

Note: The OECD data base, the main source of the data, has been revised as of 1982 with a new data base. Therefore, the series for 1975 and 1980 are not strictly comparable with the new time series 1986–89.

Sources: UNCTAD, *Handbook of International Trade and Development Statistics: 1991*, United Nations, New York, 1992, pp. 424–25. The debt figure for 1992 is from the *Annual Report* of the Reserve Bank of India as reported in *Economic Times*, 7 September 1992.

The performance of the large private sector companies and their contribution to net foreign exchange earnings (foreign currency earnings *less* the utilization) continues to be a relevant area of enquiry. The policy emphasis is on the large private corporations to play an important role in helping India realize higher levels of exports. For long, the assumption has been that with the given level of domination of markets of the advanced countries, TNCs' involvement in India's export efforts would prove to be beneficial to the country.[12] There is fresh emphasis on foreign private capital for reducing the deficit on current account. Therefore, apart from studying the large Indian companies the performance of TNCs in earning net foreign exchange needs to be examined more closely.

Export performance of large private sector companies

The reference years for the company-wise analysis in the main study were 1975–76 and 1983–84. Eight years have lapsed since then and this is a reasonably long period to undertake a review of the trends. Most of the policy changes of the 1980s, and especially the recent ones, have sought to meet the long standing demands of the large private corporations. One would, therefore, expect that the large private corporate sector would reciprocate and strive for higher levels of exports. Similarly, one has reason to expect that the composition of Indian exports would have undergone a noticeable change, with the engineering and chemical sectors taking the lead as these two sectors have better and easy access to foreign technology and capital imports. The 1980s witnessed a substantial increase in the number of approved foreign collaborations and investments. Chemical and engineering industries accounted for more than 80 per cent of the total approved collaborations at the beginning of the 1980s and for over three-fourths of the total towards the end. Payments for technology imports increased substantially. Average annual remittances, on account of technical know-how, were to the tune of Rs 42.5 crores during the period 1977–78 to 1979–80 and Rs 342.3 crores during the period 1984–85 to 1986–87.

The export performance and net foreign exchange earnings of different sets of companies during the recent past are shown in Table 24.[163] Though the data refer to two different years, it may be noted that foreign controlled rupee companies (FCRCs) showed a lower export propensity compared to the large public limited companies.[164] In terms of financing their requirements of foreign exchange, the large companies performed better, though only marginally.[165] Private limited companies, though they engage in foreign trade on a modest scale, show favourable results in terms of net earning of foreign exchange and export orientation.

The combined results of the foreign exchange transactions of 312 large private sector companies, each having a paid-up capital of Rs 1.00 crore or above in 1980–81 are presented in Table 25. These results confirm the trends observed in Table 24. The large Indian private sector did not become more export-oriented during the remaining period of the 1980s as exports continued to account for a small percentage of their overall sales turnover. The net

TABLE 24

Export Performance of Different Constituents of the Indian Corporate Private Sector* (in Rs crores)

Item	*Category of Companies*			
	Public Ltd Cos (1988–89)	*Large Public Ltd Cos (1989–90)*	*Foreign Controlled Rupee Cos (1987–88)*	*Private Ltd Cos (1988–89)*
Number of Companies	1678	604	298	869
Exports	2934.4	3145.9	674.8	177.8
Net Sales	61710.1	52257.7	13061.2	2590.0
Exports to Sales Ratio (%)	4.8	6.0	5.2	6.9
Total Earnings	3490.2	3697.1	779.3	196.0
Total Expenditure	5951.1	5157.7	1116.0	117.3
Net Earnings	−2460.9	−1460.6	−336.7	78.3
Earnings/Expenditure Ratio (%)	58.7	71.7	69.8	166.8

Note: * The presentation excludes trading, tea plantation, electricity generation and shipping companies in the first three categories; tea, trading, land and estate, road transport and shipping companies in the case of private limited companies.

Source: Based on the company finance studies published in *Reserve Bank of India Bulletin*, February 1992, November 1991, March 1992 and June 1992.

earning capacity of the large corporate private sector, while fluctuating widely, further weakened as these companies reported increasing net losses of foreign exchange. The average loss during the first three years was Rs 321.2 crores and it was Rs 1,128 crores during the final three years.

More detailed information is now available on the composition and nature of exports of large corporations. The larger companies, whether Indian or foreign affiliates, seem to be increasingly involved in trading activity instead of emerging as manufacturer exporters. Garments, leather goods, marine products, spices, rice etc. have become favourite items of export. Even in the case of the largest TNCs based in India no direct relationship has been observed between products exported and their main line of manufacturing activity. Indeed, one could hardly distinguish a foreign export house from an Indian one.

In view of the evidence available for company level exports, a

TABLE 25
Export Performance of 312 Large Private Sector Companies During 1980–81 to 1988–89 (in Rs crores)

Year	*Exports*	*Sales*	*Export/ Sales Ratio (%)*	*Earnings*	*Foreign Exchange*	
					Expenditure	*Net Earnings*
1980–81	723.70	13,367.91	5.41	795.06	983.79	−188.73
1981–82	838.12	16,337.08	5.13	936.41	1,287.17	−350.76
1982–83	863.86	18,047.19	4.79	1,027.83	1,451.83	−424.00
1983–84	769.19	19,814.41	3.88	958.19	1,370.69	−412.50
1984–85	993.66	22,737.13	4.37	1,228.75	1,591.25	−362.50
1985–86	1,067.32	26,176.91	4.08	1,334.58	2,106.12	−771.54
1986–87	1,051.67	28,671.82	3.67	1,345.92	2,525.24	−1,179.32
1987–88	1,319.55	31,554.98	4.18	1,683.14	2,484.45	−801.31
1988–89	1,890.00	37,885.21	4.99	2,182.91	3,586.16	−1,403.25

Source: Computed from an ISID data base on company level statistics.

serious doubt has been raised whether non-related exports were not third party exports for which credit documents were bought in the market. For example, the exports of marine products from India increased substantially during the recent years. Many companies belonging to or associated with large houses have been engaged in exports of marine products. However, these companies have exhibited large fluctuations in exports of marine products.[166] Had these exports been based on the company's own manufacturing/processing, there would have been a more sustained pattern of exports. Moreover, the export data from Bombay, Calcutta and Cochin ports show that none of the large companies was a significant exporter of marine products.[167]

Composition and direction of India's exports

To understand the structure of India's exports and major markets for different groups of items, an analysis was done of the exports averaged over the three years 1987–88 to 1989–90 (see Table 26).[168] During this period, textiles and related articles[169] ranked highest in India's exports, followed by pearls and precious stones and vegetables products, in that order. These three product groups accounted for over half of the total exports from India. The combined share of the OECD countries in the first two categories was more than three-fourths. Moreover, the OECD countries accounted for over three-fourths of the exports of animal products and hides and skins and had nearly 60 per cent share in the footwear category and metals and metal products and nearly half of mineral products.

Chemicals and engineering exports which are important from the industrial policy point of view together accounted for about one-fifth of the total exports.[170] In these items[171] the OECD and East European countries (hereinafter referred to as the socialist bloc) have almost equal shares—a little over 32 per cent each. The erstwhile USSR accounted for the bulk of the exports to the socialist bloc. At the section level, however, the two country groups behave differently. In the case of chemical and chemical products there seems to be a clear division. Nearly two-thirds of the synthetic dyes (falling under the heading 3209) were exported to the OECD countries. The corresponding share of the socialist bloc was only 11 per cent. Paints and varnishes were almost entirely (97.4 per cent) exported to the socialist bloc. Markets of the socialist bloc were also important for soap and washing preparations (87.5 per cent) and perfumery and toilet preparations (71 per cent). The engineering category had a combined share of 11.2 per cent. In the case of metals and metal products, the OECD countries had a 60 per cent share, while the socialist bloc had substantial shares in instrument and apparatus and machinery and parts — 62.6 per cent and 48.4 per cent respectively.

Excluding the high import content category of pearls and precious stones, and textile items which are subjected to quota restrictions, the OECD countries had high shares in industries which are either primary or semi-processed in character (mineral products, hides and skins and base metals) or which are known to be environmentally disadvantageous (dyes, hides and skins and base metals). In contrast, India's dependence on the socialist bloc was more for the export of consumer products: vegetable products, foodstuffs and tobacco, paints and varnishes, drugs and pharmaceuticals, soaps and detergents, toiletries, footwear. The socialist bloc was also a major market for engineering items.

The share of the socialist bloc showed an increasing trend as is evident from the fact that in 1989–90 these countries had higher shares compared to the three year average. In 1990–91 their share

TABLE 26

Industry and Destination-wise Exports of India During 1987–88 to 1989–90 (in Rs crores)

Section	*Description*	*Average Exports During the Period*		*% Share of the Group of Countries*			
		Amount	*% to Total*	*OECD*	*Socialist Bloc*	*Asia*	*Rest incl. Unspecified*
1	Live Animals, Products	767.32	(3.67)	79.66	0.41	10.77	9.16
2	Vegetable Products	2507.10	(12.00)	33.94	36.17	10.31	19.59
3	Animal or Vegetable Fats & Oils etc.	38.32	(0.18)	54.73	34.76	5.21	5.30
4	Prepared Foodstuffs, Beverages and Tobacco	665.34	(3.18)	15.00	58.15	10.62	16.23
5	Mineral Products	1451.01	(6.94)	49.44	6.99	15.10	28.46
6	Products of Chemical or Allied Industries	1472.20	(7.05)	35.09	37.34	17.59	9.98
7	Plastics & Rubber	199.91	(0.96)	32.49	19.05	29.49	18.97
	Sub-total Chemicals & Plastics: (6 + 7)	**1672.11**	**(8.01)**	**34.18**	**35.15**	**18.41**	**11.05**
8	Hides & Skins, Leather Products, Fur Skins and Articles Thereof etc.	1109.25	(5.31)	77.42	14.26	7.54	0.79
9	Wood, Cork & Articles Thereof etc.	22.81	(0.11)	44.01	11.93	25.53	23.02
10	Paper & Paper-Board and Articles Thereof	42.85	(0.21)	18.07	9.16	34.55	38.22
11	Textile and Textile Articles	5119.35	(24.50)	72.74	12.45	7.78	7.04
12	Footwear, Headgear, Umbrellas etc.	559.10	(2.68)	60.80	36.82	1.14	1.23
13	Stone, Cement, Ceramic and Glass Products	75.87	(0.36)	49.33	16.47	21.70	12.49
14	Pearls, Precious or Semi-precious Stones/ Metals & Articles Thereof	4103.59	(19.64)	78.22	0.21	19.45	2.13
15	Base Metals & Articles of Base Metal	738.28	(3.53)	59.97	7.86	15.71	16.46
16	Machinery & Their Parts, Electrical & Electronic Equipment, Parts Thereof	1089.24	(5.21)	17.36	48.36	18.26	16.03

17	Instruments & Apparatus, Clocks &	380.76	(1.82)	20.22	10.37	32.57	36.83
18	Watches etc.						
	Watches, etc.	134.47	(0.64)	23.55	62.58	6.29	7.58
	Sub-total Engineering: (15 to 18)	**2342.75**	**(11.20)**	**31.60**	**30.24**	**19.09**	**19.08**
19+	Miscellaneous Goods & Manufactured						
	Articles and Unspecified	418.37	(2.00)	76.79	5.62	5.44	12.14
	Total	**20095.14**	**(100.00)**	**38.06**	**18.00**	**13.13**	**10.81**

Notes: (*a*) The section grouping follows the DGCI&S classification. (*b*) Figures in parentheses indicate the percentage share of the different sections in the total. (*c*) Composition of the country groups is: OECD—Australia, Austria, Belgium, Canada, Denmark, Finland, France, the FRG, Greece, Iceland, Ireland, Italy, Japan, Luxembourg, the Netherlands, New Zealand, Norway, Portugal, Spain, Sweden, Switzerland, Turkey, the UK and the USA; Socialist bloc—Bulgaria, Czechoslovakia, GDR, Hungary, Poland, Romania, the USSR and Yugoslavia. (*d*) 19+ covers sections 19 to 21, miscellaneous and project goods and unclassified ones.

Source: Based on the data tape supplied by the Directorate General of Commercial Intelligence & Statistics (DGCI&S).

was 19.8 per cent compared to the three year average share of 18.0 per cent.[172] The important individual groups which had higher shares in 1989–90 compared to the average were: vegetable products (42.1 per cent); prepared foodstuffs, beverages and tobacco (62.2 per cent); chemicals and chemical products (42.9 per cent); and machinery and parts (50.4 per cent).

The growth in chemical and engineering exports from India could, to a significant extent, be attributed to the reliance on markets of the socialist bloc. The break-up of the USSR and the collapse of the important markets of East European countries is, therefore, significant for these exports. During April-June 1992 exports to the Commonwealth of Independent States (CIS)—the erstwhile USSR—stood at Rs 461 crores compared to Rs 880 crores during the corresponding months of 1991 i.e. a decline of 45 per cent.[173] A similar decline in exports was also noticed in the case of Romania, Hungary and Poland. The major export items which suffered were pharmaceutical products, cosmetics and toiletries, tea, transport equipment, leather footwear etc.[174] Who were the main suppliers of these items to the socialist bloc? There are various possibilities, though not mutually exclusive. If TNCs were the main suppliers, it depends upon the TNC strategy whether to continue to supply from India or from other locations. Hitherto, TNCs were probably taking advantage of India's special relationship with the bloc. If the main suppliers were other companies, the CIS countries could opt for other sources.

While at the aggregate level the OECD countries and the socialist bloc accounted for over three-fourths of India's total exports, Asian countries had 13.1 per cent share. This was primarily due to a 29.5 per cent share in the exports of plastics and rubber products; 32.6 per cent in transport equipment; 18.3 per cent in machinery and parts; and 19.5 per cent in pearls and precious stones. The high share in machinery could be due to the concentration of Indian joint ventures in this region.[175]

Composition and direction of exports of foreign affiliates from India

To understand the phenomenon of exports to the socialist bloc as also to examine the direction and pattern of TNC exports from

India, a separate exercise was undertaken. An attempt was also made to compare the behaviour of the TNCs and their Indian counterparts in a few industries.[176] For this study we used a data base generated at the Institute for Studies in Industrial Development from the Daily Trade Returns (DTR) of various custom houses.[177] The custom houses covered are Bombay (Air & Sea), Calcutta (Air & Sea), Delhi (Air & ICD) and Cochin (Air & Sea).[178] The DTR is a record of individual export/import transactions of specific trading parties. The analysis was based on the country of destination and the year of reference was 1990–91. In view of the large size of the data file the party-wise exports were aggregated at the industry and country levels. Out of the resulting data records all those amounting to less than Rs 1.00 lakh were dropped to bring the data file to a manageable size.[179] The exporters were then categorized into those with 25 per cent or more foreign equity and branches of foreign companies. The results are presented in Table 27. The foreign affiliates accounted for Rs 959 crores of the total exports of Rs 19,686 crores from these ports or about 5 per cent of the total. The foreign affiliates, therefore, do not seem to be making a significant contribution to India's exports.[180] Other evidence also supports this observation. At the aggregate level foreign affiliates accounted for only about 6–7 per cent of India's total exports. According to a RBI study on finances of foreign controlled rupee companies (FCRCs), the exports of FCRCs totalled Rs 1,587 crores in 1986–87 and 1987–88 which constituted 5.6 per cent of India's exports during the corresponding years.[181]

The share of the OECD in the exports of foreign affiliates was somewhat lower than at the aggregate level as seen in Table 26. Comparatively the dependence on the socialist bloc was slightly higher at 20 per cent. The share of Asian countries was also a shade higher at 20 per cent. Machinery, vegetable products and chemicals and chemical products accounted for nearly 70 per cent of the exports of foreign affiliates. Tea accounted for nearly 90 per cent of the exports of vegetable products.

When seen together, the OECD and the socialist bloc had almost equal shares in the exports of chemical and engineering categories—35 per cent each. There are, however, wide differences in the shares of the two groups of countries within the chemical and engineering categories and even at the product group level. In the machinery category, important export products and markets

TABLE 27

Industry and Destination-wise Exports of Foreign Affiliates During 1990–91 from Four Major Ports of India (in Rs crores)

Section	*Description*	*Exports*		*OECD*	*Socialist Bloc*	*Asia*	*Rest incl. Unspecified*
		Amount	*% to Total*				
1	Live Animals, Animal Products	37.07	(3.86)	88.02	0.00	4.53	7.44
2	Vegetable Products	234.29	(24.42)	66.40	1.06	6.07	26.48
3	Animal or Vegetable Fats & Oils etc.	8.25	(0.86)	99.76	0.00	0.24	0.00
4	Prepared Foodstuffs, Beverages and Tobacco	7.32	(0.76)	28.55	16.12	2.05	53.13
5	Mineral Products	0.13	(0.01)	46.15	0.00	53.85	0.00
6	Products of the Chemical or Allied Industries	187.85	(19.58)	35.41	42.42	17.10	5.86
7	Plastics & Rubber	28.94	(3.02)	58.53	21.15	5.56	14.72
	Sub-Total Chemicals & Plastics: (6 + 7)	**216.79**	**(22.60)**	**38.50**	**39.58**	**15.56**	**6.36**
8	Hides & Skins, Leather Products, Fur Skins and Articles Thereof	2.34	(0.24)	94.02	2.14	0.43	3.41
9	Wood, Cork & Articles Thereof etc.	1.83	(0.19)	74.86	0.00	20.22	4.92
10	Paper & Paper-board and Articles Thereof	16.59	(1.73)	92.93	0.42	3.01	3.74
11	Textile and Textile Articles	59.88	(6.24)	69.12	0.90	14.90	15.10
12	Footwear, Headgear, Umbrellas etc.	25.84	(2.69)	97.17	0.19	0.27	2.37
13	Stone, Cement and Glass Products	3.66	(0.38)	27.32	2.73	27.32	42.63
14	Pearls, Precious or Semi-precious Stones/Metal Articles Thereof	4.65	(0.48)	90.54	0.00	9.46	0.00
15	Base Metals & Articles of Base Metal	38.79	(4.04)	31.40	8.71	40.47	19.39
16	Machinery & Their Parts, Electrical & Electronic Equipment etc.	237.08	(24.72)	33.96	37.63	16.77	11.64
17	Transport Equipment	25.68	(2.68)	11.37	14.80	36.33	37.50

18	Instruments & Apparatus, Clocks & Watches etc.	12.41	(1.29)	44.08	46.09	5.24	4.60
	Sub-Total Engineering: (15 to 18)	**313.96**	**(32.73)**	**32.20**	**32.52**	**20.84**	**14.44**
19+	**Miscellaneous Goods & Articles and Unspecified**	**26.62**	**(2.78)**	**32.63**	**2.84**	**57.59**	**6.94**
	Total	**959.23**	**(100.00)**	**50.30**	**20.14**	**14.80**	**14.76**

Note: See Table 26.
Source: Generated from the Daily Trade Return (DTR) data on exports. The data analysed refer to Custom Houses of Bombay, Calcutta, Delhi and Cochin.

were rubber and plastic machinery (almost entirely to the socialist bloc); air and vacuum pumps (two-thirds to the OECD); carbon electrodes (more than half to Asia); insecticides (about 70 per cent to the socialist bloc); and wires and cables (more than half to the socialist bloc and a little more than one-third to Asia).

In the chemicals category too, similar specialization could be observed. More than 60 per cent of the pharmaceuticals exports (chapter 30)* were directed to the socialist bloc. The share of the OECD in these was a little over one-fourth. In sharp contrast, more than half of the exports of this product group by non-affiliates were directed to the OECD while the share of the socialist bloc was only one-fifth. In the case of cosmetics, soap and washing preparations, the affiliates' dependence on the socialist bloc markets was almost total. In contrast, only half of the non-affiliates' exports were directed to the socialist bloc. Of the total exports of dyestuff of foreign affiliates 62 per cent were to the OECD countries.

The analysis of exports of foreign affiliates presents some interesting patterns, particularly noteworthy is the fact that for certain items of capital and consumer goods the affiliates depended heavily on the socialist bloc markets. The results of this exercise corroborate the observations of the main study. There is a need to conduct similar exercises to bring out inter-temporal changes. Such studies may profitably take explicit note of the home country of the affiliate, period of its entry into India, type of industry, size and spread of the parent company's operations, extent of integration of the host country affiliate with the parent organization etc. The analysis also could be extended to technology licencing arrangements.

In view of the meagre contribution of foreign affiliates to India's exports, their potential for contributing positively to India's balance-of-payments becomes a matter of serious debate. International experience has shown that net inflows of foreign direct investment, after taking note of outflows due to profits, have generally been negative in the case of developing countries. This was more so in the case of moderately indebted low income countries.[182] The negative balance-of-payment impact of affiliates of transnational corporations has been proved time and again in the case of India.

* Schedule I of the Customs Tariff Act, 1975 is divided into 99 chapters. Chapter 30 relates to pharmaceutical products.

In the light of this, withdrawal of export restrictions, scrapping of the phased manufacturing programme and withdrawal of dividend balancing provision—all elements of the new strategy—may not work to the advantage of India.

Summing up

This note examined the structure and direction of India's exports and the export performance of the large private sector companies as well as their ability to earn net foreign exchange. An additional feature of the presentation is an examination of the nature of exports of foreign affiliates in India.

The performance of private sector companies suggests the continuation of the trends observed in the main study. This is in spite of the liberalization measures of the 1980s and increased access to foreign capital and technology. The performance of foreign controlled companies in the recent past does not appear to be better than that of the large Indian private sector companies.

The composition and direction of India's exports is such that developments in the East European countries would not be uniformly felt across all the product groups. Certain product groups, notably, some consumer products and engineering items would be most adversely affected. The latest available trade data reflect this reality. The export processing zones whose exports are closely linked to the bloc would suffer serious dislocation in their operations. The exports of individual companies in the domestic tariff area depending upon the socialist bloc would also be affected similarly.

Since the mid-1970s there has been a special emphasis on promoting engineering exports. The excessive reliance on the East European markets for machinery and instruments belies the intrinsic failure on this front. It is likely that the Indian joint ventures were responsible for export of machinery to regions other than the socialist bloc and the OECD. In such a case, it may reflect the implicit relationship between investment and direction of trade.[183]

At present foreign affiliates do not seem to be contributing to India's export efforts in any significant manner. Their share is merely 6–7 per cent. If the fact that a few of the larger ones among these turned export houses—one hardly finds any difference in the exports of Indian and foreign export houses—which implies that their exports are not closely related to their main line of manufacturing and that some of these happen to be in low technology consumer goods industries is given the recognition, the contribution of foreign affiliates would seem to be even smaller. The desirability of the policy of encouraging exports through foreign trading houses from the point of India's long-term interests needs to be examined closely.

Foreign affiliates in India tended to depend more on the socialist bloc markets for export of certain chemical and engineering products than on their home markets. Interestingly enough, non-affiliates i.e. Indian exporters exported pharmaceutical products more to the OECD markets than to the socialist bloc. There is a need to explore if outright technology purchases by Indian companies would be more advantageous for enhanced exports and positive BOP impact in the long run than depending on TNCs or foreign controlled or associate corporations.

The new policies are basic in nature and it is only too early to make a detailed and objective assessment of their impact on India's export potential and development. But in view of the observed performance of the large private sector companies in India, a movement towards the emergence of trade blocs, collapse of the East European markets, and experience of many other developing countries with foreign investments, it is difficult to visualize a reduction in foreign debt through an acceleration in exports. At present one only hears of the optimistic view. The evidence, however, does not support the confidence.

NOTES

1. This study is exclusively based on the data available in the Corporate Information System (CIS) of the Corporate Studies Group (CSG) which has since been integrated with the Institute for Studies in Industrial Development (ISID). Prof. S.K. Goyal, Director of the CSG programmes, and presently Director of ISID, has been a constant source of encouragement and guidance. The author benefited extensively from the suggestions and comments made by Prof. Goyal, Prof. G. Junne of the University of Amsterdam, and B. Evers, Director of IVO in Tilburg (the Netherlands). The author also benefited from the comments and suggestions of the reviewers of IDPAD and Sage.

   Thanks are due to Dr Pitou van Dijck for carefully going through the manuscript and for making many useful suggestions and to Umesh Kumar Singh for word processing the manuscript at the ISID Computer Centre. The responsibility for any errors in presentation and the views expressed is, however, entirely that of the author.

The author's debt to his colleagues at the CSG who shared the responsibility of establishing the CIS is immense. These include Dr Nagesh Kumar, Dr K.V.K. Ranganathan, M.R. Murthy, E.M. Gupta, Biswajit Dhar, Sudha Sachdeva, D.N. Sharma, Farrukh Riaz, D.S. Ram Vijji, Dr Harbans Singh Sidhu, M.G.S. Yadav and Rajiv Khera. Thanks are also due to colleagues at the Institute for Studies in Industrial Development for going through the draft and offering critical comments.

2. For a discussion on the international set-up that emerged during the mid-1940s, see, J.P. Pronk, Political conditions for a new international economic order, in *The New International Economic Order: Problems and Perspectives*, ICSSR Publication No. 137, New Delhi, 1983.
3. G. Myrdal, *Economic Theory and Underdeveloped Regions*, Vora and Co., Bombay, 1973, p. 19.
4. See, S.K. Goyal, The new international economic order and transnational corporations, in ICSSR, *op. cit*, pp. 64–68.

   The Brandt Commission placed finance as the most important need of the South. Commenting on the slowing down of growth of the developing countries, the Commission stated: 'However great their (South's) own efforts, huge sums will be needed to enable the countries of the South to regain their momentum, to provide jobs and incomes to overcome poverty, and to enable them to become more self-sufficient and to take a fuller part in the world's trading system'. See Report of the Independent Commission on International Development Issues, *North-South: A Programme for Survival*, Pan Books, 1980, p. 221.
5. O. Lange, Planning economic development, in H. Bernstein (ed), *Underdevelopment and Development: The Third World Today*, Penguin Books, Harmondsworth, 1973, pp. 207–15.
6. The experience of India with regard to oil exploration is a case in point. India still depends on external sources for mining and other technologies. For instance, Coal India Ltd, a public sector holding company for coal mining operations has contracted for technology purchases from Canada, the United Kingdom, the erstwhile USSR, France, Poland and the Federal Republic of Germany.
7. Nearly all low and middle income countries were recipients of food aid (cereals). See World Bank, *World Development Report*, 1986, p. 190. The socio-economic implications of food aid are sharply brought out in S. George, *How the Other Half Dies: The Real Reasons of World Hunger*, Penguin Books, Harmondsworth, 1983.
8. The situation in the Indian subcontinent is a typical example of this phenomenon. India and Pakistan have had strained relations since their independence from the British. Acquiring of sophisticated arms by one country sends the other shopping for arms to maintain the balance. For instance, when Pakistan tried to get AWACS planes from the US, India on its part tried to get equipment which could neutralize Pakistan's advantage. Similarly, the so-called Islamic Bomb of Pakistan has resulted in many Indian politicians urging the Indian government to change its stand on nuclear weapons and to go in for the production of nuclear weapons.

9. The following table shows that education and health claimed a lower share in the national budgets in 1983 than in 1972. The decline is particularly large in low income countries.

Shares of Selected Categories of Expenditure in Central Government's Expenditure (in percentages)

Countries	*Defence*		*Education*		*Health*	
	1972	*1983*	*1972*	*1983*	*1972*	*1983*
Low Income Countries	17.2	19.5	12.7	4.7	4.6	27
Middle Income Countries	15.1	11.4	12.8	12.1	6.3	45
High Income Countries	13.0	27.7	13.6	9.4	5.6	60
Developed Market Economies	20.8	14.3	5.4	4.7	10.0	112

Source: World Bank, *World Development Report 1986*, Oxford University Press, Oxford, 1986, pp. 222–23.

10. For instance, the UNESCO Commission on TNCs observed that exports of developing countries have been 'adversely affected not only by protectionism but also by the dramatic falls in commodity prices that have accompanied the weak demand in the industrialized economies'. One of the instances cited in this regard was the decline in oil prices as a result of which some of the oil-producing developing countries have become major debtors to international banks. See UNESCO, Commission on Transnational Corporations, *Recent Developments Related to Transnational Corporations and International Economic Relations: Report of the Secretary General*, 30 January 1987.
11. The World Bank stated in its *Policy Agenda for Developing Countries* that:

> Trade policy reform is a top priority. The fundamental goal should be to increase competitiveness in world markets. This has shown that the countries which adopted outward-oriented trade strategies have out-performed those that followed inward-oriented trade strategies—in income growth, export growth, employment and savings. An outward-oriented trade strategy means lowering trade barriers, replacing quantitative restrictions with tariffs, and adopting realistic exchange rates. The objectives are to improve resource allocation, to force domestic firms to compete with foreign firms, and to open the economy to new opportunities.

See World Bank, *World Development Report 1987*, Oxford University Press, Oxford, 1987, p. 169.
12. For the planning strategy adopted by India see the documents of the First and Second Five-Year Plans.
13. One model was provided by *A Plan of Economic Development for India*, also called the Bombay Plan, by tne prominent industrialists of the time. The other alternative was suggested in the *Peoples' Plan*, reflecting the point of view of

Indian labour. The former laid emphasis on the establishment of basic industries on which 'ultimately the whole economic development of the country depends'. It proposed that the sterling balances of the country amounting to nearly Rs 800 crores should be spent on importing capital equipment. It envisaged that the drawing up of the plans would be entrusted to a National Planning Committee under the authority of the central government and their execution to a Supreme Economic Council. See: A plan of economic development for India (Part I), reproduced in *Young Indian*, Special Independence Number, 1972, pp. D45–D62. The *Peoples' Plan* which followed soon after, discounted the inference that an increase in national income would necessarily lead to an improvement in the standard of living of the people. The *Peoples' Plan* laid primary emphasis on restructuring of the economic system and directing policies for the formation of human capital as a priority. This was in sharp contrast to the point of view presented in the Bombay Plan. The foreign exchange implications of both plans differed significantly. See Peoples' Plan, reproduced in *Young Indian*, Special Independence Number, 1972, pp. D72–D95.

14. Government of India, Industrial Policy Statement, 1948, para. 2.
15. The Bombay Plan proposed controls on (*a*) production, (*b*) distribution, (*c*) consumption, (*d*) investment, (*e*) foreign trade and exchange, and (*f*) wages and working conditions. The production controls were to operate 'chiefly through a system of licences for establishing new units and for expanding existing ones'. The objective of controlling investments was to 'secure proper distribution of available resources, to prevent inflation, to provide for the orderly development of new enterprises and generally to maintain and promote the interests of Indian nationals.' Control on foreign trade and exchange was to serve the dual purposes of conserving foreign exchange and protecting Indian industries. See, *A Plan of Economic Development for India*, Part II, *Distribution—Role of State*, 1944, p. 32.
16. The foreign exchange requirements of the Second Five-Year Plan were estimated at nearly one-fourth of the Plan expenditure. See Government of India, Planning Commission, *The New India: Progress Through Democracy*, Macmillan, 1958.
17. In 1946 the sterling balances were estimated at Rs 1,724 crores as against Rs 64 crores in 1939. See Reserve Bank of India, *Report on the Census of India's Foreign Liabilities and Assets as on 30th June 1948*, 1950, p. 13.
18. The need for foodgrain imports had persisted over the past four decades. While it is true that at the end of 1986 food reserves were of the order of 23.60 million tonnes, it is equally true that during the 1979–88 period the total quantum of cereal imports was 8.86 million tonnes. See Government of India, Ministry of Finance, *Economic Survey: 1988–89*. Though the country is considered 'self-sufficient' in foodgrains, viewed from another perspective, the foodgrain reserves represent surpluses arising out of denial of basic food consumption level for nearly two-fifths of the national population. FAO forecasted that despite increased production, India would need 'significant' rice imports in 1989 to rebuild depleted stocks. In its *Food Outlook* report, FAO also forecasted 2.5 million tonnes of wheat imports by India. See, *Indian Express*, 3 April 1989.
19. The PL 480 foodgrain supplies generated huge rupee funds with the US

administration. The impact of these funds on the promotion of US private investments in India has been carefully examined by a number of scholars. See, for instance, B.R. Shenoy, *PL 480 Aid and India's Food Problem*, East-West Press, New Delhi, 1974.

20. Expenditure on defence accounted for as much as 33.08 per cent of total revenue expenditure of the Government of India in 1970–71. Though its share declined in subsequent years, it continued to account for about 20 per cent of expenditure. See Reserve Bank of India, *Report on Currency and Finance*, 1985–86, Vol. II, *Statistical Statements*, Statement 81.
21. Government of India, *Economic Survey: 1962–63*, pp. 40–41.
22. Government of India, Ministry of Commerce, *Report of the Export Promotion Committee*, 1949. The Committee was headed by A.D. Gorwala, a distinguished member of the Indian Civil Service. After retirement he took up the editorship of *Opinion*, a magazine of the Forum for Free Enterprise.
23. For a brief review of the foreign exchange position during the First and Second Plans, see Government of India, *Third Five Year Plan*, 1961, pp. 107–15.
24. Government of India, Ministry of Commerce and Industry, *Report of the Export Promotion Committee*, 1957, p.1.
25. *Ibid.*, p. 29.
26. *Ibid.*, pp. 136–42.
27. The chairman of the Committee was Mr A. Ramaswami Mudaliar, who was Chairman of India Steamship Co. Ltd belonging to the Birla House and Tube Investments of India Ltd, then a foreign subsidiary forming part of the Murugappa Chettiar House. Among the other members were Mr G.L. Bansal, Secretary General of the Federation of Indian Chambers of Commerce and Industry (FICCI), Mr P.A. Narielwala, Chairman, Ceat Tyres and Director, Tata Industries Pvt. Ltd. and other Tata companies, and Mr N.M. Wagle, Managing Director, Greaves Cotton and Co. Ltd of the Thapar House.
28. Government of India, Ministry of Commerce and Industry, *Report of the Import and Export Policy Committee*, 1962.
29. Government of India, Ministry of Industries, *Final Report of the Industries Development Procedures Committee*, 1964. The final report contains the intermediate report and the decisions of the government on the Committee's recommendations.
30. See Indian Investment Centre, *Industrial Licensing: A Guide on Procedures*, 1969.
31. J.N. Bhagwati and T.N. Srinivasan, *Foreign Trade Regimes and Economic Development: India*, Macmillan, 1976, p. 83; see also, S.K. Verghese, *Export Assistance Policy and Export Performance of India in the Seventies*, Centre for Policy Research, 1978 (mimeo).
32. Government of India, Ministry of Industrial Development and Company Affairs, *Report of the Committee on Foreign Collaboration*, May 1967, p. 13.
33. *Ibid.*
34. *Ibid.*
35. Government of India, Ministry of Industrial Development, Internal Trade and Company Affairs, *Report of the Industrial Licensing Policy Inquiry Committee* (Main Report), July 1969, p. 135. The Chairman was S. Dutt.
36. *Ibid.*, p. 32.

37. See Export Policy Resolution 1970, as cited in Government of India, Ministry of Commerce, *Annual Report: 1973–74*, 1974. It is interesting to note that the IBRD described the Resolution as 'an admirable document' as it stated that 'in no uncertain terms the resolve of the Authorities to promote exports and to amend, if necessary, some rules of the existing economic policy in order to achieve that goal'. See IBRD and IDA, *India's Export Prospects*, Vol. I, *Prospects for Industrial Exports*, May 1971, p. 55.
38. Government of India, *Report of the Committee on Engineering Exports*, 1974. The chairman was M. Sondhi.
39. *Ibid.*, p. 21.
40. Government of India, Ministry of Commerce, *Report of the Committee on Import-Export Policies and Procedures*, 1978.
41. *Ibid.*, p. 73.
42. One of the main factors responsible for the stagnation of Indian industry was identified as 'the industrial policy framework, including both domestic industrial policies and trade policies and their effect in creating a high cost industrial structure in the economy' See Isher Judge Ahulwalia, *Industrial Growth in India: Stagnation Since the Mid-sixties*, Oxford University Press, Delhi, 1985, p. 168. The Committee set up by the government to examine the possible shifts from physical to financial controls recommended that 'a greater measure of competition within the domestic economy and greater exposure to international competition are important in order to develop costs and quality consciousness' among the industrial producers. See Government of India, *Report of the Committee to Examine Principles of a Possible Shift from Physical to Financial Controls*, 1985, p. 24. The chairman was M. Narasimham.
43. These arguments have been put forth by a number of responsible persons in government. Broadly speaking, this is what provides a justification for policies which have been included under the 'liberalization' approach of the government.
44. Government of India, Ministry of Commerce, *Report of the Committee on Export Strategy: 1980s* (Final Report), December 1980. The chairman was P.L. Tandon.
45. *Ibid.*, p. 72.
46. *Ibid.*, p. 88.
47. *Ibid.*, p. 88.
48. Industrial Policy Statement, 23 July 1980, in Government of India, Ministry of Industry, *Guidelines for Industries*, Part I, 1982.
49. *Report of the Committee on Export Strategy: 1980s, op. cit.*, pp. 178–201.
50. *Ibid.*, p. 178.
51. *Ibid.*, p. 193.
52. *Ibid.*, p. 196.
53. Government of India, Ministry of Commerce, *Committee on Free Trade Zones and 100 per cent Export Oriented Units* (Final Report), August 1982.
54. *Ibid.*, p. 51.
55. *Ibid.*, p. 96.
56. Government of India, Ministry of Commerce, *Report of the Committee on Trade Policies*, 1984, p. 5.

57. Government of India, Ministry of Industry, *Report of the Committee on Perspective Plan and Strategy for Export of Engineering and Capital Goods*, 1984.
58. Taken from Government of India, Ministry of Finance, *Economic Survey, 1986–87*, p. 97.
59. *Ibid.*, p. 35
60. *Ibid.*, p. 72.
61. M. Narasimham, Chairman of the committee, held many important positions in the government. He was Finance Secretary in 1983. In 1977 he was the Governor of Reserve Bank of India. He also served as Executive Director, IMF, in 1980. See, *Who's Who in India*, Business Press, Bombay, 1986.
62. Government of India, Ministry of Finance, *Report of the Committee to Examine Principles of a Possible Shift from Physical to Financial Controls*, 1985.
63. Government of India, Ministry of Commerce, *Report of the Committee on Trade Policies*, 1984.
64. One can cite any number of cases of repetitive imports of technology. Of the recent cases mention may be made of the automobile and the telecommunications sectors. Technology was obtained by different Indian parties from various foreign collaborators or sometimes from a single collaborator for basically a single product. For example, Jeumont Schneider of France has supplied technology for the manufacture of Electronic Private Automatic Business Exchanges (EPABX) to (*a*) Blue Star Ltd, (*b*) Escorts Ltd, (*c*) Indian Telephone Industries Ltd, (*d*) Larsen & Toubro Ltd, (*e*) U P Electronics Ltd, (*f*) West Bengal Electronics Industry Dev. Corpn, (*g*) Artel Communications Pvt. Ltd, and (*h*) Usha Computers & Peripherals Ltd. The case of technology import for the manufacture of light commercial vehicle is another good example in this context. Four different joint venture companies were incorporated with the help of financial collaborations with four Japanese vehicle manufacturers, the details are as follows:

Joint Venture Company (Annual Capacity)	*Collaborator and Country*	*Foreign Equity (Rs Lakhs and %)*	*Vehicle Specification (Tonnes)*	*Payments (Royalty and Lump Sum)*
1. Allwyn Nissan Ltd (10,000)	Nissan Motor Co., Japan	250 (15%)	Range of 3 tonnes	Yen 300 mn. *plus* 3% royalty
2. DCM Toyota Ltd (15,000)	Toyota Motor Corp., Japan	390 (26%)	Range of 3 tonnes	Yen 611.5 mn. *plus* 3% royalty
3. Eicher Motors Ltd (12,000)	Mitsubishi, Japan	150 (15%)	Range of 3 tonnes	Yen 330 mn. *plus* 3% royalty
4. Swaraj Mazda Ltd (10,000)	Toyo Kogyo Co., Ltd, Japan	299 (26%)	3.5 tonnes	

Note: . . Not available.

Source: Prospectuses of companies and company write-ups in the Bombay Stock Exchange Official Directory.

65. Narasimham Committee, *op. cit.*, pp. 4–5.

66. There are several problems with respect to some other suggestions of the Committee. The arguments in favour of economic levels of capacity could be accepted on the basis of sheer economic logic. However, in practice one expects a number of problems to be encountered. The Narasimham Committee specifically recommended that new investments should be at levels of capacity which are economic at international prices. In practice, it might be the case that the needed capacities were so high that unless exports were resorted to, domestic demand would not be able to absorb the full production from such plants both in the short as well as medium terms. In view of the uncertain export market it would be difficult to foresee any domestic manufacturer preparing to saddle himself with idle capacity. The logical step for the country would then be either to force the public sector to fill the gap in the industrial structure or to rely on imports.
67. In this case, mention may be made of PEICO (chokes, condensers, chokes fittings), NELCO (transistors, voltage stabilizers), MICO (filter inserts), Godrej (toiletries), Bata (footwear), Britannia (biscuits), HMM (biscuits), Colgate (toiletries), Singer (sewing machines and domestic appliances), Bajaj (domestic electrical appliances), Jay Engineering (fans and sewing machines), Hindustan Lever (soaps), Parry & Co. (sweets), Blow Plast (toys), Lucas TVS (components and parts), Rallis (insecticides and toiletries), Goodlass Nerolac (paints), Dalmia Dairy Industries (garments, matches), Parley (aerated water) and a number of pharmaceutical companies (drug formulations). Hindustan Lever Ltd was in fact a recipient of the ASSOCHAM Award 'in recognition of its efforts in promoting *exports of products of small scale and ancillary industries*'.
68. Narasimham Committee, *op. cit.*, p. 21.
69. Would the Indian party be denied fresh collaborations? Would his (group's) other companies also be subjected to similar treatment? Would the foreign collaborator be blacklisted for future technology purchases? In case the decision depended on the merit of the case who was to decide it? Would it not be at the discretion of the bureaucrats?
70. Narasimham Committee, *op. cit.*, p. 21.
71. Of particular importance is the opinion regarding the licencing system and the associated controls. The general pattern is to accept the usefulness of the system in the industrialization of the country and then to seek changes in the industrial policy. For instance, the Committee on Trade Policies noted: 'We were convinced that three decades of planned economic development in India have yielded many valuable dividends . . . . The time has come to think anew and afresh. This is true in the sphere of foreign trade . . .' (p. v).

    The Committee on Physical Controls followed:

    > Over the past thirty years, there has been considerable success in achieving these objectives (as a result of the industrial licensing system under the IDRA, the objectives being effective utilization of natural resources in accordance with national priorities, reducing foreign dominance, encouraging small scale industry, bringing about regional dispersal, prevent concentration of economic power, expand the public sector, etc.) . . . Indian industry had also made impressive strides in the range and sophistication of output manufacture . . . . *While considerable progress has thus been made in*

> *Indian industry since Independence and we now have a reasonably well diversified industrial structure*, the development of our industry has exacted a heavy price in terms of a high cost structure . . . . The high cost structure, in turn, may be ascribed to an element of technological obsolescence as well as market conditions . . . (p. 2).

A similar view was expressed by the World Bank in its *Background Note* prepared for the India Consortium.

> India's industrial policies have been largely successful in accomplishing some of the country's fundamental development objectives. High protection of domestic producers, large scale government investment, and widespread controls and incentives have interacted to encourage a sector that develops a wide variety of products, that is increasingly regionally dispersed, and has given the country considerable self-reliance. '*Nevertheless, this policy framework carried with it some important costs:* (1) output growth, productivity increase and employment expansion have been below the expectations of the nation's policy makers; (2) many products do not approach international standards for price, quality and reliability; and (3) technology has lagged behind the rapidly advancing technology in the industrial countries'(emphasis added).

See World Bank, *India Consortium: Background Note*, prepared for the meeting of the India Consortium held during 22–23 June 1987.

72. 'Exports' may in fact be compared with *open sesame* of the Arabian Nights' fame. Practically all restrictions and regulations are set aside in the name of export promotion.
73. Government of India, Ministry of Finance, *Budget at a Glance: 1987–88*, February 1987. Budget estimates for 1989–90 in this regard were placed at Rs 1,621 crores accounting for 19.17 per cent of the total subsidies of Rs 8,454.25 crores. Figures taken from Government of India, *Receipts Budget*, 1989–90, Vol. 1. It has been suggested that the budgeted figures are misleading as nearly half of the cash assistance granted comes back to the government in the form of corporate income tax. See V.L. Kelkar, Export subsidy: theory and practice, in *Economic and Political Weekly*, Vol. XV, No. 23, 7 June 1980.
74. The problem of trade deficit gets deeper particularly after 1983–84, if one goes by the Reserve Bank of India's (RBI) figures. Against the Rs 5,390.5 crores reported by the Directorate General of Commercial Intelligence and Statistics (DGCI&S) for the year 1984–85, the RBI's figures indicated a deficit of Rs 6,721 crores. The corresponding deficit for 1987–88 was Rs 6,657.7 crores and Rs 9,296 crores respectively. The cumulative trade deficit for the period 1980–81 to 1987–88, according to the DGCI&S figures, was Rs 51,632.7 crores. On the other hand, the RBI figures showed a deficit of Rs 58,692 crores for the same period. Figures taken from Government of India, Ministry of Finance, *Report of the Economic Advisory Council on the Current Situation and Priority Areas for Action*, 1989.
75. The note only informs that the item 'engineerng goods' includes 'machinery including transport equipment and metal manufactures excluding iron and

steel'. See Government of India, Ministry of Finance, *Economic Survey: 1986–87*, pp. S-62–S-63.

76. Including iron and steel (prime).
77. Exports of pearls and precious stones were worth Rs 98.4, Rs 148.5 and Rs 287.0 crores during 1974–75, 1975–76 and 1976–77, respectively. The corresponding imports of the items were Rs 53.0 , Rs 84.2 and Rs 180.6 crores, respectively. During 1983–84, 1984–85 and 1985–86 India exported Rs 1,207.4, Rs 1,153.3 and Rs 1,429.9 crores worth of precious stones and pearls, respectively. During these years India's imports in this regard were Rs 1,097.9, Rs 1,032.1 and Rs 1,106.3 crores, respectively. See Government of India, Ministry of Finance, *Economic Survey* for the years 1981–82 and 1986–87.
78. See Government of India, Ministry of Finance, *Economic Survey: 1984–85*, p. 77.
79. Government of India, *Economic Survey: 1986–87*, p. 96.
80. Recent data indicate that India's share declined from 0.5 per cent in 1985 to 0.4 per cent in 1986. Figures taken from Government of India, *Economic Survey, 1988–89*.
81. Government of India, Development Commissioner for Small Scale Industries, *Annual Report of the Small Industry Development Organisation* (SIDO), 1985–86. According to the SIDO, the reported figures do not include the indirect exports of the small-scale units effected through export houses and other merchant exporters. The Ministry of Industry also observed that 'the share of small scale sector in total exports would be more if its contribution in the form of indirect exports is also taken into account as the small units supply a large volume [of] parts and components that go into assembly of finished products by the medium and large scale sector.' The small-scale sector also accounts for 30 per cent of engineering exports from the country. See Government of India, Ministry of Industry, Department of Industrial Development, *Report: 1986–87*, pp. 48–49.
82. These comments are irrespective of the fact that the public sector in India was not seen as an agency to promote exports. The rationale of the sector, from the viewpoint of planning, lay in establishing basic and key industries to ensure inter-sectoral balances. For a discussion on this issue, see S.K. Goyal, *Public Sector in India*. Paper presented at Canada–India Conference on Public Economy, Carlton University, Ottawa, Canada, 24–25 February 1986. One also needs to take a close look at the composition of the sector's exports.
83. Even the Export Promotion Committee in 1957 suggested that canalization of exports through a single agency should be considered as an exceptional measure. The Alexander Committee in 1978 disfavoured canalization and recommended decanalization of a number of export items (p. 47). The Committee on Trade Policies in 1984 recommended that canalization of imports should be an exception rather than a rule (p. 86).
84. For instance, the World Bank identified the ill effects of the industrial licencing system on Indian industry in the following manner:

> But India's capacity licensing system has constrained competition between domestic firms. High rejection rates, long delays and changing sub-sector priorities have made it a significant barrier to entry and growth. It has

contributed to the high concentration in Indian industry, sub-optimal scales of production and slow technical progress.

See World Bank, *World Development Report, 1987*, Oxford University Press, Oxford, 1987, p. 116.

85. This was mainly possible with the de-licencing of investmens below certain limits. These limits were raised upwards progressively. The exemption limit which stood at Rs 10 lakhs in 1960 was raised to Rs 25 lakhs in 1964 and further to Rs 1 crore in 1970. This limit was raised to Rs 3 crores in 1978 and to Rs. 5 crores in 1983.

86. In 1973 time-limits were set for disposing applications for new investments in order to reduce time-lags. During 1974–75 diversification into related areas of production was allowed in a number of industries (machinery, machine tools, electrical equipment, steel castings, cement machinery by cement manufacturers, steel forgings, steel ingots, passenger cars, non-ferrous alloys and semis). Foreign collaboration policy was relaxed at the end of 1973 to allow imports of designs and drawings for the manufacture of machinery which was extended to the electrical industry in early 1975. During the same year the policy of re-endorsing of capacities on the basis of maximum utilization of plant and machinery was introduced. This was done to enable manufacturers to utilize their installed capacities in case they were constrained by capacity restrictions. Later in 1975, medium level entrepreneurs were exempted from the provisions of the IDRA, 1951 in respect of 21 industries. It was announced that medium level entrepreneurs would have full freedom to utilize thier installed capacities 'without limit even though this may be in excess of their licensed capacity' in respect of 29 engineering and chemical industries. There was, however, the qualifying criterion that the industrial unit should not place any further burden on the foreign exchange resources whether in the form of imported raw materials and capital goods or foreign collaboration. This concession was available to MRTPA and FERA companies provided they agreed to export or distribute, according to the directions of the government, the resulting excess production.

To enable industrial units to modernize their machinery a provision was made for liberal re-endorsement of capacities arising out of modernization and replacement of equipment. Such increases in capacities were to be allowed even if they were in excess of the normal permissible limit of 25 per cent of production over the authorized capacities. MRTPA and FERA companies were also eligible for availing this facility. On the basis of the recommendations of the Committee on Engineering Exports in 1974 it was accepted by the government that automatic growth of capacities over and above the normal permissible limit of 25 per cent excess production over the authorized capacity would be allowed in 14 engineering industries.

In 1980, relaxations in the licencing system were extended to all Appendix I industries. However, the policy of imposing export obligations on imported capital equipment continued.

87. For an understanding of the extent of non-registration of recognized large house companies under the MRTPA, see S.K. Goyal, *Monopoly Capital and Public Policy*, Allied Publishers, Delhi, 1979. The registrations under the Act

after the 1984 amendment also demonstrate the extent to which large houses were able to remain outside the purview of the MRTPA for a long time.

88. In response to a question in the Indian Parliament it was stated that: 'The MRTP Act is not aimed at total prevention of growth of MRTP companies as such but is designed to regulate their expansion in accordance with national priorities ensuring that such expansion does not lead to concentration of economic power and is not prejudicial to public interest'. See, Reply to the Unstarred Question Number 485 answered on 28 February 1984.
89. The assets under the control of the 20 largest industrial houses increased from less than Rs 3,000 crores in 1972 to approximately Rs 7,500 crores in 1980. This figure more than doubled in just four years to Rs 15,744.80 crores by 1984. See S.K. Goyal, *Nature and Growth of Private Corporate Sector*, Brij Narain Memorial Lectures delivered at Panjab University, Chandigarh, 12–14 January 1987.
90. The companies were in fact deriving undue advantage as they were able to benefit from special concessions provided to the small-scale sector besides being able to circumvent the licencing policy. See S.K. Goyal, K.S. Chalapati Rao and Nagesh Kumar, *Small Scale Sector and Big Business*, Indian Institute of Public Administration, New Delh, 1984 (mimeo). See also, Lok Sabha Secretariat, Public Accounts Committee (Eighth Lok Sabha), *Forty-Ninth Report: Union Excise Duties—Irregular Grant of Exemption on Production in Small Scale Sector for and on Behalf of Large Scale Units, 1986.*
91. The export obligation in respect of non-Appendix I products to be manufactured by MRTPA and FERA companies was reduced from 60 per cent to 50 per cent in the case of category B and C districts and to 30 per cent in the case of category A districts. In December 1985 this was further reduced to 25 per cent in the case of B and C districts and was completely dispensed with in the case of category A districts. See Press Note of the Ministry of Industry dated 31 December 1985.
92. Out of the 1963 companies registered under the MRTPA at the end of 1984 in only 98 cases clauses relating to market dominance were applicable. (A note on industrial policy prepared by the Planning Commission, however, placed this number at 120). A majority of these companies were registered under the MRTPA in 1970. There have been very few additions since then. In fact, in the later years there were a number of de-registrations. In nearly one-third of the cases the respective companies were also producing products in which they were not dominant.
93. The practice of excess production over licenced capacities was brought out by the ILPIC. Surprisingly even till 1982 the government claimed that no action could be taken against the violators of licencing restrictions due to a loophole in the Criminal Procedure Code. See Corporate Studies Group, *Functioning of Industrial Licensing System*, Indian Institute of Public Administration, New Delhi, 1983 (mimeo).
94. See Corporate Studies Group, *op. cit.*, for an understanding of the extent of variations between the licenced and installed capacities on the one hand and between the licenced capacities and actual production of the private sector companies on the other hand. It was observed that companies registered under the MRTPA and FERA (including those that were no longer under FERA

because of equity dilution) had excess capacities and were producing beyond the licenced capacities even in the case of items reserved for the small-scale sector and industries that were specially regulated.

95. See S.K. Goyal, K.S. Chalapati Rao and Nagesh Kumar, *op. cit.*
96. For the ways in which de-reservations have been effected see S.K. Goyal, K.S. Chalapati Rao and Nagesh Kumar, *op. cit.*
97. For details, see the discussion on policy changes presented in the previous section.
98. These were prepared by (*a*) the Committee on Trade Policies; (*b*) the Committee on Perspective Plan and Strategy for Export of Engineering and Capital Goods; and (*c*) the Committee to Examine Principles of a Possible Shift from Physical to Financial Controls.
99. Government of India, Planning Commission, *Seventh Five Year Plan*: 1985–90, Vol. I, p. 77.
100. The first export promotion committee in 1949 included K.D. Jalan of the Soorajmull Nagarmull House as one of its members. In the 1957 Committee the private sector was represented by Karam Chand Thapar of the Thapar House and P. Chentsal Rao of the Federation of the Indian Chambers of Commerce and Industry (FICCI). For particulars, in the case of the Mudaliar Committee (1962), see Note 27. P.L. Tandon, former chairman of Hindustan Lever during the period 1961–68, headed two committees, viz. the Committee on Export Strategy: 1980s and the one on Free Trade Zones and 100 per cent Export-Oriented Units. Rahul Bajaj of the Bajaj house and the then President of the Association of the Indian Engineering Industry (AIEI) was a member of the former. The D.V. Kapur Committee (1984) included the President of the AIEI as one of its members. It is interesting to note that D.V. Kapur joined DCM Ltd of the Shri Ram House as an adviser after retirement from government service. Upon retirement, M. Sondhi, Chairman of the Committee on Engineering Exports (1974), was appointed Chairman of several TNCs *viz.* Ennore Foundries Ltd, Ashok Leyland Ltd, Asea Ltd, Molins of India Ltd and ICIM Ltd.
101. For this, we have mainly followed the official classifications. The studies conducted by the Corporate Studies Group and the information available with the Corporate Information System have also been taken advantage of.
102. For the rationale and methodology of classifying companies as 'foreign controlled' see Biswajit Dhar, *Foreign Controlled Companies in the Indian Corporate Sector: An Attempt at Identification*, Corporate Studies Group Working Paper No. 14, 1987. Companies like Amines and Plasticizers Ltd. and Skol Breweries Ltd. were classified as foreign controlled companies on the basis of the controlling shareholder being itself a foreign controlled company. One company viz. Lucas India Services Ltd. has been classified as a foreign subsidiary as the parent company Lucas TVS Ltd itself is a foreign subsidiary.
103. Registrations under the Act take place nearly continuously. A new company gets registered under the Act if: (*a*) it exceeded the prescribed asset limit, (*b*) it becomes interconnected (as defined under the Act) with an already registered company, (*c*) its interconnection is established and registration can no longer be avoided, and (*d*) total assets of the company and its interconnected

companies exceed the prescribed limit. Similar provisions are also applicable to product monpolies and their interconnected companies. A company can be de-registered from the MRTPA if it can be proved that the grounds for establishing the interconnection with the already registered companies no longer exist. A hike in the prescribed asset limit also frees companies from the purview of the Act. As a result, one finds that the MRTPA companies at a particular point of time got themselves registered during the course of a long period beginning from 1970. The registrations as taken note of in the study indicate their relationship with the large houses rather than reflecting the effect of MRTPA legislation on their export orientation. (Groups of interconnected companies under the MRTPA are often referred to as large houses or monopoly houses).

104. The top 20 houses covered under the MRTPA at the end of 1984 were: Birla, Tata, J.K. Singhania, Mafatlal, Thapar, Reliance, Modi, ACC, Bangur, Larsen and Toubro, Sarabhai, Bajaj, ICI, Mahindra, Shri Ram, Walchand, Kirloskar, ITC, TVS Iyyengar, and Hindustan Lever.

105. The large private corporate sector in India is highly diversified. Many of its constituents produce more than one product often unrelated to one another. See also, S.K. Goyal, *op. cit.*, January 1987, for an account of the diversified nature of industrial activities undertaken by large industrial houses and companies. This type of diversification makes industrial classification of companies difficult and at times meaningless. This became more complicated as some of the manufacturing companies entered trading activity (*a*) to avoid industrial regulations, (*b*) to benefit from the lower costs of production and overheads in the small-scale sector, and (*c*) in direct response to governmental incentives like the export and trading house schemes. On their part a few trading companies entered manufacturing activities (e.g. Tata Exports, Voltas). This often leads to complications in classifying companies in a particular industry. This phenomenon has a strong bearing on the industry-wise analysis carried out in the present study. The exports of a company need not always be in its major area of production. In extreme cases, the products exported may be completely bought from the open market or captive small units and as such are in no way related to the company's manufacturing activity. Another problem encountered in classifying companies has been the changes in the sales basket of the companies over the period of the study. For the sake of uniformity, these companies have been classified according to their original industrial groups.

106. For this purpose one has used the list of recognized export houses provided in (*a*) Federation of Indian Export Organisations (FIEO), Annual Report & Accounts, 1985–86. (Recognized Member Houses as on 15 July 1986); and (*b*) separate lists of recognized export houses by the FIEO. Since July 1983 the FIEO has been acting as the agency to disburse Market Development Assistance (MDA) to export trading houses for their expenditure abroad on sales-cum-study tours, participation in fairs, bringing out publications and on advertising. Registration with the FIEO is a precondition for recognition/renewal of Export House Certificates as per the export-import policy of 1985–88. These lists were used because (*a*) year-wise lists of recognized export houses were not available for the entire period; and (*b*) recognition as an

export house is granted on the basis of past performance. The import-export policy of 1985–88 informs that '(t)he eligibility for grant of Export House Certificates shall be determined on the basis of the export actually made in the *preceding three financial years which shall be treated as the base period*'. In specific terms, '(t)he annual average F.O.B. value of exports in the prescribed base period of select products should not be less than Rs. three crores or those of non-select products Rs. seven crores'. In view of this it may be reasonable to take the export houses reported in the above publications, as having been recognized for their performance during the later period of the study. Two trading houses—Hindustan Lever Ltd and Tata Exports Ltd—have been included in the export houses for purpose of analysis.

107. The Government of India vide Notification No. G.S.R. 494 (E) dated 30 October 1973 introduced a number of changes in the items on which information has to be disclosed in the 'Balance Sheets' and 'Profit and Loss Accounts' of corporate bodies. The Notification, *inter alia*, requires companies to furnish details regarding their licenced and installed capacities, actual production during an accounting period, and earnings and expenditure of foreign exchange as part of the 'Notes' to the 'Profit and Loss Account'.

108. An amendment to the Companies Act, 1956, enacted in May 1988, made it possible for companies whose shares are listed on the stock exchanges to bring out abridged Annual Reports. The abridged reports can withhold vital information on the companies' physical functioning. One of the important items that was withdrawn as a result is the particulars of earnings and utilization of foreign exchange. It is sufficient if the aggregates are given in the Directors' Report to the shareholders. This renders detailed analysis of the present form difficult as the tendency of the private sector companies would be to send abridged reports instead of full accounts.

109. Marine products, garments, leather products and carpets are some of the items which are traded in this way.

110. The Sixth Plan envisaged an annual average growth rate of 9 per cent at constant prices of 1978–80. See Government of India, Planning Commission, *Sixth Five Year Plan: 1980–85*, p. 70.

111. However, since the behaviour of international markets will not be uniform in respect of all commodities and manufactured products, this line of argument has its own limitations.

112. The unit value index of exports (base 1978–79 = 100) increased to 151 by 1983–84. See Government of India, Ministry of Finance, *Economic Survey: 1986–87*, Statement 6.5, p. S–60. However, this type of comparison has serious limitations as the exports basket of the companies under study may be—and indeed is as seen later—quite different from the composition of national exports. Even among the different export items one notices substantial variation in the movement of the unit value index. While the index of food articles (base 1978–79 = 100) increased to 117 by 1982–83, the index of chemical and chemical products increased to 123. Similar indices for machinery, transport equipment and crude materials (except fuels) were 134 and 149 respectively. See Reserve Bank of India, *Report on Currency and Finance: 1985–86*, Vol. II, *Statistical Statements*, Statement 105, p. 147.

113. See Note 106.

114. For further details on 'deemed exports' see Government of India, Ministry of Commerce, *Import and Export Policy*, April 1985–March 1988 (as amended up to 31 October 1986), Vol. I, *Import and Export Promotion*, 1986, pp. 60–61.

115. For instance, Bajaj Auto Ltd reported that during 1983–84, the rupee equivalent of foreign exchange earned by the company was Rs 51.17 crores while direct exports were worth Rs 4.84 crores only. See Bajaj Auto Ltd, *39th Annual Report: 1983–84*, p. 21.

116. India's indices of unit values of exports, imports and net terms of trade (base 1978–79 = 100) and the index numbers of wholesale prices (base 1970–71 = 100) are as follows:

Year	*Unit Value Index*		*Net Terms of Trade*	*General Index of Wholesale Prices*	*Price Index for Manufactures*
	Exports	*Imports*			
1975–76	83.9	99.1	84.7	173.0	171.2
1976–77	89.4	96.3	92.9	176.6	175.2
1977–78	100.3	88.0	114.0	185.8	179.2
1978–79	100.0	100.0	100.0	185.8	179.5
1979–80	105.4	114.1	92.4	217.6	215.8
1980–81	108.5	134.2	80.8	257.3	257.3
1981–82	124.1	133.1	93.2	281.3	270.6
1982–83	132.0	136.3	96.8	288.7	272.1
1983–84	151.0	125.8	120.0	316.0	295.8

117. This phenomenon seems to be continuing for quite some time. It was observed that in 1975–76 the operations of 133 foreign subsidiaries resulted in a net outgo of Rs 98.34 crores. See S.K. Goyal, *The Impact of Foreign Subsidiaries on India's Balance of Payments*. Study prepared for the Joint CTC-ESCAP Unit, Bangkok, 1979.

118. This suggests that one needs to be cautious while interpreting the results of company level studies brought out by official agencies such as the Industrial Development Bank of India and the RBI. These studies, it appears, are biased towards showing better export and foreign exchange earning capability of the companies under study. Their results in this regard can be accepted better for the pre-1980 period. The possibility of double counting, even in the case of manufacturing companies, increased considerably during the 1980s. This is further supported by the case studies presented later.

119. For a discussion on the implications of the foreign equity dilution strategies of the FERA companies see S. Chaudhuri, FERA appearance and reality, *Economic and Political Weekly*, Vol. XIV, No. 16, 21 April 1979, pp. 734–44.

120. The fact that foreign controlled enterprises in the Indian economy did not show significant differences in export performance in comparison with their local counterparts was brought out in Nagesh Kumar, *Multinational Enterprises in India*, Routledge, London, 1990.

121. Reserve Bank of India, Finances of public limited companies, 1986–87, in

Reserve Bank of India Bulletin, Vol. XLIII, No. 9, September 1989. The importance of 1,942 companies can be understood from the fact that they accounted for 64.2 per cent of the paid-up capital of non-financial, non-government public limited companies at the end of March 1987.

122. Industrial Development Bank of India, *Financial Performance of IDBI Assisted Companies in the Private Sector: 1987–88*, 1989.
123. According to the company, this was in recognition of its 'collaboration with small scale and cottage sector'. See Hindustan Lever Ltd, *Report and Accounts, 1981*, p. 3. It is interesting to find that exports of fruits, vegetables, cut flowers and decorative plants are treated *on par* with exports of selected products manufactured by the small-scale units for purposes of extending recognition as a trading house. See Government of India, Ministry of Commerce, *Import and Export Policy, April 1984–March 1985*, Vol. I, *Imports and Export Promotion*, p. 67.
124. A few other Unilever associates in India have converted themselves into export houses. These are Lipton India Ltd, Brooke Bond India Ltd and Pond's (India) Ltd.
125. Hindustan Lever Ltd, *Hamara*, September 1986, p. 17. *Hamara* is an in-house journal of the company. Surprisingly, the list of approved foreign collaborations published by the Indian Investment Centre does not include any of these collaborations entered into by Hindustan Lever Ltd. The company has entered into licence agreements for manufacturing Nino, Cerruti, Atkinsoms and Lanvin brands of cosmetics also. See, *Hamara*, February 1986, p. 5.
126. Hoechst Pharmaceuticals Ltd (now Hoechst India Ltd), *26th Annual Report, 1981*, p. 7.
127. Hoechst India Ltd, *30th Annual Report, 1985*, p. 2.
128. Annual Reports of the company for the years 1981 and 1985, p. 21 and p. 25 respectively.
129. Glaxo Laboratories India Ltd, *Annual Reports and Accounts: Year Ended 30th June 1983*.
130. Glaxo Laboratories India Ltd, *Glaxo Business Review*, Vol. III, No. 3, January, February and March 1981, p. 7.
131. Siemens India Ltd, *Annual Report: 82/83*, p. 2.
132. Siemens India Ltd, *Annual Report: 81/82*, p. 3.
133. Siemens India Ltd, *Annual Report: 82/83*, p. 2.
134. Siemens India Ltd, *Annual Report: 80/81*, p. 3.
135. Siemens India Ltd, *Annual Report: 1986/87*, p. 6.
136. Siemens India Ltd, *Annual Report: 1979/80*, p. 2.
137. Union Carbide India Ltd, *Annual Report, 1985*, p. 4.
138. Union Carbide India Ltd, *Annual Report, 1984*, p. 3.
139. Union Carbide India Ltd, Annual Reports for the years 1987 and 1988–89.
140. Industrial Cables India Ltd, *27th Annual Report*, 1982–83, p. 4.
141. Industrial Cables India Ltd, *24th Annual Report*, 1979–80, p. 3.
142. Philips India Ltd, *Annual Report, 1977*, p. 3.
143. Peico Electronics and Electricals Ltd, *Annual Report, 1987*, p. 2.
144. Peico Electronics and Electricals Ltd, *Annual Report, 1986*, p. 39.
145. Dunlop India Ltd, *Annual Report, 1982*, p. 3.

146. Dunlop India Ltd, *Annual Report, 1986–87*, p. 8.
147. Export of marine products seems to have been adopted by companies as an easy way of showing quick export earnings. Some of the important companies registered with the Marine Products Export Development Authority are Baroda Rayon Corpn Ltd, Bombay Oxygen Corpn Ltd, Britannia Industries Ltd, Ceat Tyres of India Ltd, Cimmco Ltd, Dunlop India Ltd, Escorts Ltd, Ethnor Ltd, GTC Industries Ltd, Greaves Cotton & Co. Ltd, HMM Ltd, Hindustan Lever Ltd, ITC Ltd, Indexport Ltd, Indian Organic Chemicals Ltd, Infar India Ltd, Lalbhai Exports Ltd, MRF Ltd, Mahindra & Mahindra Ltd, Metal Box India Ltd, Nava Bharat Ferro Alloys Ltd, Needle Industries India Ltd, Orkay Silk Mills Ltd, Peico Electronics and Electricals Ltd, Ponds India Ltd, Proctor and Gamble India Ltd, Rallis India Ltd, Raymond Woollen Mills Ltd, Searle India Ltd, Southern Petrochemicals and Industries Corpn Ltd, T.I. & M. Ltd, Tata Exports Ltd, Tata Iron & Steel Co. Ltd, Voltas International Ltd, WIMCO Ltd, and Zenith Ltd. Apart from Hindustan Lever Ltd and Nava Bharat Ferro Alloys Ltd all these companies are registered as merchant exporters. Rallis India Ltd claimed that it was one of the five largest exporters of seafoods in the country. These cases are selected from Marine Products Export Development Authority, *Directory of Exporters of Marine Products from India*, 1989.
148. The foreign exchange transactions (in lakhs) of the company during the period 1981–85 were as follows:

Year	*Exports*	*Sea Food*	*Other Earnings*	*Imports*	*Other Expenditure*	*Dividends*	*Net Earnings*
1981	1219.50	670.19	47.11	4867.15	457.06	—	−4058.10
1982	1839.72	1667.01	10.59	5708.10	2998.29	—	−6856.08
1983	521.25	299.26	9.33	3131.98	582.96	54.55	−3298.91
1984	418.00	336.00	—	5194.00	1878.00	87.54	−6741.54
1985	564.00	494.00	—	16712.00	3939.00	121.00	−20208.00

It is interesting to note that during the period 1981 to 1985 the company received Rs 375.88 lakhs as export incentives and duty drawback.

149. Foreign exchange transactions and export incentives (in Rs crores) received by the company during the three years 1981–82, 1982–83 and 1983–84 were as follows:

Exports	147.08
Total Earnings in Foreign Exchange	156.94
Imports	125.84
Other Expenditure in Foreign Exchange (incl. Dividends)	23.18
Total Expenditure	149.02
Net Earnings in Foreign Exchange	7.92
Export Incentives	33.39

Based on the company's Annual Reports for the years 1982–83 and 1983–84.

150. Tata Engineering and Locomotive Co. Ltd, *Annual Report: 1985–86*, p. 14.
151. Annual Reports of the company for various years.
152. Tata Iron and Steel Co. Ltd, *Annual Report, 1988–89*, p. 4.
153. Recognized export/trading houses of the Tata House include Tata Exports, TISCO, Tata Tea, Rallis India, Voltas International Ltd, Gokak Patel Volkart Ltd, Tata Unisys Ltd, Taj Trade and Transport Co. Ltd, and Tata Consultancy Services. If each company of Tata House exported on its own, probably most of them could not have been able to get recognition as an export house. But by routing the group's exports through a selected number of companies export houses are created without any addition to the net exports of the group.
154. Mahindra and Mahindra Ltd, *Annual Report: 1983–84*, p. 5.
155. The company stated that there was 'large potential for further improving exports to the Soviet Union, Australia, and South East Asia where reasonable success have been achieved'. See Greaves Cotton & Co. Ltd, *Annual Report and Accounts, 1988–89*, p. 5.
156. See the Annual Reports of Greaves Cotton and Co. Ltd for various years.
157. One finds a number of other companies which have entered into export of items which are wholly unrelated to their main lines of activity. For instance, in *Exporters from India*, published by the Federation of Indian Export Organisations, one finds cases like Amco Batteries Ltd (readymade garments, marine products), CIMMCO Intl.—export division of Central India Machinery Manufacturing Co. Ltd (handloom, readymade garments, fabrics, handicrafts), Dalmia Udyog—of Dalmia Dairy Industries Ltd (garments, hoisery, woollen carpets), Escorts Ltd (coir and coir made-ups, canvas, military software web sets and felts), Grindwell Norton Ltd (readymade garments and hoisery, leather goods, handicrafts), Madura Coats Ltd (leather goods, tea), Industrial and Structurals Pvt. Ltd (fabrics of cotton, silk and rayon, handloom, readymade garments, hosiery, made-ups), Oberoi Exports—export division of East India Hotels Co. Ltd (cotton and silk textiles, readymades, carpets, processed foods including meat, seafood, fruit and vegetables, spices, cashew, cardamom and rice, leather and sports goods, handicrafts and brassware), Rallis India Ltd (textiles including made-ups, garments, marine products, finished leather and leather goods), Shaw Wallace & Co. Ltd (jute, handloom, readymade garments, processed foods, spices, leather goods, footwear, sports goods), Expo Machinery Ltd (fish and fish meal), Imkemex India Ltd (mango products and other canned food products, animal feeds), Industrial Perfumes Ltd (spices and oils, oil resins), Kelbex International Ltd (frozen fish, dry fish of all varieties), Standard Batteries Ltd (marine products). See FIEO, *Exporters from India*, n.d.
158. For instance, the Ministry of Commerce, in response to a query by the Estimates Committee of the Indian Parliament as to whether any assessment was made to ascertain the profitability of exports, replied that it 'has not undertaken any study of this type . . . . While a more thorough assessment is considered necessary for exports to ensure that the exports are really meaningful it has been found difficult to undertake in-depth studies of this type due to practical difficulties and limitations of the available data'. See Lok Sabha Secretariat, *Twenty-Third Report of the Estimates Committee: Ministry of Commerce—Export Promotion*, 1982, p. 13.

159. For instance, a survey of foreign collaborations conducted by the Reserve Bank of India finds that the 'most common type of restriction imposed (in collaboration agreements) was that of prohibition or regulation of exports'. More than 80 per cent of restrictive clauses related to exports. It was further noted that

> . . . of the 594 export clauses, 445 clauses forming 74.9 per cent of the total, prohibited exports to collaborator's country or to countries in which the collaborator operates through branches/subsidiaries/affiliates or is having similar collaboration agreements or to certain other specified countries . . . . Though the Government views with disfavour any restrictions on the right of Indian companies to export freely to any country, it makes certain exceptions in respect of countries where the foreign collaborator has existing licensing agreements to manufacture.

For further details see Reserve Bank of India, *Foreign Collaboration in Indian Industry: Fourth Survey Report*, RBI, 1985.

160. Government of India, Ministry of Finance *Economic Survey: 1986–87*, p. 97. It was explained that 14 broad sectors were identified for making *special thrust* in export markets. Similarly, the 'select list of export products' whose exports have a special significance for granting export house status also contains a number of agriculture and forest-based products, handicrafts and garments.
161. Indian companies do not seem to be under any obligation to indicate separately the accounts of their foreign branches and offices in their Annual Reports. They club the information pertaining to foreign branch operations with the aggregate accounts for the company as a whole. See, for instance, the Annual Reports of Greaves Cotton and Co. Ltd and Tata Oil Mills Co. Ltd.
162. Such an assumption is also implicit in the Statement on Industrial Policy, July 1991. It states:

> (f)oreign investment would bring attendant advantages of technology transfer, marketing expertise, introduction of modern managerial techniques and new possibilities for promotion of exports . . . . Promotion of exports of Indian products calls for a systematic exploration of world markets possible only through intensive and highly professional marketing activities. To the extent that expertise of this nature is not well developed so far in India, Government will encourage foreign trading companies to assist us in our export activities.

163. Companies engaged in shipping, electricity generation, trading, and tea plantations were not included in the analysis in order to present the results more realistically. Exclusion of trading companies still does not take care of double counting, trading and export of items not related to the main line of manufacture of the companies.
164. A study of 144 foreign controlled rupee companies showed a declining export propensity as also declining net earnings over a period of 13 years (1975–76 to 1987–88). Since the study attempted to cover a consistent set of companies for

the entire period, it had to exclude the ones incorporated after 1975. The results should, therefore, mean to represent the performance of older companies. The decline in performance is in spite of the fact that a number of larger among these have converted themselves into export/trading houses. See Candra Shekhar, *Political Economy of India*, Vikas, New Delhi, 1992.

165. If the fact that the set of large public limited companies would include some foreign controlled companies is also taken note of, the performance of large Indian companies would turn out to be more favourable than that of the FCRCs.

166. See S.K. Goyal *et al., India's Imports and Exports: Some Insights (An Analysis of Daily Trade Register Data)*, Institute for Studies in Industrial Development, New Delhi, 1991 (mimeo). The annual reports of some of the large companies confirm that they only trade in marine products.

167. Large companies including foreign controlled ones accounted for about 6 per cent of the total marine product exports of Rs 583 crores. This data set will be discussed later.

168. This analysis is based on the data file supplied by the Directorate General of Commercial Intelligence & Statistics (DGCI&S), Ministry of Commerce. The section grouping follows the DGCI&S classification. The DGCI&S classification matches the Harmonised System of Commodity Description and Coding System up to the six-digit level.

169. Apart from the vagaries of changing fashions in the international markets, once the North American Free Trade Agreement (NAFTA) comes into effect, it is difficult to imagine to what extent the textile exports could be sustained.

170. The Eighth Five-Year Plan while envisaging an increase in exports from Rs 44,292 crores to Rs 83,869 crores, does not foresee any substantial change in the share of engineering and chemical sectors. Their share is expected to remain at about 20 per cent during the entire plan period (20.33 per cent in 1991–92 and 21.57 per cent in 1996–97). Cumulated trade deficit for the plan period is projected to be Rs 69,497 crores and after taking note of the expected net inflow of invisibles the current account deficit is expected to be to the tune of Rs 54,863 crores. (See India, Planning Commission, *Eighth Five Year Plan, 1992–97*, Vol. I, 1992). The plan projection of a static share of chemicals and engineering exports is in contrast to the expectation that large amounts of foreign investment would flow in during the plan period, as a result of the new trade and investment policies. Obviously, the new foreign investment should contribute to technology intensive exports.

171. Here the reference is to chemical and chemical products and plastics and rubber in the first category and base metals and metal products, machinery, transport equipment, instruments and apparatus in the latter.

172. During the first nine months of 1990–91 i.e. from April-December 1990 their share was 19.44 per cent. However, during the corresponding nine months of 1991 the share fell sharply to 11.53 per cent. See India, Ministry of Commerce, *Annual Report: 1991–92*.

173. See, India, Ministry of Commerce, Directorate General of Commercial Intelligence & Statistics, *Foreign Trade Statistics of India* (Principal Commodities and Countries), June 1992.

174. It has been reported that Kandla Free Trade Zone which was mainly catering to the Socialist bloc market—during 1985–86 to 1987–88 out of the total exports of Rs 658.15 crores as much as Rs 586.04 crores (89.04 per cent) were directed to the USSR—was on the verge of closure as exports from the zone fell steeply. See Kandla: A trading zone sans trade, *Times of India*, 27 August 1992. The newly established Madras Export Processing Zone also shows a similar tendency. (See Lok Sabha Unstarred Question No. 2527 answered on 12 August 1988).
175. South and Southeast Asia account for more than half of the investment in Indian joint ventures abroad. See, K.V.K. Ranganathan, Exports and Indian joint ventures, unpublished doctoral thesis submitted to the Kurukshetra University, Kurukshetra, 1990.
176. This exercise has a few limitations. One of them is the identification of exporters and the coverage. The publicly available information base is weak in identifying companies with foreign equity and the nature of the foreign shareholder. Second, this exercise does not represent all TNCs exports as it was based on only selected ports. It also does not represent the total exports of the TNCs covered as they could be exporting from other locations too.
177. The Annual Report of the Ministry of Commerce for the year 1991–92 carries a description of the Daily Trade Return data. The DTR data have a number of shortcomings and disadvantages for analytical purposes. These are discussed in detail in S.K. Goyal, *et. al.*, *op. cit.* and S.K. Goyal, *Exchange Rates, Trade Policy and Tariff Structure*, Institute for Studies in Industrial Development, New Delhi, 1991 (mimeo). In spite of the many limitations, the DTR data have extensive scope for policy analysis and for checking a number of policy and theoretical assumptions and identifying the emerging trends. First is the analysis of export products and markets of different groups of companies. Next is the impact of foreign technology on the import pattern as also on export production. Yet another area where this data could be useful is in the identification of transfer pricing practices and their extent. These data have a distinct advantage over company annual report data as one could avoid double counting as also the effects of window-dressing. The main problem at present is that not all the ports computerize the DTR data.
178. These ports account for nearly half of the total exports from India.
179. The left out records accounted for Rs 360 crores.
180. Tentative estimates place the contribution of companies of large houses at about 7.5 per cent of the exports from these ports. One could extend this exercise to cover other categories of exporters as well.
181. While it may be possible to argue that the RBI studies may not cover all FCRCs in India, and therefore, this is an underestimate of their contribution, it is reasonable to assume that all foreign subsidiaries and large sized affiliates, more so the public limited ones, would have been included in the RBI study.
182. See Nagesh Kumar, Resource flows and foreign direct investments in developing countries: trends and prospects, *RIS Digest*, Research and Information System for the Non-Aligned and Other Developing Countries, Vol. 9, No. 3, September 1992, pp. 43–56.
183. It sounds paradoxical if India expects both her investment in other countries and foreign investment in India to promote her exports.

ANNEXURE: LIST OF COMPANIES COVERED IN THE STUDY

1 A P Paper Mills Ltd. (M, T)
2 ACC Babcock Ltd. (M, 1, T)
3 Adarsh Chem. & Fertilizers Ltd.
4 Aditya Mills Ltd.
5 Advani Oerlikon Ltd. (5)
6 Ahmedabad Mfg. Calico Ptg Company Ltd. (M, T)
7 Ahmedabad New Cotton Mills Company Ltd.
8 Albright Morarji & Pandit Ltd. (1)
9 Alembic Chemical Works Company Ltd. (M)
10 Alembic Glass Inds Ltd.
11 Amar Dye-chem Ltd. (M, 5)
12 Amines & Plasticizers Ltd. (M, 4)
13 Amrit Banaspati Co Ltd.
14 Andhra Cement Co Ltd.
15 Andhra Sugars Ltd. (M)
16 Anglo India Jute Mills Company Ltd. (M)
17 Angus Co Ltd. (M, 2)
18 Anil Starch Products Ltd. (M)
19 Antifriction Bearing Corporation Ltd. (5)
20 Apte Amalgamations Ltd.
21 Aruna Mills Ltd.
22 Aruna Sugars Ltd.
23 Asea Ltd. (1)
24 Ashok Leyland Ltd. (M, 3, T, E)
25 Asian Cables Corpn Ltd. (5)
26 Asian Paints India Ltd.
27 Asoka Mills Ltd. (M)
28 Assam Carbon Products Ltd. (4)
29 Associated Bearing Company Ltd. (M, 3, T)
30 Associated Cement Company Ltd. (M, T, E)
31 Atic Industries Ltd. (M, 2, T)
32 Atlas Copco (I) Ltd. (1)
33 Atul Products Ltd. (M, E)
34 Audco India Ltd. (M, 2, T)
35 Automobile Products (I) Ltd. (M)
36 Avery India Ltd. (1)
37 Bajaj Auto Ltd (M, T)
38 Bajaj Tempo Ltd. (M, 4)
39 Bakelite Hylam Ltd. (2)
40 Ballarpur Industries Ltd. (M, T)
41 Baroda Rayon Corporation Ltd. (M, 5, E)
42 BASF India Ltd. (2)
43 Bata India Ltd. (M, 1, E)
44 Bayer India Ltd. (M, 3)
45 Beardsell Ltd. (1)
46 Belapur Sugar & Allied Inds Ltd.
47 Belpahar Refractories Ltd. (M, T)
48 Berger Paints India Ltd. (M, 1, T)
49 Best & Crompton Engineering Ltd (M, E)
50 Bharat Bijlee Ltd. (5)
51 Bharat Commerce & Industries Ltd. (M, T)
52 Bharat Forge Co Ltd. (M)
53 Bharat Gears Ltd. (M)
54 Bharat Steel Tubes Ltd. (M, E)
55 Bharat Vijay Mills Ltd. (M)
56 Bharatiya Electric Steel Co Ltd.
57 Bhoruka Steel Ltd. (M)
58 Bihar Alloy Steels Ltd. (M, T)
59 Bimetal Bearing Ltd. (M, 1)
60 Binny Ltd. (M)
61 Birla Jute & Industries Ltd. (M, T, E)
62 Blow Plast Ltd. (E)
63 Blue Star Ltd. (M, E)
64 Boehringer Knoll Ltd. (1)
65 Bombay Burmah Trading Corporation Ltd. (5)
66 Bombay Dyeing & Manufacturing Co Ltd. (M, 5)
67 Bombay Malleable Iron Castings & Allied
68 Bombay Oxygen Corpn Ltd.

69 Boots Co India Ltd. (3)
70 Borosil Glass Works Ltd. (1, T)
71 Bowreah Cotton Mills Co Ltd. (M, T)
72 Brakes India Ltd. (M, 2, T)
73 Buckau Wolf India Ltd. (2)
74 Cable Corpn of (I) Ltd. (M, 4)
75 Calcutta Steel Co Ltd.
76 Camphor & Allied Products Ltd.
77 Caprihans India Ltd. (M)
78 Carborundum Universal Ltd. (M, 1)
79 Cellulose Products of (I) Ltd.
80 Central India Machine Mfg Co Ltd. (M, T, E)
81 Central India Spinning Weaving & Manufacturing Co (M, T)
82 Central Pulp Mills Ltd. (M)
83 Century Enka Ltd. (M, 1, T)
84 Century Spinning & Mfg. Co Ltd. (M, T, E)
85 Chemicals & Plastics (I) Ltd. (4)
86 Chettinad Cement Corpn Ltd.
87 Chloride India Ltd. (M, 3, E)
88 Cibatul Ltd. (M, 4)
89 Coates of India Ltd. (M, 1, T)
90 Colour Chem Ltd. (M, 4)
91 Cominco Binani Zinc Ltd. (M, 2)
92 Consolidated Pneumatic Tool Company (I) Ltd. (3)
93 Crompton Greaves Ltd. (M, 4, T, E)
94 Cummins Diesel Sales & Services (I) Ltd. (M, 2, T)
95 Cyanamid India Ltd. (3)
96 D C M Ltd. (M)
97 D L F Universal Ltd. (5)
98 David Brown Greaves Ltd. (M, 4, T)
99 Deepak Insulated Cable Corporation Ltd.
100 Deepak Nitrite Ltd.
101 Dharamsi Morarji Chemical Co Ltd. (M)
102 Dhrangadhra Chemical Works Ltd. (M, E)
103 Dr Beck & Co (I) Ltd. (2, T)
104 Duncan Bros & Co Ltd. (M)
105 Dunlop India Ltd. (M, 1, E)
106 E I D Parry (I) Ltd. (M)
107 East Anglia Plastics (I) Ltd.
108 East India Hotels Ltd. (M, E)
109 Elecon Engineering Co Ltd. (M)
110 Electric Construction & Equipment Corporation (M, T)
111 Enfield India Ltd (M, 4)
112 Engine Valves Ltd.
113 English Electric Company of (I) Ltd. (M, 3)
114 Ennore Foundries Ltd. (M, 3, T)
115 Escorts Ltd. (M, E)
116 Escorts Tractors Ltd. (M, 4)
117 Excel Industries Ltd. (T)
118 F G P Ltd. (1)
119 Facit Asia Ltd. (1, T)
120 Fenner India Ltd. (1, E)
121 Firth India Steel Co Ltd.
122 Fit Tight Nuts & Bolts Ltd. (M)
123 Flakt India Ltd. (3)
124 Flender Macneill Gears (I) Ltd. (M, 2)
125 Food Specialities Ltd. (1)
126 Forbes Forbes Campbell & Co Ltd. (M, T)
127 Fort Gloster Inds Ltd. (M, T, E)
128 G T C Industries Ltd. (M)
129 Gabriel India Ltd. (M, 1)
130 Gammon India Ltd. (5)
131 Gangappa Industries Ltd.
132 Gangeshwar Ltd.
133 Garware Nylons Ltd. (M, E)
134 Garware Paints Ltd. (M)
135 Geep Industrial Syndicate Ltd.
136 General Electronic Co of (I) Ltd. (M, 3)
137 Geoffery Manners & Co Ltd. (1)
138 German Remedies Ltd. (4)
139 Glaxo Laboratories (I) Ltd. (M, 1)
140 Godfrey Philips (I) Ltd. (1, T)
141 Goetze India Ltd. (M, 4)
142 Gokak Patel Volkart Ltd. (M, 5, T)

143 Goodlass Nerolac Paints Ltd. (M, 1, T, E)
144 Goodyear India Ltd. (M, 3)
145 Graphite India Ltd. (M, 5, T)
146 Grasim Industries Ltd. (M, T, E)
147 Greaves Cotton & Co Ltd. (M, T)
148 Grindwell Norton Co Ltd. (2)
149 Groz-beckert Saboo Ltd. (3, T)
150 Guest Keen Williams Ltd. (M, 2)
151 Gujarat State Fertilisers Co Ltd.
152 Gujchem Distillers (I) Ltd.
153 Herbertsons Ltd. (M)
154 Herdillia Chemicals Ltd. (M, 2)
155 Hind Lamps Ltd. (M, 1, T)
156 Hindoostan Spinning & Weaving Mills Ltd. (M, E)
157 Hindustan Aluminium Corpn. Ltd. (M, 4, T)
158 Hindustan Brown Boveri Ltd. (M, 4, T)
159 Hindustan Ciba-Giegy Ltd. (M, 3, T)
160 Hindustan Construction Company Ltd. (M, T)
161 Hindustan Development Corpn Ltd. (M)
162 Hindustan Ferodo Ltd. (M, 3)
163 Hindustan Gas & Inds Ltd. (T)
164 Hindustan Lever Ltd. (M, 3, T, E)
165 Hindustan Motors Ltd. (M, T)
166 Hindustan Sugar Mills Ltd. (M, T)
167 Hindustan Wires Ltd.
168 Hoechst India Ltd. (M, 2, E)
169 Hukamchand Mills Ltd.
170 Hyderabad Industries Ltd. (M, T)
171 I D L Chemicals Ltd. (M, 2)
172 I T C Ltd. (M, 1, T, E)
173 I V P Ltd. (M)
174 India Carbon Ltd. (M, 4)
175 India Cements Ltd. (M)
176 India Sugars & Refineries Ltd.
177 Indian Aluminium Co Ltd. (M, 3)
178 Indian Cable Co Ltd. (M, 4)
179 Indian Duplicator Co Ltd. (M, 1)
180 Indian Dyestuff Industries Ltd. (M, 5, T, E)
181 Indian Organic Chem. Ltd. (M)
182 Indian Oxygen Ltd. (M, 1)
183 Indian Rayon Corpn. Ltd. (M, T, E)
184 Indian Tube Co Ltd. (M, T)
185 Indo Asahi Glass Co Ltd. (1)
186 Indofil Chemicals Ltd. (M, 3, T)
187 Industrial Cables India Ltd. (M, E)
188 Infar India Ltd. (2, E)
189 International Computers India Ltd. (1)
190 J K Synthetics Ltd. (M, T)
191 Jagatjit Cotton Textile Mills Ltd. (M, T)
192 Jardine Henderson Ltd. (M)
193 Jay Engineering Works Ltd. (M, E)
194 Jay Shree Tea & Industries Ltd. (M, T)
195 Jayant Vitamins Ltd.
196 Jayshree Chemicals Ltd. (M, T)
197 Jenson & Nicholson (I) Ltd.
198 Johnson & Johnson Ltd. (3)
199 Jyoti Ltd. (M)
200 K C P Ltd. (M, E)
201 K E C International Ltd. (M, E)
202 K S B Pumps Ltd. (3)
203 Kalyanpur Lime & Cement Works Ltd.
204 Kamani Metals & Alloys Ltd.
205 Kelvin Jute Co Ltd.
206 Kerala Electric Lamp Works Ltd. (M, 4, T)
207 Kesar Enterprises Ltd. (M)
208 Khatau Makanji Spinning and Weaving Mills Co Ltd. (M)
209 Killick Nixon Ltd.
210 Kinetic Engineering Ltd.
211 Kirloskar Brothers Ltd. (M, T)
212 Kirloskar Cummins Ltd. (M, 2, T)

213 Kirloskar Electric Co Ltd. (M, 5, T)
214 Kirloskar Oil Engines Ltd. (M, T, E)
215 Kores India Ltd. (T)
216 Kothari Industrial Corporation Ltd. (M)
217 Kunal Engineering Co Ltd.
218 L & T Macneill Ltd. (M, 4, T)
219 L G Balkrishnan & Bros Ltd.
220 Lakhanpal National Ltd. (4)
221 Lakshmi Machine Works Ltd. (M, 5)
222 Lucas India Services Ltd. (M, 3, T)
223 Lucas TVS Ltd. (M, 3, T)
224 M R F Ltd. (M, E)
225 Machinery Manufactures Corporation Ltd. (M, T)
226 Mackinnon Mackenzie & Co Ltd. (1)
227 Madras Aluminium Co Ltd. (M, 4)
228 Madras Cements Ltd. (M)
229 Madras Petrochem Ltd.
230 Madura Coats Ltd. (M, 1)
231 Mafatlal Dyes & Chemicals Ltd. (M, 4, T)
232 Mafatlal Engg. Co Ltd. (M, T)
233 Mafatlal Fine Spinning and Manufacturing Co Ltd. (M, T)
234 Mafatlal Inds Ltd. (M, T, E)
235 Maharaja Shree Umaid Mills Ltd. (M, T)
236 Maharashtra Sugar Mills Ltd.
237 Mahendra Mills Ltd.
238 Mahindra & Mahindra Ltd. (M, 5, E, T)
239 Mahindra Spicer Ltd. (1, T)
240 Martin Burn Ltd.
241 Mather & Platt (I) Ltd. (3)
242 Matulya Mills Ltd. (M, T)
243 Merind Ltd. (3, T)
244 Metal Box India Ltd. (M, 1, E)
245 Metal Powder Co Ltd.
246 Mettur Chemical and Industrial Corporation Ltd.
247 Modern Mills Ltd.
248 Modi Rubber Ltd. (M, T, E)
249 Modi Spinning and Weaving Mills Co Ltd. (M, T)
250 Modipon Ltd. (M, 4, T)
251 Mohan Meakin Ltd. (M)
252 Molins of India Ltd. (3)
253 Morarjee Goculdas Spg & Wvg Co Ltd. (M)
254 Motilal Padampat Udyog Ltd. (T)
255 Motor Industries Co Ltd. (M, 3)
256 Mukand Iron & Steel Works Ltd. (M, T)
257 Multimetals Ltd. (4)
258 Mysore Cements Ltd. (M, T)
259 Mysore Kirloskar Ltd. (M, T)
260 Mysore Paper Mills Ltd.
261 National Insulated Cables Co
262 National Organic Chml Inds Ltd. (M, 4, T)
263 National Peroxide Ltd. (M, 4)
264 National Radio & Electronics Co Ltd. (4, T)
265 National Rayon Corpn Ltd. (M)
266 National Standard Duncan Ltd. (1)
267 Needle Roller Bearing Co Ltd. (4)
268 New India Inds Ltd. (M, 4)
269 Nicholas Laboratories India Ltd. (1)
270 Nirlon Synthetic Fibres & Chemicals Ltd. (M, E)
271 Nuddea Mills Co Ltd. (M, 4)
272 Oriental Paper & Inds Ltd. (M, T)
273 Oriental Carpet Manufactures Ltd. (M, T, E)
274 Oriental Hotels Ltd. (T)
275 Orissa Cements Ltd. (M)
276 Orissa Industries Ltd.
277 Otis Elevator Co (I) Ltd. (M, 3, T)
278 Oudh Sugar Mills Ltd. (M, T)
279 Panyam Cements and Minerals Industries Ltd. (M)
280 Paper Products Ltd.
281 Parke Davis and Company (2)
282 Patel Engineering Co Ltd.
283 Peico Electronics & Electricals (M, 1, E)

284 Pfizer Ltd. (M, 3)
285 Phillips Carbon Black Ltd. (M, 4)
286 Plastic Resins and Chemical Ltd. (M)
287 Podar Mills Ltd.
288 Polychem Ltd. (M, 4)
289 Polyolefins Industries Ltd. (M, 4, T)
290 Precision Bearings (I) Ltd. (4)
291 Premier Automobiles Ltd. (M, T)
292 Premier Cable Co Ltd.
293 Premier Cotton Spg Mills Ltd.
294 Premier Instruments Coimbatore Ltd.
295 Premier Mills (CBE) Ltd.
296 Premier Tyres Ltd.
297 Pudumjee Pulp and Paper Mills Ltd.
298 R H Windsor (I) Ltd. (M, 2)
299 Raigarh Jute Mills and Industries Ltd.
300 Raipur Manufacturing Company Ltd. (M)
301 Rajasthan Spinning and Weaving Mills Ltd. (M)
302 Rallis India Ltd. (M, 4, E)
303 Ralliwolf Ltd. (M, 4)
304 Rane (Madras) Ltd.
305 Rane Brake Linings Ltd. (4)
306 Rathi Alloys & Steel Ltd.
307 Raymond Woollen Mills Ltd. (M, T, E)
308 Reckitt & Colman of (I) Ltd. (1)
309 Reliance Industries Ltd. (M, T, E)
310 Remington Rand of (I) Ltd. (M)
311 Richardson Hindustan Ltd. (3)
312 Roche Products Ltd. (3)
313 Ruston & Hornsby (I) Ltd. (M, 5, T)
314 Sakti Sugars Ltd.
315 Sandoz India Ltd. (M, 3, E)
316 Sandvik Asia Ltd. (M, 3)
317 Sankey Wheels Ltd. (M, 4)
318 Sarangpur Cotton Manufacturing Co Ltd. (M)
319 Saraspur Mills Ltd. (M)
320 Saurashtra Cement and Chemical Industries Ltd. (2)
321 Searle India Ltd. (1)
322 Seshasayee Paper & Boards Ltd. (M)
323 Shalimar Paints Ltd. (1)
324 Shree Bhawani Cotton Mill & Inds Ltd.
325 Shree Digvijay Cements Co Ltd. (M, 5, T)
326 Shree Digvijaya Woollen Mills Ltd. (T)
327 Shree Ram Mills Ltd. (M)
328 Shree Synthetics Ltd. (M, 5, T)
329 Shree Vindhya Paper Mills Ltd. (M, T)
330 Shri Dinesh Mills Ltd.
331 Shriram Fibres Ltd. (M)
332 Siemens India Ltd. (M, 3, E)
333 Simpson & Co Ltd. (M)
334 Sindu Resettlement Corpn Ltd.
335 Sir Shadi Lall Enterprises Ltd.
336 Sirpur Paper Mills Ltd. (M, T)
337 Sirsilk Ltd. (T)
338 Skol Breweries Ltd. (M, 4)
339 South India Sugars Ltd.
340 South India Viscose Ltd. (M, 5)
341 Spencer & Co Ltd.
342 Sree Meenakshi Mills Ltd. (M)
343 Sri Chamundeshwari Sugar Mills Ltd.
344 Standard Batteries Ltd. (5, E)
345 Standard Mills Co Ltd. (M, T)
346 Standard Motors Prdts of (I) Ltd.
347 Stewarts & Lloyds of (I) Ltd. (M, 1, T)
348 Straw Products Ltd. (M, T)
349 Sudarshan Chemical Industries Ltd. (E)
350 Suessen Textile Bearings Ltd. (4)
351 Sundaram Clayton Ltd. (M, 2, T)
352 Sundaram Fastners Ltd. (M, T)

353 Sundaram Industries Ltd. (M, T)
354 Super Spinning Mills Ltd.
355 Svadeshi Mills Co Ltd. (M, T)
356 Swadeshi Polytex Ltd. (M)
357 Swan Mills Ltd. (M, E)
358 Swil Ltd.
359 Sylvania & Laxman Ltd. (4)
360 Synbiotics Ltd. (M, 1, T)
361 Synthetics & Chemicals Ltd. (M, 5)
362 Tata Chemicals Ltd. (M, T)
363 Tata Engineering and Locomotive Co Ltd. (M, 5, T)
364 Tata Exports Ltd. (M, T, E)
365 Tata Finlay Ltd. (M, T)
366 Tata Iron & Steel Co Ltd. (M, T)
367 Tata Robins Fraser Ltd. (M, 5, T)
368 Tata Yodogawa Ltd. (M, 4, T)
369 Texmaco Ltd. (M, T, E)
370 Textool Co Ltd.
371 Thiru Arooran Sugar Ltd.
372 Tinplate Co of (I) Ltd. (M, 1, T)
373 Titaghur Paper Mills Co Ltd. (M)
374 Tractors & Farm Eqpt Ltd. (M, 2)
375 Tractors (I) Ltd. (5)
376 Travancore Chemical and Manufacturing Co Ltd.
377 Travancore Electro Chemical Industries Ltd. (M, T)
378 Travancore Rayons Ltd.
379 Tribeni Tissues Ltd. (M, 3, T)
380 Triveni Engg Works Ltd. (M, E)
381 Tube Investment of (I) Ltd. (M, 1)
382 U P Hotels Ltd.
383 Ugar Sugar Works Ltd.
384 Union Carbide (I) Ltd. (M, 3, E)
385 United Carbon India Ltd. (M, 2)
386 Usha Alloys & Steels Ltd.
387 Usha Martin Black Ltd. (M, 5, E)
388 Vardhman Spinning & Genl Mills Ltd. (M)
389 Vickers Systems International Ltd. (2, T)
390 Voltas Ltd. (M, T, E)
391 VST Industries Ltd. (M, 1, T)
392 Vulcan Laval Ltd. (1)
393 W H Brady & Co Ltd.
394 W S Insulators of (I) Ltd.
395 Warner Hindustan Ltd. (2)
396 Wavin India Ltd. (1, E)
397 West Coast Paper Mills Ltd. (M, T)
398 Western India Erectors Ltd.
399 Wheels India Ltd. (M, 1, T)
400 Widia India Ltd. (3, T)
401 Willard India Ltd.
402 Wimco Ltd. (M, 1, E)
403 Woodcraft Products Ltd. (M, T)
404 Woolcombers of (I) Ltd. (5)
405 Zuari Agro Chml Ltd. (M, 2, T)

Note: 'M' within parenthesis denotes that the company was registered under the MRTP Act at the end of 1983.
'T' within parenthesis denotes that the company belongs to one of the top 20 houses.
'E' within parenthesis indicates that the company is a recognized export/trading house.
'1' within parenthesis indicates that the company was an ex-FERA company.
'2' denotes FERA company with less than 51 per cent foreign equity.
'3' indicates subsidiary of a foreign company.
'4' denotes a company with 25–40 per cent foreign equity.
'5' denotes a company with 10–25 per cent foreign equity.